THOMAS HARDY

IRVING HOWE

THOMAS HARDY

MACMILLAN

First edition 1967
Reprinted with a new preface 1985

Published by
THE MACMILLAN PRESS LTD
Houndmills, Basingstoke, Hampshire RG21 2XS
and London
Companies and representatives
throughout the world

Printed in Hong Kong

The author wishes to make grateful acknowledgement to the following for
permission to reprint material first published by them: *The Hudson Review*,
for "A Note on Hardy's Stories," Vol. XIX, No. 2. Summer, 1966; *The
Southern Review*, for "The Short Poems of Thomas Hardy," Vol. II, No. 4
(new series) Autumn, 1966; and to Fawcett Publications, Inc., for portions
from the author's Introduction to *The Selected Works of Thomas Hardy*.

Acknowledgement is also made to the following for permission to quote
from copyrighted material: to St. Martin's Press, Inc., The Macmillan Press
Ltd., for permission to quote from *The Life of Thomas Hardy* by Florence
Emily Hardy; to Macmillan London Ltd., and the Trustees of the Hardy
Estate for permission to quote from *The Dynasts* by Thomas Hardy and to
Macmillan Publishing Company, for permission to quote from *The Collected
Poems of Thomas Hardy*.

British Library Cataloguing in Publication Data
Howe, Irving
Thomas Hardy.—(Masters of world literature
series)
1. Hardy, Thomas, *1840–1928*—Criticism and
interpretation
I. Title   II. Series
823'.8   PR4754
ISBN 0–333–39537–9 (hardcover)
ISBN 0–333–39503–4 (paperback)

For Arien

Contents

CONTENTS

Preface to the 1985 Edition

FEW PLEASURES·CAN BE KEENER for a writer than to see a long-unavailable book returned to print. It gives one all sorts of happy illusions about a second life.

The first edition of my book appeared sixteen years ago, and rereading it now I find myself somewhat bemused about the man who wrote it—someone, evidently, who is both I and not I. The primary analyses and judgments in this book I still hold to. The affection for Hardy as novelist and poet I feel, if anything, still more strongly. But if I were to write this book now I would do it somewhat differently. About "critical methodology," too often a substitute for critical perception, I remain quite as skeptical as in 1966. I would, however, try for a somewhat more just distribution of space and a more austere style. I would want to write in greater detail about Hardy's poetry, and I would try for a somewhat less epigrammatic or "lapidary" style, convinced as I am that in criticism lucidity is all. Were I able to confront the author of this book face-to-face, I would say in all friendliness: You have probably overestimated the critical value to be extracted from a nicely turned subordinate clause.

When I wrote this book, the influence of the New Criticism

was still strong and the force of T. S. Eliot's depreciation of Hardy still felt by serious literary people. That may explain why at a few points this book has a somewhat combative edge and in one or two footnotes becomes downright pugnacious. Eliot's attack had already been parried, quite brilliantly, by Katherine Anne Porter, and Hardy's poetry had been praised by W. H. Auden in an influential essay. Still, one must remember how enormous—and I think, merited—was Eliot's authority in our literary life a few decades ago. For him to attack Hardy as he did was an act of some cultural importance, and anyone proposing to assess Hardy's work had to confront it—which, directly and indirectly, I tried to do.

Today that would no longer be quite so necessary. The kind of criticism that faulted Hardy's novels for their structural and tonal irregularities—a criticism that in a less sophisticated version faulted Hardy for not adhering to the disciplines of the Flaubertian "art novel"—has receded in influence. Critics do not seem so concerned with "unity" in a work of fiction as they were during the high point of the New Criticism, and they certainly have a greater awareness of, and tolerance for, kinds of "unity" that don't necessarily manifest themselves as structural compactness and economy. The more open, mixed and experimental forms of fiction that have recently flourished give us a better appreciation for the heterodox ways in which Hardy put together his novels. We have learned to see what experienced nineteenth century readers must have grasped intuitively: that episodic fictions can be held together through a unity of voice and that novels can be marked by values at least as significant and attractive as the kind of structural unity so greatly prized a few decades ago.

As for Hardy's poetry, that now seems more secure in its literary position than it was two or three decades ago. Not many of us are worried—some never were—about Hardy's alleged heresies as a lapsed Christian. We know, as both Ms. Porter and other critics before her have pointed out, that in Hardy's loving-kindness of voice, his compassion for all living creatures, he embodied the Christian virtues far better than a good many later writers conspicuously striving for orthodoxy. We are now also likely to have a greater responsiveness to Hardy's gnarled romanticism; to his unorthodox opinions, drawn from both a "churchy" youth and mature experiences; and to the verse techniques with which he kept experimenting. Some of his ideas may seem a little dated, the remains of late nineteenth century skepticism and "scientism"; but his underlying sense of things, the profound gravity and doubts of a man unsure of his place in the world, is closer to us than the more strident assertions of many later poets.

There has never been another voice in English poetry like Hardy's and there probably never will be. Hardy, I believe, is one of the few "classical" English poets who retain a strong following among nonacademic and nonprofessional readers, those who turn to poetry for pleasure and feel toward him a deep sense of friendship.

Still another reason for the recent growth of interest in Hardy's work ought to be noticed here, and that is the rise of feminist approaches in literary criticism. The new sensibility to which these approaches have contributed teaches us that in both literature and criticism there is often an unexamined sexual bias, sometimes asserted with a conscious will to domination, more often emerging unwittingly as part of that structure of values by which we order our lives. Whether developed with measure or excess, feminist criticism has forced us to look at our intellectual premises and moral prejudices, questioning the previously unquestioned. That such a criticism should take a keen interest in Hardy's fiction is understandable, since there is hardly another English novelist in the nineteenth century who has drawn such striking yet radically different figures as Bathsheba, Tess and Sue. My book was written before the recent upsurge of feminist opinion, but parts of it, such as the opening to Chapter VI, touch upon the kinds of problems with which feminist opinion concerns itself.

In the years since this book first appeared there has been a good deal published about Hardy. Let me mention just a few of the books that seem essential for bringing up to date the "Suggestions for Further Reading" on p. 195.

There is, first of all, a new *Complete Poems* edited by James Gibson and the first volume of a *Collected Poems* edited by Samuel Hynes. Several volumes of Hardy's letters have also appeared.

Perhaps the foremost addition to the Hardy literature is Michael Millgate's *Thomas Hardy*, a careful and thorough piece of work that may now be regarded as the definitive biography. It is one of those "old-fashioned" biographies that allow narrative to unfold at a steady, leisurely pace. A critical work I have found especially interesting is Donald Davie's *Thomas Hardy and English Poetry*, 1972, which contains acute criticism of Hardy's poetry and argues that it is he, rather than Yeats or Eliot, who has been the central influence on twentieth century English poetry. Davie sees Hardy as a "liberal" poet, by which he has in mind not so much a political opinion as a style of response, a humane and tolerant way of dealing with our experience. Perhaps a bit excessive at some points, Davie's book has a virtue not always present in critical studies: it is completely interesting.

A critical work I have found stimulating is Joseph Hillis Miller's *Thomas Hardy: Distance and Desire*, 1970. Among the feminist studies of Hardy, two are especially notable: Mary Jacobus, "Sue the Obscure," *Essays in Criticism*, #25, 1975, and Elaine Showalter, "The Unmanning of the Mayor of Casterbridge," in Dale Kramer, *Critical Approaches to the Fiction of Thomas Hardy*, 1979. Ms. Showalter's essay includes a disagreement with portions of my book, and while appreciating her concern I must report that it has not shaken my belief in the book you are now about to read.

—IRVING HOWE, 1984

Preface

I think this is a good time to be writing about Thomas Hardy. He is an acknowledged classic of English literature, but a classic not secure. During the last few decades he has been subjected to severe critical attack, at times to blunt dismissal. The novels have suffered most, the poems least; the stories have been ignored. In any case, it can no longer be assumed—it must now be argued —that Hardy is a great writer. Even the most friendly estimates of his work have implied a shift so radical in their terms of appraisal, they have surely left Hardy's more traditional admirers—the vicarious sojourners of Wessex, the bemused spectators of rusticity, the awed students of philosophy—almost as dismayed as have the attacks. To write criticism about such nineteenth century figures as Jane Austen, George Eliot and Joseph Conrad is largely to confirm established views; to write criticism about Hardy is to encounter uncertainties, embarrassments, challenges and revisions. Yet, for precisely that reason, he lives as a writer. Being problematic he can be discussed almost as if he were a contemporary, in a way that most of his contemporaries cannot.

The amount of Hardy criticism is enormous, and there might be little point in adding to it but for a wish to confront the questions I have just mentioned. A good part of the Hardy criticism is, in the unhappy sense, academic: treatises on his philosophy. Another part is genteel: tours of his landscape. But some of it is distinguished: the early books by Lionel Johnson and Lascelles Abercrombie, the fierce essay by D. H. Lawrence, the tough-minded "revisionist" study by Albert Guerard. To all these critics I am indebted.

The amount of attention paid in this book to Hardy's biography is slight. I have no fresh information to add, and the unexciting facts about Hardy's life are easily available in the standard biographies of Carl Weber, Evelyn Hardy and Edmund Blunden. I have chosen to discuss only those aspects of his life which seem to have a direct bearing upon a consideration of his work.

Most of the material available to Hardy's biographers comes from the standard biography written under the name of the second Mrs. Hardy: *The Early Life of Thomas Hardy* and *The Later Years of Thomas Hardy*. The quotations concerning Hardy's life in my first chapter are drawn from this source.

I. H.

Background and Profile

THE WORLD OF THOMAS HARDY'S YOUTH—he was born in the
village of Higher Bockhampton near Dorchester, June 2, 1840—
was another world, an earlier England. It was rural, traditional,
fixed in old country ways, rituals and speech. England was then
deep into the convulsive transformations of the Industrial Revolution; the reform movement known as Chartism was stirring
many people and frightening many more; but in the Dorset
countryside at the southwest corner of the island (Wessex, in
the novels) one might almost have supposed that human existence was changeless, unaffected by history or technology, flowing
through the centuries like a stately procession of verities and
recurrences. Changes did come, of course. When Hardy was a
boy of seven Dorchester saw its first railroad, and all through
the second half of the century new machines, new methods, new
men would be reaching into the countryside. The slow incursion
of such novelties and threats forms a major theme in Hardy's
fiction. But during the years of his childhood these novelties and
threats were not yet dramatically visible; and for a man who
would experience the turning from country faith to modernist
skepticism in the most personal way, there was an urgent need

to recall the earlier days as a time of charm, peace and social unity. In Wessex, wrote Hardy,

> three or four score years were included in the mere present, and nothing less than a century set a mark on its face or tone. Five decades hardly modified the cut of a gaiter or the embroidery of a smock-frock by the breadth of a hair. Ten generations failed to alter the turn of a single phrase.

In the book from which these sentences are taken, *Far from the Madding Crowd,* Hardy speaks with evident feeling about "the attachment to the soil of one particular spot by generation after generation." Such sentiments, at least among writers of the past hundred and fifty years, have rarely been enough to inspire great works: for they are sentiments too unshaded, too much at ease with themselves, too lacking in dramatic turmoil. A regional consciousness, left to itself, seldom results in anything but tiresome romanticizing of the past. In the modern era, serious writing seems to require some rupture of faith and connection, and if the novelist of provincial rootedness is to achieve an art of universal interest he must choose (or be driven) to uproot himself. Still, the "attachment to the soil of one particular spot" can be a starting point for that stringent and self-conscious nostalgia which animates the work of Hardy, George Eliot and Faulkner, thereby making possible an interplay between past and present in which each becomes a premise for the criticism of the other. This nostalgia, so different from the indulgence usually passing under that name, is available to the writer only upon reaching the point of sophistication at which he can surrender the fantasy of returning home. It is as if some deracination in real life were necessary for enabling him to summon the remembered homeland in literature. Confined now to the geography of imagination, the writer releases his nostalgia through a fabled reconstruction, a balked piety, which he then sets off against the ruthlessness of historical change. His possession of a slowly fading world, remembered with pathos and unrivaled knowledge, is for the writer an advantage comparable only to an unhappy childhood: it makes for tension, memory and a brief monopoly of legend.

As a boy Thomas Hardy was sufficiently at home with "local hearts and heads" to absorb the unspoken assumptions of the traditional Dorset culture. Growing older, into his late adolescence, he found himself gradually moving away from that culture: not at all what we might today call "alienated," but aware that he was marked by some personal and social differences. His father was a master-mason, life-holder of a house and reasonably prosperous; but in the past Hardy's family had stood higher on the social scale and now it wobbled, not too uncomfortably, between the gentry above and the peasants below.

The boy Thomas Hardy spent much of his free time with the educated members of local society. Noticed as bright and sensitive, he was a favorite of the lady of the manor, Julia Augusta Martin, who, he would later recall, was "passionately fond of him" and for whom his own feeling was "almost that of a lover." In the Dorset of the 1840s and 1850s the harshest line of social distinction was drawn between those working on the land as farmers or laborers and everyone above them; but among the latter, class differences were still relaxed, not very sharp or wounding. Yet throughout his life Hardy would retain a strong feeling of social inferiority, caused not so much by his sense of where he stood in Dorset as by his sense of where Dorset stood in relation to London. Even when he married the niece of an archdeacon and became a literary figure sought after by London hostesses, he still thought of himself as a country man, the son of simple and hardworking people. One fact is central to his life and career: Thomas Hardy did not go to a university, he would never feel quite at ease in either the wealthy or the educated circles he later met in London, and he came from a segment of the English people that had not yet fully entered the cultural life of the nation. Though not "class conscious" in a political way, Hardy's strongest ties—ties knitting together affection, pride and some estrangement—would always be with the world of his youth.

Hardy's most gratifying memories, vividly preserved into old age, were of the customs, work and pleasures of this country world. As a boy he was of "an ecstatic temperament," and danced to "the endless jigs, hornpipes, reels, waltzes and country-dances" that his father would play on the violin; sometimes he too would scrape away at weddings, an adolescent fiddler; once, in a flare of ecstasy, he kept playing for three-quarters of an hour, to the beat of couples dancing "The New Rigged Ship." That music could lure and intoxicate, Hardy had known since childhood. Certain tunes played by his father would make him weep even as they made him dance, and later, in one of his finest short stories, "The Fiddler of the Reels," he would depict the impassioned helplessness of a young woman when assaulted by melody. Music was enormously important to Hardy, not merely in its own right but as a token of the old days when his father had played in the Stinsford Parish choir, as *his* father had played in a neighboring church band. In the biography of Thomas Hardy which appears under the signature of his second wife, Florence Emily, but was in large measure dictated by Hardy himself, there is a charming passage that recalls how his mother would describe the family players of an earlier time:

> They were always hurrying, being rather late, their fiddles and violin-cello in green baize under their left arms. They wore top hats, stick-up shirt collars, dark blue coats with great collars and gilt buttons, deep cuffs and black silk 'stocks,' or neckerchiefs. . . . My grandfather wore drab cloth breeches and buckled shoes, but his sons wore trousers and Wellington boots.

For Hardy the musical tradition of his family was more than a source of pride and affection: it signified an active, self-contained and humane culture, rich with local associations and rooted in a local past. Mostly it was a music of passionate hymns, familiar tunes for dancing, ballads marked by the voices of generations. In the parish where the Hardys had played for close to a century, untrained but devoted musicians would practice their instruments two or three times a week, to play at church on Sundays, at weddings upon request, and for the whole community during Christmas.

This community was still a religious one. If it knew little about the fervors of piety and was deaf to the nuances of theology, it accepted without question the language of Christianity. In his early teens Hardy had taught Sunday school; in his late teens he worried about problems of religious doctrine; throughout his youth he seriously considered entering the ministry; and deep into his years of age, when he had long been a skeptic, he continued to love the simple and sometimes passionate music of the church. In the second Mrs. Hardy's biography there appears this telling passage:

Although invidious critics had cast slurs upon [Hardy] as Noncomformist, Agnostic, Atheist, Infidel, Immoralist, Heretic, Pessimist . . . they had never thought of calling him what they might have called him more plausibly—churchy; not in any intellectual sense, but insofar as instincts and emotions ruled.

In the actual course of Hardy's experience, his "churchiness" and his attachment to the Dorset countryside were inseparable, woven together into a single piety. The idea of an "organic culture" was at the center of his view of Dorset and his vision of Wessex. Not always certain whether it was an actuality of the historical past or a myth that could usefully be fixed upon the past, Hardy longed for a culture in which work and pleasure, practice and norm, body and spirit, substance and decoration would be united. And the idea of such a culture was not a mere figment of his will, it came from the depths of his own experience. It was an idea he could glimpse whole in his stories and poems, as though in snapshots freed from time; while in his novels, where the passage of time had to be acknowledged and its consequences reckoned, he could seldom avoid portraying the ways in which the culture of Wessex betrayed signs of division. In real life Hardy grasped with an intimate assurance how Dorset was moving away from even the possibility of an organic culture: he describes a "harvest home" (or supper) which was

among the last at which the old traditional ballads were sung, the railway having been extended to Dorchester just then, and the orally transmitted ditties of centuries being slain at a stroke by the London comic songs that were introduced. The particular ballad which he remembered hearing that night from the lips of the farm-women was that one variously called "The Outlandish Knight," "May Colvine," "The Western Tragedy," etc. He could recall to old age the scene of the young women in their light gowns sitting on a bench against the wall in the barn, and leaning against each other as they warbled the Dorset version of the ballad. . . .

What today can at best be vaguely suggested by the term "organic culture," Hardy experienced as a powerful reality. We have no need to fabricate an idyll: the culture of Dorset was limited, and if its strengths were drawn from local communities and traditions, so too were its weaknesses. It was a culture notably at a distance from—though not, of course, untouched by—the great crises and passions of nineteenth century history; it had little active relationship to high art or literature of the past; its religion, when not simply routine, tended to go slack; and by the middle of the nineteenth century it lacked the resilience to withstand the penetrations of industrialism. But what it did have, as evinced in work and communal life, was likely to be authentic and well-worn, controlled by the experience of generations. Limited as this culture might be, it was neither sleazy nor jaded nor exhibitionist. Solid reading was encouraged in the Hardy family, especially by Thomas's mother, a woman of firm character and ranging memories, who allowed the boy his indulgences as a "born book-worm" and helped him start a library with a gift of Dryden's Virgil, *Rasselas* and *Paul and Virginia*.

Mrs. Hardy had the even greater good sense to allow her son a measure of neglect. Often solitary and almost always shy, he would wander for hours through the countryside, learning to love —it might be more accurate to say, coming to be at one with— birds and small animals, much like the sensitive young Jude Fawley who could not bear to harm the birds he had been hired to chase from the fields. At the age of eight Thomas went to a local school, being kept near home because he had been a very frail child, but a year later he was transferred to an excellent day school in Dorchester, run by a non-conformist master. The boy was a good scholar but not a prodigy, anticipating a little the ruminative mind, at once tender and aloof, that would shine through his novels and poems.

Not all was idyll, nor even pleasant. In his last years Hardy could still remember the shock he had felt in boyhood when a Dorset child laborer was found under a hedge, dead of starvation. "Nothing my father ever said drove the tragedy of life so deeply into my mind" as the recollection of witnessing the hanging of a farm boy to whose feet weights had been tied in order to speed his death. And Hardy himself, while still a boy, watched through a telescope the hanging of a convict in Dorchester:

> At the moment of his placing the glass to his eye the white figure dropped downwards, and the faint note of the town clock struck eight. The whole thing had been so sudden that the glass nearly fell from Hardy's hand. He seemed alone on the heath with the hanged man, and crept home wishing he had not been so curious.

To regard such incidents as "traumatic" seems an exaggeration of the kind to which the twentieth century mind is prone; it is also to ignore the old, unpleasant English tradition, likely to be still vigorous in an area like Dorset, of treating public hangings as spectacles of excitement. As a boy Thomas Hardy no doubt shared in this attitude, but he had his own sensibility, his own readiness for pain. At the very least, these incidents suggest a predisposition to identify himself with the victims of justice and injustice alike—the germ, perhaps, of his feeling as a mature writer that in the democracy of suffering moral distinctions fade away. Yet neither his early encounters with social violence nor any other discoverable childhood pains and traumas can plausibly be cast as the source of that darkness of spirit which encloses Hardy's work. If in his outer biography there is a crucial event explaining why he saw human experience largely as a chain of disaster and mischance, it seems probable that this shock or break occurred after his boyhood—a boyhood, as it happens, that was far less unhappy than those of many writers far less inclined to pessimism.

At Isaac Last's school, elevated to the rank of academy shortly after Thomas's enrollment, the boy first became acquainted with the possibilities of serious intellectual work. He began to study Latin and after a time could read slowly in Virgil, a writer he would love throughout his life, and in Lucretius, a writer with whom he had affinities of temperament. The boy was diligent, and won prizes from his teacher; he began to acquire that habit of self-education which would remain with him to the death. At sixteen, "though he had just begun to be interested in French and the Latin classics," Hardy was taken out of school and apprenticed to John Hicks, a Dorchester architect distinguished by kindliness of nature and a knowledge of the classics. For Hardy the several years he spent with Hicks not only marked the beginning of a lifelong absorption with church architecture, particularly untampered Gothic; these years also provided a kind of miniature college, with another apprentice, a few young people from town and Hicks himself transforming the office into a seminar where everything from pedobaptism to classical declensions was discussed. Pockets of vigorous provincial culture could at this time still be found in England. Local schoolmasters, self-educated citizens, earnest young men with varying amounts of education (the sort who in later decades might be scholarship boys) read and discussed the books and magazines that came from London, sometimes even from the Continent. The struggle between those wishing to "modernize" Christianity toward a partial reconcilement with science and those holding to a traditionalist faith was fierce and continuous; it had its delayed but strong repercussions in a town like Dorchester; and at times it veiled unexamined differences of social allegiance. Hardy's experience as a youth encountering echoes of contemporary thought is notably similar to that of George Eliot twenty years earlier in Coventry, where her friendship with the Hennells and Charles Bray caused her to question the faith of her youth.

These were good years. The young Hardy lived in "a world of shepherds and ploughmen in a hamlet . . . where modern improvements were still regarded as wonders," yet worked in a town which had advanced to railways, telegraphs and daily papers from London. His life was happily divided among the professional, the scholarly and the rustic, all in a single day. Much of his reading "was done between five and eight in the morning before he left home for the office. In the long summer days he would even rise at four and begin. In these circumstances he got through a moderately good number of the usual classical pages. . . . He also took up Greek, which he had not learnt at school, getting on with some books of the *Iliad*."

In Dorchester Hardy made two friendships that would prove decisive in turning him to literature and the intellectual life. The first was with the Reverend William Barnes, dialect poet ("Woak Hill," "A Sly Bit o' Coorten") and philologist, who for many years had been conducting a fine school near Hicks's office. Barnes was the first poet Hardy ever knew, and in many ways an excellent model—more a model than an influence. He was a conscientious teacher, kind and unassuming; he was close to folk life and sources, yet a well-educated man; he liked to experiment with little-known, especially Welsh, verse forms; he had a good eye for the twists and charms of local personality, if not for the depths of human character. What Hardy gained from Barnes was a conviction that the life of obscure country people could provide a sufficient subject, or at least a sufficient occasion, for writing poetry. Barnes might keep his journal in

Italian and study Persian faithfully, yet he felt it no threat to his dignity that in his verse he should take pains to record local speech exactly. And he suggested a useful lesson for a post-Romantic period: that quietness and modesty are traits not necessarily unbecoming in a poet.

Barnes was a minor figure deserving a modest space in anthologies, Hardy could now and again reach the level of great poetry; but there is a clear and happy relationship between the two as writers, just as there was a long friendship between them as men. When Barnes died, Hardy printed a tribute which suggests in passing the difference in scope between the two poets:

> Mr. Barnes never assumed the high conventional style; and he entirely leaves alone ambition, pride, despair, defiance and other of the grander passions. . . . His rustics are, as a rule, happy people, and very seldom feel the sting of the rest of modern mankind—the disproportion between the desire for serenity and the power of obtaining it. One naturally thinks of Crabbe in this connection; but though they touch at points, Crabbe goes much further than Barnes in questioning the justice of circumstance. Their pathos, after all, is the attribute upon which the poems must depend for their endurance. . . .

The mention of Crabbe is very much to the point, since at least part of Hardy's verse can be regarded as, roughly, a bringing together of Barnes and Crabbe (who was, Hardy later told a friend, "the earliest influence in the direction of realism" upon him). When Hardy remarks that Crabbe goes further than Barnes "in questioning the justice of circumstance," he is also tacitly noting the extent of his own enlargement upon Barnes.

The example of Barnes would in time help Thomas Hardy to write novels and poems about the life of Dorset, and to write them in a way quite transcending Barnes's limited *genre* pieces; the influence of Horace Moule, a young man Hardy also met in Dorchester, would bring him into an active relationship with the possibilities of modern thought. The son of a local clergyman, Moule had been raised a good Anglican. During and after his years at Cambridge he was shaken by the radical philosophic and theological writings of mid-nineteenth century England, particularly the Higher Criticism which had begun to corrode Christian belief through its demand that sacred history be subject to the same criteria of evidence as secular (in effect, though not intent, a way of dislodging the category of the sacred). Gradually Moule abandoned his orthodoxy, though not, in any formal sense, his Christianity. The belief he now held was increasingly "liberal" in nature, proposing to free Christian doctrine of superstitious and dogmatic accretions. To Moule, as to many other serious men of the day, only some such radical operation could save the faith in which he had been brought up. He was wrong, though hardly in a position to know it. He did not realize that once begun, the disintegration of a religious system can rarely be halted at a chosen point.

Though still in his twenties when Hardy first met him, Moule was already launched on an intellectual career of some distinction. He helped Hardy with his studies in Greek, encouraged and criticized his early attempts at verse, and most important of all, opened up to him the whole vista of intellectual life. He guided Hardy into that arena of controversy where inherited pieties cannot be protected from the acids of reason and doubt.

It was Moule who persuaded Hardy to read *Essays and Reviews,* a powerful and influential collection of polemical studies, published in 1860 by a group of dissident churchmen and caustic dons, which assailed the encrusted dogmas of the Church of England; and it was probably Moule who a year earlier brought to Hardy's notice a book still more damaging to his faith, Darwin's *The Origin of Species.* Men like Horace Moule appear and reappear throughout the latter part of the nineteenth century. Brilliant, erudite and unstable, they are modern intellectuals somewhat in advance of modernity. Catalysts of the very disbelief toward which they hesitate to yield themselves, they are torn by the struggle between youthful pieties and mature intelligence, and they end by paying dearly for their heresies and doubts— Moule, like a good many other English intellectuals of the day, was given to bouts of severe melancholia. Upon Hardy his effect was to crack, once and for all, the surface of orthodoxy, thereby opening him to the harsher batterings of outright skepticism. Hardy's youthful idea of preparing himself for the church was now forever abandoned.

At twenty-two, his architectural training completed and his mind beginning to fire with literary ambitions, Hardy left Dorchester for London, where he again worked in an architect's office.[1] The four years he now spent in London were extremely valuable as a time in which to learn, to soak up impressions of cosmopolitan life, to form the complex of opinions he would retain throughout his life and to begin writing poetry. He read widely in the Greek tragedians, who left upon him a profound though not easily distinguishable mark, and in such recent and contemporary English writers as Shelley, Browning, Bagehot, Darwin, Huxley, Swinburne and Mill. He attended lectures and galleries. He went through a brief phase as a Radical, though politics would never be important in his life or work. He wrote some thirty poems during these years, a few of which, like "Hap" and "Neutral Tones," are not merely distinguished in their own right but anticipate the voice of his later poetry. He worked too hard, reading through the early morning and far into the night, and "when he visited his friends at Dorset they were shocked by the pallor which sheeted a countenance formerly ruddy with health." By his mid-twenties Hardy was convinced that architecture was not for him. He wished to be a poet, as he would continue to wish throughout his life, and for a while he dropped his intellectual studies in order to devote himself entirely to reading verse.

1. Since this chapter was written, there has appeared in England a curious book, *Providence and Mr. Hardy,* by Lois Deacon and Terry Coleman, which claims to have discovered a previously unknown episode in Hardy's life: that as a young man he was secretly engaged for five years to his cousin Tryphena Sparks, who then threw him over for another man. Miss Deacon and Mr. Coleman argue that Tryphena was really Hardy's niece, and to do that they have to posit two illegitimate births in the family. They further speculate that the suicide of Hardy's closest friend, Horace Moule, was precipitated by a dispute between the two men over Miss Sparks. And they claim, finally, that Miss Sparks gave birth to Hardy's illegitimate son, an event that was carefully hushed up.

The only evidence, other than speculative "readings" out of Hardy's work, offered by the authors is the testimony of a lady, Mrs. Bromell, declaring herself to be Tryphena Sparks's daughter. Mrs. Bromell first disclosed these revelations at the age of eighty, and the alleged illegitimate child she mentioned only in 1965, when she was eighty-six and as the authors gravely remark, "beginning to fail."

There is, thus far, no other evidence to support any of these claims, and even if they turn out to be true, it is of very small importance indeed, in no serious way changing one's sense of Hardy the man or the writer. But whatever the fate of this book and its allegations, one sentence that appears in it deserves to become immortal. "Hardy's marriages," write the authors, "were childless, but he was probably not altogether without issue."

It was, nevertheless, during these years in London that Hardy completed his apprenticeship to the advanced thought of his time. There is something admirable and touching in the sight of this country youth as he pores over Darwin and Spencer, Huxley and Mill, striving to provision his mind and discover the truth about God, man and nature, no matter how damaging that truth might be to the remaining fragments of his faith. Hardy's gradual slide into skepticism he felt, at least in part, as a kind of liberation. Years later, in 1910, in the course of an elegy for Swinburne, whose iconoclasm gave him vicarious pleasure, Hardy would recall

> O that far morning of a summer day
> When, down a terraced street whose pavements lay
> Glassing the sunshine into my bent eyes
> I walked and read with a quick glad surprise
> New words, in classic guise

The very act of abandoning Christianity revealed, as perhaps nothing else could, how powerful its hold remained upon his imagination. A turn of such consequence made him unavoidably anxious as to its ethical dangers and seemed to threaten the belief in the virtues of devotion (or as we might now say, commitment) which he had inherited from Christianity. In the 1860s —it may be necessary to remark—religious faith was a serious option for thoughtful Englishmen, and not the mere social propriety or period fashion it later would often become. To be forced, through the pain of integrity, to surrender a faith by which childhood had been warmed and moral sentiments forged could constitute a terrible drama of the soul. For Hardy, because this drama did not entail a severe family quarrel, it was not so immediately anguished as for George Eliot and Edmund Gosse; but being less exhaustingly personal it also persisted through the years, acting itself out on the sunken stage of his consciousness, with delayed reactions and reverberations, and never quite allowing him to resolve emotionally what he had resolved in his mind.

The agnostic intellectuals, though winning debates and anticipating moods of the future, were still a minority in England and probably among the educated classes too. Earnest and disinterested, they were among the first English writers consciously to regard themselves as intellectuals: men for whom the life of ideas had become a controlling passion and who saw their task as the defense of free inquiry and high culture against a philistine society. The passage of time has been somewhat unkind to the agnostics and rationalists of the mid-nineteenth century, and few of us can now wholly share their soaring optimism or their confidence in the idea of progress; but one need not wholly accept their doctrines—one need only appreciate their seriousness and their abilities—to see why a young man like Hardy should have declared himself a disciple.

Darwin, who kept himself aloof from the polemics of the time, damaged the world-view of conventional Christianity and confirmed Hardy in his feeling that pain and cruelty are built into the very structure of existence. Spencer taught him that "the Power which the Universe manifests to us is utterly inscrutable" and also provided the germ of Hardy's later notions about Immanent Will or Emergent Consciousness. Huxley and Mill nudged him toward open disbelief: the universe being unsponsored, it contains neither inherent purpose nor moral quality. What Hardy kept searching for was not merely, and not even so much, a metaphysical system that might replace Christian theology. What he wanted and needed most were philosophical cues by means of which ethical discipline and human solidarity might be maintained in the frigid universe postulated by the skeptics. Toward this end Huxley and Mill spoke more powerfully to him than Darwin and Spencer. "There is no alleviation for the sufferings of mankind," wrote Huxley, "except veracity of thought and wisdom, and the resolute facing of the world as it is." Hardy too wished to face the world as it is, or at least as it struck him, and repeatedly he echoed Huxley: "If a way to the Better there be, it exacts a full look at the Worst."

Mill was probably the strongest influence of all, since Hardy admired him not merely as a thinker but also as a man of rectitude and courage. In his study of Hardy's intellectual development William Rutland has paired a key passage from Mill with one from Hardy, in order to underline the similarities between their thought. Mill, in his "Essay on Nature," attacks those "natural theologians" who argue that "all the suffering in the world exists to prevent greater" suffering:

a thesis which . . . could only avail to explain and justify the works of limited beings, compelled to labour under conditions independent of their own will; but can have no application to a Creator assumed to be omnipotent, who, if he bends to a supposed necessity, himself makes the necessity to which he bends. If the maker of the world *can* all that he will, he wills misery, and there is no escape from the conclusion.

In a letter dated 1902 Hardy echoes part of what Mill has said:

Pain has been, and pain is: no new sort of morals in Nature can remove pain from the past and make it pleasure for those who are its infallible estimators, the bearers thereof. And no injustice, however slight, can be atoned for by her future generosity, however ample, so long as we consider Nature to be, or to stand for, unlimited power. The exoneration of an omnipotent Mother by her retrospective justice becomes an absurdity when we ask, What made the foregone injustice necessary to her omnipotence?

Dr. Rutland's juxtaposition is neat, but what he does not add is that the two passages also reveal a characteristic difference between Mill and Hardy. Though sharing a line of thought with Mill, Hardy is most concerned with its experiential consequences ("Pain has been, and pain is"). What Mill says in exposition Hardy personalizes, intensifies and renders subjective, for even when engaged in abstract discourse Hardy bends and shapes his thought to the possibility of creative use.

Fruitful as these years in London may have been for Hardy, they were not particularly happy ones. He never felt at home in London, where he was "among strangers and strange things," and he found it easier to accept the radical views of the city's intellectuals than to accustom himself to its mode of life. In his diary for 1865 there is an entry: "My 25th birthday: not very cheerful. Feel as if I had lived a long time and done very little." Yet these years in London helped prepare Hardy for his career as a novelist and even, paradox as it may seem, for writing novels that deal with rural life. London and everything it stood for gave him the vantage point of critical distance from which to turn back to his formative experience; it gave him a range of ideas and impressions which saved him from the self-satisfied provincialism frequent among "regional" novelists. For the creator of Clym Yeobright and Jude Fawley it was immensely valuable to have stood one day in 1865 and listened at Covent

Garden to John Stuart Mill campaign for a seat in the House
of Commons:

> The appearance of the author of the treatise *On Liberty* (which we
> students of that date knew almost by heart) was so different from the
> look of persons who usually address crowds in the open air that it
> held the attention of people for whom such a gathering in itself had
> little interest. Yet it was, primarily, that of a man out of place. The
> religious sincerity of his speech was jarred on by his environment—
> a group on the hustings who, with few exceptions, did not care to
> understand him fully, and a crowd below who could not. He stood
> bareheaded, and his vast pale brow, so thin-skinned as to show the
> blue veins, sloped back like a stretching upland . . . The picture of
> him as personified earnestness surrounded for the most part by care-
> less curiosity derived an added piquancy . . . from the fact that the
> cameo clearness of his face chanced to be in relief against the blue
> shadow of a church, which, on its transcendental side, his doctrines
> antagonized.

In July 1867 Hardy returned to Bockhampton. ("Town life,"
we read about one of Hardy's early heroes, "had for some time
been depressing him . . . The perpetual strain, the lack of that
quiet to which he had been accustomed in early life, the absence
of all personal interest in the things around him, was telling
upon his health of body and mind.") He went back to Hicks's
architectural office, now working part time, and began to write
a novel, *The Poor Man and the Lady*, the full text of which
has not been preserved, but some idea of which can be had from
Hardy's recollections, from an emasculated version of the novel
called upon publication *An Indiscretion in the Life of an
Heiress*, and from a thoughtful letter the publisher Alexander
Macmillan wrote upon rejecting the manuscript. Strongly auto-
biographical and tensed by Hardy's momentary Radicalism, *The
Poor Man and the Lady* contrasts the trivialities of fashionable
London life with the naturalness of the country. George Meredith, then employed as a publisher's reader, advised Hardy to
abandon social satire—good advice, even if justified by reasons
ingloriously prudential—and to try something more popular, in
the line of Wilkie Collins. The result, quite as sensational as
Collins's fiction but with sections foreshadowing Hardy's genius,
appeared in 1871 as *Desperate Remedies*.

A year earlier, while undertaking a journey to Cornwall on

an architectural mission, Hardy had met a young woman, Emma Lavinia Gifford, who impressed him with her "aliveness." Interested in books, active in parish affairs, brisk with physical vitality, she won and returned Hardy's love. They married, after a lengthy engagement, in 1874. For a time it was a happy union, with Hardy working steadily and his wife a sympathetic helper, though the absence of children was keenly felt by both. Later, after Hardy had become famous and his wife ambitious, there were serious troubles.

Between about 1868 and 1896 Hardy proved to be an enormously productive writer, turning out fourteen novels, many of them first appearing in bowdlerized form as magazine serials, as well as three volumes of short stories. Hardy was inclined to look down upon prose fiction as an inferior—perhaps because popular—art. By no means sharing the reverent attitude toward the novel held by writers like James and Conrad, he was all too ready to follow the advice of editors that he trim his serials to late Victorian taste. Once, however, the novels appeared in book form, he was careful that his text should be quite as he wished. During the years of his fame Hardy returned briefly to live in London, but again found it depressing; most of his life was to be spent in home country, though with regular trips to London. In 1883 he began to build a house near Dorchester, and there he spent the remainder of his years.

We have reached the point where the two strongest influences upon Hardy's work—the formative experience of Dorset and the pressures of nineteenth century thought—have made themselves felt. Before turning to the novels and poems directly, it should be useful to look at these influences not as facts in his biography but as forces in his writing, so that in place of Dorset we now consider Wessex and in place of Hardy's ideas, their role in his books.

Like many great or near-great writers, Thomas Hardy is an elusive, almost protean figure. The more one reflects upon his work, the more it seems to grow into multiplicity. We can read him as a philosopher spinning fables of determinism, an elegist of rural simplicities, a poet of tenderness, a Christian whose faith has been hollowed by skepticism, a country pagan whose

mind is covered over with Christian pieties, an imaginati
torian of the revolutionary changes in nineteenth century
consciousness, an autodidact who keeps stumbling into sublimi-
ties of intuition, a troubled modernist trying to come to terms
with the malaise of our life. Each of these figures corresponds
to a portion or strand of Hardy's work, each has been celebrated
during the past seventy years in accordance with the cultural
bias of the moment. Not all are of equal value. By now, far
into the twentieth century, we are not nearly so impressed with
Hardy's discovery that the cosmos is a trap of fatality as we are
with his humane brooding upon the difficulties that follow from
this point of view.

One part of Hardy—it comes through most easily in *Far from
the Madding Crowd* and *The Woodlanders*—would always know
and love the world of Wessex as nothing else: it represented for
him the seemliness of an ordered existence, of all that is natural,
rooted and tried. This Hardy is a traditionalist writer whose
deepest affinities are with the farmlands, animals, rocks, hills
and simple people who live among them. It is almost as if the
natural world, both in its wildness and its cultivation, were
meant to represent the principle of a non- or supra-historical
permanence; things and places that make us realize with a resignation beyond pain how great is the distance between the rhythms
of the earth and the beat of human affairs.

In the world of Wessex there survives the memory of a life
in which nature and society are at peace. A sense of the past,
like a heavy aroma, lingers over this land, sometimes as a controlling discipline behind classes and customs, sometimes in such
painful evidence as words repeated and folkways re-enacted but
both no longer understood. Perceptions of time and space are
both radically divergent and closely linked. Time stretches out
as a vast gray corridor into and beyond the historical past. Space
is cramped, precisely defined and worn. Yet in the perceptions
of Wessex, the two come together through the experiencing and
apprehension of local particulars. The past lives on, a repository
of history but also something else, something not always to be
grasped through the categories of history. For here in Wessex
long stretches of the past can be seen as embodying the sameness
and continuity, the unifying rhythms, of a human existence that

extends beneath or beyond the agitation of the historical process. For Wessex, and most of the time for Hardy, what is essential in life is that which is repeated.

The land shows evidence of generations working the soil mostly with age-old methods, and handing down pretty much the same moral and social precepts. The people of Wessex, writes Hardy, "are the representatives of antiquity. Many of these laborers about here bear Norman names; many are descendents of the squires in the last century, and their faces even now strongly resemble the portraits in old manor-houses." Such sentences evoke the curve of families rising and falling, but they do this from a distance in time that suggests not the turbulence of immediate disaster but a retrospective calm.

Casterbridge, writes Hardy, "announced old Rome in every street, alley and precinct." Old Rome, in its roads, amphitheaters and street plans, forms one layer in the thickness of Wessex history: a history which resembles a series of geological strata exposed by a cut in depth. And further back, beyond the most remote segments of history, there lurks a pre-historic antiquity, its remains scattered across the land, perhaps a few of its customs and rites mysteriously preserved. While the streets in the town and the farms on the land speak of historical accumulation and density, Hardy's novels gain their special quality from his capacity for breaking past the limits of history and suggesting the faintly haunting presence of a time before, a space beneath, history. Hardy invokes the echoes of forgotten centuries together with the voices of the historical past, all lingering into the present, and thereby he creates one of his most powerful effects: that of the essential unity of human life. Lionel Johnson, in his study of Hardy's novels, presents an image of Wessex marvelously evocative of this effect:

> A rolling down country, crossed by a Roman road: here a gray standing stone, of what sacrificial, ritual origins I can but guess; there a grassy burrow, with its great bones, its red brown jars, its rude gold ornaments, still safe in earth: a broad sky burning with stars: and a solitary man.

A solitary man: the Hardyan hero and his "experiencing nature." For not only does Hardy transform the Wessex landscape into a scene of vastness and echo, he also lends it an aura of contemplativeness, coloring it with subdued tints and shadows. And it is this aura of contemplativeness—far more than any explicit philosophical statements—which produces the true Hardy note: plangent and deep, ruminative and awestruck, fraternal and uncensorious; patient before the monotony of change and the sameness of novelty.

In his own life Hardy found himself, both in spirit and style, close to the ways of farmers, woodcutters, village artisans; they had not yet been infected with the diseases of restlessness, the peculiarly—as Hardy thought—modern diseases. He felt that working with one's hands had both esthetic propriety and re-demptive value, that there is health in a life close to the earth, and that it is folly to dismiss the old ways that have survived from centuries past. With the major exception of *Jude the Obscure,* the Wessex novels form a prolonged celebration, if at times dropping into a minor key, of the English countryside. In *Under the Greenwood Tree* Hardy evokes the charm of an "unspoiled" village; in *Far from the Madding Crowd* the cura-tive freshness of farm life; in *The Return of the Native* the permanence of the heath.

One reason Hardy felt so nostalgic toward this country life was that during his own lifetime he had been a reluctant witness to its gradual dissolution under the assaults of commerce and industrialism. "Dear, delightful Wessex," he wrote, "whose statu-esque dynasties are even now only just beginning to feel the shaking of the new and strange spirit without, like that which entered the lonely village of Ezekiel's vision, and made the dry bones move, where the honest squires, tradesmen, clerks and people still praise the Lord with one voice for His best of all possible worlds." So secure is Hardy in his relationship toward Wessex, he knows that the distance he permits himself from it entails no danger that he will be cut off. Regardless of what he says or thinks, he remains a man of this countryside. The result is a characteristic passage, in which a mild irony reinforces the dominant note of affection.

The more Hardy became aware of the thrust of social change, the more he felt a need to turn back to those memories of the past which could yield him a fund of stories, legends, supersti-tions, folk sayings and fragments of wisdom. Hardy came to this

material with a doubleness of vision. He commanded it completely, it was inseparable from the store of impressions he had
hoarded from his youth, and hardly a critic or reader would dare
challenge its authenticity. Yet in his use of this material he could
not avoid a certain self-consciousness, partly because he was no
longer simply at home in his culture and partly because he
seems to have come under the influence of late nineteenth century folklorists busily trying to relate the customs of the countryside to pagan and ancient sources. The easy grace of a Herrick
in using folk festivals as emblems of dissolution and recreation
was not always available to Hardy: since for Herrick such ceremonies were organically rooted in the life from which he drew,
while for Hardy they became in part subjects for critical scrutiny
and didactic inference.

Folk material freezes the characteristic gestures of a culture,
perhaps its gestures of yesterday: awkward, half-articulate, fixed
in unchanging choreographies. It contributes tokens of the past,
blurred remnants of history, brought with loss and distortion to
the threshold of the present. It brings antiquity into oblique,
sometimes comic relation with the modern. It creates an illusion
of time suspended, the earth as a setting for a sluggish repetition
of dramas of desire and frustration. It reveals the underpinning
of paganism and superstition beneath the visible appearance of
rural Christianity. It yields a surface piquancy, the small shock
of the pleasantly strange, to set off against the grimness of Hardy's
fables. And it permits him to impute a fatalistic pessimism to
the cycle of history, the way things are and must be.

Susan Nonesuch roasts a wax image of Eustacia Vye in *The
Return of the Native,* and Michael Henchard in *The Mayor
of Casterbridge* fears his misfortune may be due to someone
stirring an unholy brew to confound him—witchcraft works beneath religion. When someone dies, folk custom requires that
his next of kin "tell the bees" lest the poor creatures cease providing honey and die of broken hearts: as in "Interlopers in the
Knap." Omens crowd through Hardy's pages: a "letter in the
candle" in *The Trumpet Major,* Christian Cantle in *The Return
of the Native* doomed to remaining a bachelor because he was
born on a moonless night. Premonitions are frequent in the
poems: a fearful gesture of crucifixion in "Near Lanivet," the

foreknowledge of death in "The Last Performance." Seasonal rites are rendered with frequent beauty: the club-walking, a survival of May rites, in *Tess of the D'Urbervilles,* sheepshearings in *Far from the Madding Crowd.* The auxiliary or choral rustics, some drawn from life and others mere copies from Shakespeare, speak in a vivid folk poetry, as when Nance Mockridge bemoans Henchard's bride ("She'll wish her cake dough afore she's done of him. There's a bluebeardy look about 'en; and 'twill out in time!"), or as in the comment of a maidservant about the marriage of Bathsheba and Troy in *Far from the Madding Crowd* (" 'Twill be a gallant life, but may bring some trouble between the mirth.").

The countryside in the Wessex novels comes to embody the accumulated richness—but since Hardy is realistic and honest, also the accumulated stagnation—of an old and stable culture. As long as that culture remains available for Hardy's protagonists to come back to, away from the pressures of ambition and thought, they need not feel entirely homeless in the world. Once it is no longer there or no longer felt to be vital, there follows the deracination of *Jude the Obscure.* Toward this decline of a sustaining community Hardy seldom displays a simple or unambiguous attitude. He regrets the loss, but believes it unavoidable; he has decidedly modest hopes for the future, and these hopes are chastened still further by his overwhelming awareness of the troubles and failures that have crowded the past. For him the prospect of social change is inseparable from the threat of personal displacement, and the two together stir up in his work a constant—though extremely fruitful—discord of approval and anxiety.

Meanwhile, in all the Wessex novels but *Jude the Obscure,* the natural world figures as a vibrant and autonomous being, in effect a "character" with its own temperament, force and destiny. Hardy's observation of nature is expert in detail, the reward of a constant and untheoretic exposure; it is often especially powerful for the way he spontaneously transmits to the external world qualities we usually take to be confined to the human. As in this sentence from *The Woodlanders:*

There was now a distinct manifestation of morning in the air, and presently the bleared white visage of a sunless winter day emerged like a dead-born child.

And this passage from *Far from the Madding Crowd:*

> The night had a haggard look, like a sick thing; and there came finally an utter expiration of air from the whole heaven in the form of a slow breeze, which might have been likened to a death. And now nothing was heard in the yard but the dull thuds of the beetle which drove in the spars, and the rustle of thatch in the intervals.

And, still more striking, this passage from *The Return of the Native:*

> Skirting the pool she followed the path toward Rainbarrow, occasionally stumbling over twisted furze-roots, tufts of rushes, or oozing lumps of fleshy fungi, which at this season lay scattered about the heath like the rotten liver and lungs of some colossal animal.

In Hardy's novels nature is not a mere backdrop, a contrivance we are invited to admire for its picturesqueness—though a charge of staginess could well be made against the opening chapters of *The Return of the Native.* Nor is nature a mere cluster of inert objects, something "out there," to be apprehended as a pleasing but mute surface. In the best of Hardy's novels, as John Holloway observes, nature emerges as "an organic whole, and its constituent parts, even the inanimate parts, have a life and personality of their own." Nature speaks, as "a cosmic agency, active, lashing, eager for conquest" in *A Pair of Blue Eyes,* "through the night-gauzes as persistently as if it had a voice" in the story "A Tryst at an Ancient Earthwork." Nature seems to live and breathe, it becomes an animated presence, it stirs and brushes against us like a pulsing hand. (Perhaps this gift for regarding the natural world as if it were an enormous living creature—for seeing, in the words of Martin Buber, not an "it" but a sentient "thou"— is the basis of Hardy's franciscan gentleness, that wonderful capacity he has for yielding to the mute and the helpless.) Only in *Jude the Obscure* does Hardy leave behind him the rural world, in a desperate realization that he has lost his "homeland" to the machine, commerce and functional rationality. The loss is a deep one, and helps explain why *Jude the Obscure* is the most disconsolate of his novels: for it is a loss that represents a radical estrangement, the death of a culture.

There is a strong Wordsworthian quality in Hardy's conviction
—perhaps one should say, Hardy's passionate intuition—that the
natural world is the source and repository of all the energies that
control human existence. Like Wordsworth, Hardy instinctively
unites nature and man, making the external setting a kind of
sharer in the human fate. Still more Wordsworthian is Hardy's
persuasion that the best life is one spent in undemanding harmony with the biological and geographic environment. In *The
Woodlanders* there is a remarkable passage describing the em-
pathic relationship of Marty South and Giles W.nterbourne with
their native milieu:

> The casual glimpses which the ordinary population bestowed upon
> that wondrous world of sap and leaves called the Hintock woods
> had been with these two, Giles and Marty, a clear gaze. They had
> been possessed of its finer mysteries as of commonplace knowledge;
> had been able to read its hieroglyphics as ordinary writing; to them
> the sights and sounds of night, winter, wind, storm, amid those dense
> boughs . . . were simple occurrences whose origin, continuance and
> laws they foreknew. They had planted together, and together they
> felled; together they had, with the run of the years, mentally col-
> lected those remoter signs and symbols which seen in few were
> of runic obscurity, but all together made an alphabet. From the
> light lashing of the twigs upon their faces when brushing through
> them in the dark either could pronounce upon the species of the tree
> whence they stretched . . . They knew by a glance at a trunk if its
> heart were sound, or tainted with incipient decay . . . The artifices of
> the season were seen by them from the conjuror's own point of view,
> and not from that of the spectator.

It is at this point that most Hardy critics are inclined to
stop, for like many urban intellectuals they are extremely susceptible to pastoral delights. But Hardy's attitude is more complex, tough-spirited and inconsistent than is usually allowed. A
strict adherence to his philosophical position would have confined him to the view, common enough among a later generation
of writers, that the natural world is neither benevolent nor
malicious but ethically neutral. In his notebook for 1865 Hardy
wrote: "The world does not despise us; it only neglects us." So
he continued formally to believe, but nevertheless found it hard,
as must anyone raised in the shadow of Christianity, to accept
a world stolidly indifferent to mankind. He had an overwhelming
need to spiritualize nature, and if he could not provide good

spirits he would settle for bad. At times he wrote as if there were lurking in nature a consciousness that schemed to harm mankind. Yet even when toying with this cosmic misanthropy—an attitude very much in conflict with his philosophical opinions— Hardy was closer to Wordsworth than, say, to Conrad, for as novelist and poet he continued to attribute meaning to the universe. A post-Romantic, he remained enthralled by romanticism.

Again like Wordsworth, Hardy favors a harmonious submission to the natural order, and such figures of suffering and patience as Gabriel Oak and Giles Winterbourne testify to the strength of that belief. It is correct to say, as does John Holloway, that in Hardy's world "the great disaster for an individual is to be *déraciné*"; but to say this and no more, is not to say enough. For in his best novels, turning sharply away from Wordsworth and the whole nature mystique, Hardy becomes emotionally entangled with such rebellious figures as Clym Yeobright and Jude Fawley, who decide to separate themselves from their environment and pay the price of estrangement. Hardy believes in the virtues of passivity, but somewhat as with Hawthorne, his strongest creative energies are stirred by the assertiveness of men defining themselves apart from and in opposition to the natural order. At the end he draws away from them and must punish their claims to self-sufficiency, yet in his heart of hearts he loves them. There is a repeated conflict between the principle of submission and the temptation of the promethean; and from this conflict derives a large part of the drama and vitality in his novels.

What Hardy gained, then, from his possession of Wessex was a fictional world sharply contoured and superbly known, so that the very setting of his novels and poems seems a force making for dramatic control and personality. He composed his works under the pressures of an inescapable subject—the fate of Wessex —as it came welling up in memory, a subject he had neither to discover nor improvise but merely submit to. Wessex was his fixed principle of order and recollection, the constant about which he could maneuver the modernist variables of rebellion and doubt—until, by *Jude the Obscure,* Wessex too began to crumble in his imagination and the further writing of fiction became, for him, impossible.

For the purpose of analysis we can distinguish among the

phases of Hardy's conviction, but in the experience of the living man, as in the texture of his best work, the Dorset countryman and the disciple of nineteenth century skepticism are closely intertwined. If there was a radical break between his Christian upbringing and his conversion to philosophical naturalism, there were also strong elements of continuity, not least of all a tie between the timeless folk pessimism that clung to Dorset Christianity and the vision he found in Darwin of life as an unrelenting struggle. The young man who composed the Wessex idyll of *Under the Greenwood Tree* was the same young man who grew excited by Herbert Spencer's doctrine of "the Unknowable." Hardy's experience was continuous and unified: the "advanced" thought of the 1860s which in effect became his lifelong persuasion allowed him to look back upon Dorset with a certain ironical distance, but this merely complicated and enriched his affections, it did not dissolve them.

Hardy continued to love the country parsons long after he had ceased to believe what they kept repeating from generation to generation. He loved the old rituals and observances, though increasingly for their own esthetic sake. He became a skeptic, not with the sneer of the disbeliever who rejoices in shaking off priestly bonds nor the indifference of a rationalist for whom faith is never an option, but with the gnawing and tender regret of the lapsed Christian. "I have been looking for God 50 years," he wrote toward the end of his life, "and I think that if he existed I should have discovered him." From the pen of a twentieth century writer such a remark might seem merely flippant; from Hardy it is simple honesty. In one of his poems, "God's Funeral," this tangle of feelings is exposed with candor:

> I could not buoy their faith; and yet
> Many I had known; with all I sympathized;
> And though struck speechless, I did not forget
> That what was mourned for, I, too, long had prized.

Even after Hardy turned away from Christianity, its modes of perception remained fixed in his consciousness. What he had ceased to believe influenced his work at least as much as what he now felt obliged to think. Yet think he did, throughout his life, with an earnestness that merits respect even when the results do not permit admiration. Had he been better educated, he would no doubt still have been a skeptic, but he might have learned to be somewhat wary of his skepticism. As it is, he was overawed by the mechanistic determinism, the vision of existence as a lawful but purposeless process, which nineteenth century science seemed to enforce. Denying the presence of a transcendent mover or primal cause, he tried to locate some principle within the universe that might explain the emergence of consciousness from insentient matter, and this he called the Immanent Will. In *The Dynasts* the Ancient Spirit of the Years announces:

> The cognizance ye mourn, Life's doom to feel,
> If I report it meetly, came unmeant,
> Emerging with blind gropes from impercipience,
> By listless sequence—luckless, tragic choice,
> In your more human tongue.

Meanwhile Hardy worried about the place of human beings in this impersonal scheme of things. The doctrine of Immanent Will allowed him to express a mild hopefulness, what he called "meliorism," in regard to the ultimate destiny of the race: consciousness, slowly creeping through the centuries, might elevate itself to higher forms. But in the immediate historical moment he could not avoid the view that man's place in the universe is pitifully small, that his possibility for freedom of choice or action is equally small, and that "Crass Casualty" rules over human affairs with a brute indifference. Plenty of statements to this effect can be extracted from Hardy's writings, yet it is important to remark that his distinguished work rests upon a vision of life that is a good deal more dramatic, complex and unsettled. Hardy's world-view—what he called his "idiosyncratic mode of regard" —is something quite different from, and far less reducible to a few leaden axioms, than his formal philosophy. The philosophy inspires and inhabits certain novels and poems; through sluggish assertion, it mars a number of them; but it is not what those novels and poems are significantly about. To reduce Hardy's work to a few stock opinions (such as can be found in any handbook of metaphysics) is a critical disservice.[2]

2. Is that not what T. S. Eliot did in his notorious attack upon Hardy? The work of the late Thomas Hardy [wrote Eliot] represents an interesting

In the thought of Mill, Huxley and Spencer, the three writers who form the decisive influence upon the young Hardy, there was little, if anything, inherently "pessimistic." These vigorous men believed they were freeing themselves and others from superstition and ignorance; most of their supporters responded with an optimism and a faith in progress that has come to seem a little naive. Why then did Hardy react so differently to ideas he too regarded as liberating?

Now the melancholy and pessimism of tone that run through Hardy's work do not in themselves require special justification. All through Western literature there is a deep current of despair, for which the experience of mankind would seem to provide a sufficient warrant. Had Hardy done no more than follow in the tradition of the Greek dramatists he loved so intensely, that would have required no special explanation and one might simply have assumed that certain elements of his temperament disposed him toward a dark vision of life. Indeed, such an assumption—even if it comes to little more than a confession of our inability to explain a writer's deepest bias—can still plausibly be held in regard to Hardy's work.

What does constitute a problem is that in accepting the general outlook of Huxley, Mill and Spencer, and while judging this to be a kind of intellectual liberation, Hardy should have responded not with their combative energy and hope but with

---

example of a powerful personality uncurbed by any institutional attachment or even by submission to any objective beliefs; unhampered by ideas, even by what sometimes acts as a partial restraint upon inferior writers, the desire to please a large public. He seems to me to have written as nearly for the sake of "self-expression" as a man well can, and the self which he had to express does not strike me as a particularly wholesome or edifying matter of communication.

This is wrong, through and through, and small-spirited as well. What happened to Hardy's "powerful personality" was precisely that it *was* curbed by an institutional attachment (something clearly different from an affiliation). A churchy man, as he called himself, Hardy lived by the imperatives of Christian morality, and perhaps a trifle better than later writers whose fretful conversions enabled them to rehearse the letter of dogma but not bend to the spirit of charity. The "self" Hardy revealed in his writings was admirably free from hauteur and snobbism, untarnished by any prejudice, and notable for its moral earnestness, natural piety and encompassing sympathy for human beings. That the author of *After Strange Gods* should have found this "self" insufficiently wholesome leaves the issue quite as every admirer of Hardy would wish.

his own low-keyed melancholy. Part of the answer is that the advanced skepticism of nineteenth century philosophers could be joined with—and serve to rekindle—the country fatalism which in Dorset lay buried beneath the surface of Christianity and which for Hardy constituted a folk heritage. There may also have been more intimate sources for Hardy's pessimism, perhaps, as some of his biographers intimate, the slow erosion of a marriage which left him childless and disconsolate. But a more fundamental explanation of his dominant temper is that his turn to skepticism shook the very foundation of his being, not as a sudden catastrophe which after a time would settle into rest, but as a constant shudder of disturbance. The truth he had found and from which, as a man of probity, he could not retreat, struck him as bleak; the struggle to liberate himself intellectually left him with a lifelong increment of sadness.

It should not be hard to see why. For someone raised in the comforts of the faith, the conviction that the cause of things is "neither moral nor immoral, but unmoral," can lead to a state of cosmic desolation. Hardy meant to depict the universe in terms of a mechanistic determinism, but so strong was the resistance created toward the new theories by his heritage of Christian feeling, that he fell back at times into a kind of gnosticism, a view of life as predetermined by bad intentions without a discernible figure or force actively intending, or at least a view of life as predetermined by bad luck. Taught to lean on God's benevolence, or at least to count on His attentiveness, a man like Hardy could well feel that the rule of impersonal law is more terrifying than if some "vengeful god" were intent upon spiting humanity—and then later, and almost imperceptibly, the belief in impersonal law might become indistinguishable from a feeling that the "vengeful god" was doing his worst. In place of Creation there was now the evolutionary process, infinitely slow and utterly indifferent to the emotions of men; and this process, as it lumbered through the centuries, left behind it a sediment of cruelty and pain, necessary results of the struggle for existence.

Hardy suspected that as men came to realize how paltry their place was in the scheme of things and how unavoidable the paltriness, they would regard consciousness itself as a burden. For what is the good of knowing when the thing one knows best is how little can be done with knowledge? Like Hardy himself, like Clym Yeobright and Jude Fawley, reflective men would be hopelessly committed to the life of ideas, and in time would learn to envy those country people rooted in the particulars of their existence and free from the torments and vanities of ratiocination. Among them happiness would find "its last refuge on earth," since "among them . . . a perfect insight into the conditions of existence" would be longest postponed. The very development of consciousness which modern life enforces upon men would, in Hardy's view, create an intense dissatisfaction with the limits and frustrations of consciousness; and ultimately the result must be torpor and weariness, the mind caught in its own motions.

This style of reflection is familiar enough in our time, even if we have found a new vocabulary for it, and all one can say in regard to Hardy's claims as a voice of pessimism is that what he lacked in intellectual finesse he made up in emotional strength. His ideas now seem a little frayed, but such as they were, he felt them with an incomparable depth and sincerity:

A woeful fact that the human race is too extremely developed for its corporeal conditions, the nerves being evolved to an activity abnormal in such an environment. Even the higher animals are in excess in this respect. It may be questioned if Nature . . . so far back as when she crossed the line from invertebrates to vertebrates, did not exceed her mission. This planet does not supply the materials for happiness to higher existences.

Those fated for thought have no choice but to suffer:

. . . what we gain by science is, after all, sadness, as the Preacher saith. The more we know of the laws and nature of the Universe the more ghastly a business one perceives it all to be . . .

As a thinker, Hardy could do no more than restate in his own idiom the assumptions dominating the advanced circles of his time. (Yet this restatement, here and again in his novels, can be curiously impressive; for the ideas of T. H. Huxley transposed or twisted into the vocabulary of Wessex take on a piquant urgency, revealing that beneath widely different styles of speech there are often profound similarities of idea and mood.) In any case, Hardy's true power derives far less from his ideas as such than from his intuitive grasp of what their triumph might mean for the nerves of sensitive men. Hardy refers, for example, to "the ache of modernism," and that striking phrase points not only to Clym Yeobright's and Jude Fawley's troubles, but also to the keenness with which he could imagine the effect of intellectual change upon exposed human beings. In *Tess of the D'Urbervilles* he speaks of "the chronic melancholy which is taking hold of the civilized races with the decline of belief in a beneficent Power," and in *Jude the Obscure* the hero remarks that a new breed of boys "unknown to the last generation" is springing up: "They seem to see all [of life's] terrors before they are old enough to resist them . . . It is the beginning of the universal wish not to live." Such insights, caught in the first of these two sentences and then dramatically fleshed in the novel itself, are more striking by far than Hardy's formal ideas; yet it must also be acknowledged that if Hardy had not struggled so earnestly and clumsily to improvise a philosophic structure as a replacement for religious faith, he would probably not have reached his insights along the way. For these come from a man who has known the torments of doubt, the pain of discovering that no idea can ever satisfy the desires that have given it birth, the whole exhausting and draining effort of the intellectual life. Hardy's very lust for metaphysics helped to enlarge and deepen his sympathies for other men, for all those who were fumbling toward some notion or intuition by which to enclose the chaos of events.

Neither as a traditionalist alone nor a modernist alone is Hardy at his best. In the first role he is sometimes too self-conscious, and in the second too uncritical. His writing, at its most distinguished, displays a unique convergence of traditional and modern, both impulses in a fruitful entanglement, neither in harmony nor struggle but in a kind of sustaining friction one with the other. The weight of the past looms large in Hardy's experience, and so too does the uncertainty of the modern world as he begins to glimpse it. Through this strange union, Hardy could brush past the conventionalities of moralism and optimism which had virtually asphyxiated official nineteenth century England: and that is one reason he continues to live for us in a way that other, more "solid" writers do not. The pessimistic anxieties of a modern intellectual rub against the stoic bias of a country mind; "modern nerves," as Hardy writes in *The Wood-landers*, against "primitive feelings"; skepticism against super-stition. And one result is that in his best work—four or five novels, a few dozen poems—Hardy achieves a rare sense of inclusiveness: the natural together with the historical, the timeless with the time-bound, the inescapable limitations of all existence with the particular troubles of the moment. Hardy may be an awkward philosopher, his ideas all too marked by the fashions of his day; but there are recurrent moments in all his Wessex novels when he achieves something far more valuable than any philosophy, his own deeply considered and contemplative wisdom. Some-times this wisdom appears in transient remarks coiling their way about a bit of narrative; sometimes in pieces of dumb show, small but revealing incidents, which display the presence of a writer who brings to bear upon his work an enormous reserve of experience and reflection.

Entertainments and Digressions

HARDY'S DEVELOPMENT AS A WRITER OF FICTION was slow and hesitant. It is easy enough to see in retrospect where his strongest talent lay: in those novels, beginning with *Under the Greenwood Tree* and ending with *Jude the Obscure,* which explore the life of Wessex while moving beyond it in range and implication. But in the experience of the young man who had begun to write novels in the 1870s there could be no such certainty. He had to fumble his way toward his true interests, and as a provincial who had come to know and admire the intellectual circles of London, he had a somewhat exaggerated respect for the advice he got from its established literary men.

When George Meredith told Hardy in 1868 to abandon his first manuscript, *The Poor Man and the Lady,* because it was too harshly satiric in tone and instead to write a story "with a purely artistic purpose, giving it a more complicated 'plot,' " the young writer soon obeyed. The result was *Desperate Remedies,* a novel groaning with plot, and published anonymously in 1871 through a subsidy provided by Hardy himself. The next novel, *Under the Greenwood Tree,* was begun after John Morley, then a reader for Macmillan, told Hardy that he admired a scene in *The Poor Man and the Lady* describing the countryfolk of Wessex. Then, while Hardy was working on the serial version of *A Pair of Blue Eyes,* he encountered Leslie Stephen, editor of the *Cornhill Magazine.* Stephen spoke well of *Under the Greenwood Tree* and asked Hardy to do a serial for his magazine that would have a similar setting but be somewhat fuller in incident: "Though I do not want a murder in every number, it is necessary to catch the attention of readers by some distinct and well-arranged plot." Again Hardy obliged, this time with *Far from the Madding Crowd,* a novel rich with incident.

The point is not that Hardy was a trimmer—he was not. It is rather that, since the days of his youth when he had begun writing poetry, he could not take the art of fiction with full seriousness. And as a young man trying to catch up with the latest advances in knowledge, he was bound to listen to men as genuinely distinguished as Meredith, Morley and Stephen—indeed, he was fortunate even to have gained their notice. The major line of Hardy's fiction begins to develop during this first decade of publication; it consists of *Under the Greenwood Tree, Far from the Madding Crowd* and *The Return of the Native,* works that are preparatory to the great novels of his later years. These three books I propose to discuss in the following chapter, while stopping here for a glance at the secondary fiction of the years 1870-80.

Unfortunately the received opinion of Hardy's minor fiction is largely correct. One can read these novels with starts of pleasure. One feels a sudden hope that there is something to be rediscovered, a claim to be staked or an injustice corrected. But the truth is that the sudden brilliance of a passage in *Desperate Remedies,* the pictorial charm of a chapter in *The Trumpet Major,* the liveliness of the opening section in *Two on a Tower* do not lead to sustained distinction. The Hardy enthusiast can patch together an imagined anthology of bits and pieces that, in isolation, would make these novels seem better than in fact they are; but there is no likelihood they will ever again come into general currency.

As a convenience I propose to consider these minor novels as entertainments and/or digressions. By an entertainment I mean what Graham Greene has said about some of his own books: they can be exciting pastimes, they are not to be despised, they are sometimes put together with craftsmanship, but finally they are not to be taken as serious works of art. The digressions are those novels in which Hardy simply wandered away from his true interests, writing about segments of experience concerning which he was ill equipped or ill attuned. The distinction is by no means inexorable, and it is clear that some of the weaker fictions can fall equally well into either group.

Un sombre récit de terreur à la Wilkie Collins—so a French literary historian has described *Desperate Remedies*. It is a good description. Sensational in every sense of the word, this book is crammed with events: a murder, a suicide, an attempted rape, a rip-roaring fight, a semi-lesbian incident, a death through falling from a church tower, a strange disease, a scene in which three characters simultaneously and unknown to one another spy on the Byronic villain, a dream by the heroine that "she was being whipped with dry bones suspended on strings," and much more. The appetite for the lurid, the violent and the mystifying, be it Victorian or not, is satisfied to the full; one can read the book as a mystery novel, a quasi-Gothic thriller (still, in spots, pretty thrilling) and a crude but forceful anticipation of Hardy's talents. *Desperate Remedies* is one of the most interesting bad novels in the English language, bad with verve, bad with passion, bad (one might even say) with distinction.

When the book first appeared in 1871, there began Hardy's lifelong ordeal under the lash of reviewers' judgments. One of these, in *The Spectator*, hurt badly: "the bitterness of that moment," Hardy would remember, "was never forgotten; at the time he wished he were dead." Yet it was an intelligent notice, particularly if some allowance is made for the priggishness of the age. *The Spectator* complained that the novel contained no original characters "to extend one's knowledge of human nature" and "no display of passion except of the brute kind" (neither charge quite true); but it added that the book showed "an unusual and very happy facility in catching and fixing phases of peasant life . . . not the manners and language only, but the tone of thought," and that "the nameless author has one other talent of a remarkable kind—sensitiveness to scenic and atmospheric effects. . . ."

The outer form of the novel is mostly nonsense, a farrago of incidents that require more ingenuity for their ordering than most readers will care to supply. From chapter to chapter, as Albert Guerard has amusingly shown, there are utterly different impulses at work: a tepid love story, a sudden dip into abnormal psychology, "a sheer delight in ingenious detection and . . . a frank delight in the macabre." But there is hardly a chapter in which remarkable happenings are absent. The figure of Miss Aldclyffe, a frustrated middle-aged tyrant, is projected with a force beyond anything else in the novel; she makes Dickens's Miss Havisham seem pallid. Miss Aldclyffe's lesbian proclivities are unmistakable and chilling:

> " 'Tis with you as it is always with girls," she said [to the young heroine, employed as her maid] . . . "You are not, after all, the innocent I took you for. No, no." She then changed her tone with fitful rapidity. "Cytherea, try to love me more than you love him—do. I love you more sincerely than any man can. Do, Cythie; don't let any man stand between us. O, I can't bear that!" She clasped Cytherea's neck again.
> "I must love him now I have begun," replied the other.
> "Must—yes—must," said the elder lady reproachfully. "Yes, women are all alike . . . Find a girl, if you can, whose mouth and ears have not been made a regular highway of by some man or another! . . . O Cytherea, can it be that you, too, are like the rest?"

Whether Hardy knew what he was doing here one cannot be sure; he certainly never wrote anything quite like this again. What is clear is that a good part of the book acquires its interest from the repeated upsurge of barely controlled psychic materials, and that these take on the force of crude revelation. If *Desperate Remedies* is not exactly a work of art, it contains the potentialities and raw evidence of art. Had Hardy been more fully in command of his imagination, he would have achieved a smoother semblance of Wilkie Collins but a less striking book. Inconceivable though it may be that the novel will ever be read by any large public, the occasional reader who, out of curiosity or accident, picks up *Desperate Remedies* will now and again be shaken by its coarse and indefensible power. Beneath the innocent bombast a novelist is at work.

At work, but by no means secure in his method or intention. Hardy's second published novel, *Under the Greenwood Tree,* comes directly from his creative strength, but there is no evidence that as yet he could sharply distinguish among his kinds and levels of achievement. At the least, however, he would never again have to face the humiliation of vanity publishing. This time Hardy's book was accepted by the publisher Tinsley under terms customary at the time—Hardy received thirty pounds for the copyright and could feel he was finally launched on a literary career. When *Under the Greenwood Tree* came out in 1872 it was amiably received by the reviewers, who could yield to its charm without having to confront the linked threats of agnosticism and innovation. But the book did not sell enough to allow Hardy to live entirely by his writing; and still not certain as to what he wished to or could make of his life, he continued to accept independent commissions as an architect. Young, energetic and reasonably ambitious, hoping that he would soon have an income sufficient for marrying Emma Gifford, Hardy worked with a will during these years, mostly as an architect by day and a novelist by night. He was, by all accounts, a talented architect who might have gone ahead to a successful career. His feelings for the profession he would soon abandon were both strong and authentic. During these years he developed his strong distaste for the "restoration" of church Gothic; he had "gone personally from parish to parish through a considerable district, and compared existing churches there with records, traditions and memories of what they formerly were." Nevertheless, he was gradually withdrawing from architecture, and at the suggestion of the shrewd Tinsley, he now tried to earn his living by the composition of magazine serials. For the next twenty-five years he would keep laboring at novel writing, first in the form of serials, with whatever truncations were required, and then as books in which his original intentions were "restored." But with the exception of *Far from the Madding Crowd*, the next few serials were singularly unimpressive.

A Pair of Blue Eyes (1873) drew both on fragments of earlier unpublished material and Hardy's recollections of courting Emma Gifford. The book seems closer to his own experience than those immediately before or after it, yet is mostly flat and lifeless. In fairness, however, it should be reported that *A Pair of Blue Eyes* has frequently been praised, by a number of Hardy's critics, by such English literary men as Tennyson and Coventry Patmore, and by Americans like William Dean Howells and William Lyon Phelps. The book seems to have a special appeal to readers with a taste for paleness.

The setting is the rough Cornish coast, where Hardy first came to know his wife. The story concerns a young architect of plebeian birth, Stephen Smith, who sets out to woo but does not win Elfride Swancourt, fickle daughter of a local clergyman. One might imagine that Hardy would be stirred by a love affair in which class snobbism trips the young lovers; but there is little evidence of emotional charge or involvement, and the writing is mostly inert. What one misses here is Hardy's personal voice, both as it makes for intensity and can slip into bad taste. Stephen is pallid, Elfride a watery anticipation of Hardy's perverse heroines, and as for the third figure, Henry Knight, he is no help at all. Imagine a man said to be a reviewer for a serious London journal, a cosmopolitan in his thirties, who has yet to kiss a girl! Perhaps in the Victorian context this is not completely implausible, yet even if barely credible, so passive a submission to the pieties of the age makes Knight a wearisome character. Replacing Stephen in Elfride's roomy heart, he is shaken to discover that in the past, through a few saucy kisses, she has been less pure than himself. Shades of Joseph Andrews.

Now it is true that in reading fiction of an earlier time we must tell ourselves that certain customs and constraints have to be accepted if we are to reach whatever is enduring in the work. But for about two-thirds of the way *A Pair of Blue Eyes* is so disconcertingly at ease with Victorian customs and constraints that little strikes the eye except the dated and the faded. And yet, as almost always with Hardy, there is a surprise in store. Having written most of the novel half awake, he finally shakes himself into life and in the second half composes two striking chapters, an adventure on a cliff and a tragi-comedy on a train.

Walking along the Cornish coast with Elfride, Henry Knight becomes entangled on "the Cliff without a Name." He slips. He is in danger of falling to his death. The thought of death energizes him as nothing in life seemed able to; he "felt himself"—the sentence could have come straight from Conrad—"in the presence of a personalized loneliness." And Hardy himself starts to write as if *his* life were at stake:

. . . opposite Knight's eyes was an imbedded fossil, standing forth
in low relief from the rock. It was a creature with eyes. The eyes,
dead and turned to stone, were even now regarding him. It was one
of those early crustaceans called Trilobites. Separated by millions of
years, Knight and this underling seemed to have met in their place
of death . . .
      The creature represented but a low type of animal existence, for
never in their vernal years had the plains indicated by those number-
less slaty layers been traversed by an intelligence worthy of the name.
Zoophytes, mollusca, shell-fish, were the highest developments of those
ancient dates. The immense lapses of time each formation represented had known nothing of the dignity of man. They were grand
times, but they were mean times too, and mean were their relics.
He was to be with the small in his death.

And then, in what Hardy must have meant as a mockery of
the Victorianism that has thus far dominated the novel, Elfride
discreetly strips herself of her "linen," makes a firm rope out of
it, and drags Knight to safety. Lucky fellow: had he been forced
to depend on what a twentieth century girl uses for "linen," he
would have hurtled straight into the abyss.

The final chapter brings Smith and Knight together on a train,
each intent upon asking once more for Elfride's hand and meanwhile arguing irritably their "rights" in courtship. Neither yet
knows that the dear girl has already married a nobleman, died
from a miscarriage, and now, in her coffin, accompanies them as a
fellow passenger. It is a mordant touch, mordant but also comic.
Rejected lovers and fateful coffin reach their destination together,
back at Cornwall, and the lovers learn that, having been dis-
placed by a man of decision, they cannot even claim the right to
intimate mourning. The one in his timidity and the other in his
righteousness must now recognize themselves as failures, and a
little foolish too, as together they walk away from Elfride's grave.
Most novels end poorly, even many good ones; this poor novel
ends well, with a fine spray of malice.

For the next decade or so Hardy's work continues on a most
uneven course, and only with the publication of *The Mayor of
Casterbridge* in 1886 will he enter his period of mastery as a
novelist. The unevenness is brought into relief by the fact that
within a space of two or three years Hardy could publish so distinguished a novel as *Far from the Madding Crowd* and something so execrable as *The Hand of Ethelberta*. And meanwhile,

all through the 1870s, Hardy was facing the problems encountered by most professional writers: he was harassed, he wrote too
much, he needed money, he raced to complete serial installments,
he was pestered by bores, he tried to keep up with new ideas, he
suffered conflicts between his career and his personal life.

In 1873 his friend Horace Moule died, perhaps a suicide, and
for Hardy the loss was shattering. He felt himself, for the first
time, without intellectual guidance, without a mentor who could
advise, correct, improve and solace. No one would ever quite replace Moule, though the man who would come closest was Leslie
Stephen, for whom Hardy quickly gained admiration and respect.
The rocky path of agnostic rationalism along which Stephen was
making his way was also Hardy's, though the exhilaration Stephen
claimed to feel upon abandoning Christian pieties Hardy by no
means shared. Austere in his own intellectual work, Stephen as
editor was quite ready to make his peace with the world; a primary criterion for choosing fiction for the *Cornhill Magazine,*
he said, was "Thou shalt not shock a young lady." Nothing but
this exalted commandment could explain the fact that, after
printing *Far from the Madding Crowd,* Stephen rejected *The Return of the Native.* No doubt there have been greater blunders in
literary history, but this one was notable enough.

With the success of *Far from the Madding Crowd,* Hardy became established as an English novelist. His books could now be
expected to sell at least moderately well and to receive steady,
often respectful attention from the reviewers. Stephen, despite his
flabbiness as an editor, was a strong and sensible influence. He
kept urging Hardy to work his own vein and not try to imitate
the masters who had come before him in nineteenth century English fiction. And aware of how pitifully thin-skinned Hardy was
to criticism, Stephen gave him some advice that makes as much
sense today as when it was first offered:

> I think as a critic, that the less authors read of criticism the better.
> You have a perfectly fresh and original vein, and I think the less you
> bother yourself about critical canons the less chance there is of your
> becoming self-conscious and cramped. . . . We are generally a poor
> lot, horribly afraid of not being in the fashion, and disposed to give
> ourselves airs on very small grounds.

The success of *Far from the Madding Crowd* also enabled

Hardy to marry Emma Gifford in the fall of 1874. For a time they were extremely happy; and only in retrospect can one measure the full irony of Mrs. Hardy's remark that in marrying the man who would compose *The Dynasts* and coin the phrase "Immanent Will," she felt herself under the guidance of "an Unseen Power of great benevolence."

Eager now to enlarge both his income and reputation, Hardy struck out in a radically new direction. He had already published an adventure story, a prose idyll, a romance and a novel about country life; he did not wish, as we would now say, to be "typed" as the man who wrote about shepherds. He would therefore try a comedy of London society, in which he had by now spent a fair amount of time. The result was a fiasco.

Behind *The Hand of Ethelberta* (1876) stands a strong array of influences—indeed, some of the major English novelists. The heroine, a talkative and rather likable adventuress, comes straight out of Thackeray: she is Becky without the sharpness, a climber without claws. Her coarse but worthy brothers, true-blue English workmen, are drawn from Dickens, but without a sufficient sweep of color or caricature. And the world into which Ethelberta elbows her way, a world of languid dinner parties and limp dialogue, is Meredith smudged—for Hardy could no more describe a sophisticated party than Meredith a Wessex milking.

Echoes do not a fiction make, but they can certainly fill several hundred pages in a serial; and the sad truth is that *Ethelberta* did better for Hardy financially than he did for Ethelberta artistically. Not that she lacks possibilities. Daughter of a butler, she rises in the world through beauty and ruse, allowing her former lover to dangle but taking care not to marry him. Ethelberta achieves a few piquant moments, but she fails to settle into a coherent figure, mostly because Hardy cannot make up his mind whether he is doing pure farce, a comedy of manners or a social documentary. None of these literary options is fully taken, and each interferes with the other.

To indicate that the book was meant as no more than an entertainment, Hardy subtitled it "A Comedy in Chapters." Unfortunately, the chapters are more noticeable than the comedy. Hardy thought the book was poorly received because of "its quality of unexpectedness—that unforgiveable sin in the critic's eyes"; but he was sadly and completely mistaken. One critical reaction, however, does throw some oblique light on his situation. Mrs. Hardy disliked the book because too many of the characters were servants.

Throughout the late 1870s the Hardys spent part of their time in Dorset and part in London. In 1876 they took a pretty cottage overlooking the Dorset Stour, at Sturminster Newton, where they lived in contentment for two years while Hardy wrote some verse and *The Return of the Native*. Hardy's notebooks for these years show scattered signs of melancholy, but these appear to be mostly of a philosophic kind, native to his temperament and not caused, or not yet caused, by the disagreements with his wife that would leave both of them distraught and estranged. There were no children, and that was reason for unhappiness. With time it became clear that there were also deep ethical and intellectual differences. Mrs. Hardy was both more pious and more worldly. Either of these alone Hardy might have been able to cope with; the two together were beyond him.

In 1878 they returned for a stay in London, where Hardy was now being treated as a famous writer, a catch for hostesses, and a peer among the dominant literary men of the day. He began his researches into the Napoleonic war that would lay the foundation for *The Dynasts* and be put to more immediate use in *The Trumpet Major* (1880), the one among his books that is most clearly meant as an entertainment. Both popular and productive, Hardy was also writing short stories, partly in response to editorial requests and partly as fragments and miniatures in his major creative enterprise, the depiction of the world of Wessex.

The Trumpet Major is a pleasant tale set in Wessex during the time of the Napoleonic wars, when Boney seemed more of a devil than Satan himself and the threat of invasion thoroughly frightened the solid villagers who pass through the book—some of them drawn to the very life, others mere copies from the English masters. Hardy worked up the period thoroughly, though its spirit he knew better than any historian could, for he was relying upon stories and legends, the oral sediment of a strong local experience, which he had kept since boyhood. And this intimacy of knowledge is a real strength: it ensures that even when the story drags, which happens more frequently than its admirers care to acknowledge, it will retain the substance of authenticity. By no means always interesting, *The Trumpet Major* is rarely false.

There hovers over the book an eighteenth century air, not so much that of Fielding as of Goldsmith: amiable domestic comedy, English ways and stuff, a moderate toying with sentiment, and a world utterly at home with itself. Hardy is for once quite without intellectual ambition, he has nothing whatever to prove and not very much to say, he can relax in the pleasures of memory and portraiture. In its mild masculinity, the prose stays comfortably close to the middle register, not at all sublime and rarely awkward. You will not find here the qualities that make Hardy an unforgettable novelist, nor those that make him an unbearable one.

The Trumpet Major yields small, steady pleasures in pictorial set-pieces and verbal charms. "My sight," says an old man, "is so gone off lately that things, one and all, be but a November mist to me." A seed cake made for the miller's son Robert is "so richly compounded that it opened to the knife like a freckled buttercup." And in describing the strong beer of Casterbridge, Hardy became rapturous:

> It was one of the most beautiful colours that the eye of an artist in beer could desire; full in body, yet brisk as a volcano; piquant, yet without a twang; luminous as an autumn sunset; free from streakiness of taste; but finally, rather heady. The masses worshipped it, the minor gentry loved it more than wine, and by the most illustrious country families it was not despised.

With equal charm Hardy sketches in local speech and manners. The miller Loveday—father of John and Robert, brothers who cross one another in love and compete, unequally, in loyalty—is a nicely recognizable Englishman of the kind that can be found anywhere in English fiction: warmhearted, well fleshed, slow-minded. John Loveday, reticent and true, is more keenly imagined, and through him Hardy pencils a thin line of controlled sadness which touches our heart, yet heartlessly serves to ratify our comfort in the happy resolution of the plot. By virtue of his character John should win the girl whom he loves more faithfully than Robert can; but Anne Garland cares more for Robert's vivacity, his bubbly talk, his *interestingness:* a quality that seems always to stir Hardy's, and usually the world's, ingenues. At the end, with a not unpleasant throb, the Trumpet Major goes off to a hero's death.

Most of the action is stock, as are all the characters except John Loveday, about whom Hardy cared more than his book required him to. But to say this is not necessarily to fault the novel, since domestic comedy depends upon steadily assuring the reader that all will end well and most prove familiar. Hardy twists the plot just enough to evoke that mild equivalent of anxiety which comedy requires if it is to have a sufficient complication; but except for the Trumpet Major's end, nothing is pushed very far, neither insight nor narrative. The plot satisfies, mostly because we need pay it no special attention, but also because it is flexible enough to allow intervals of byplay ranging from pure adventure, such as Robert Loveday's escape from a press-gang, to pure buffoonery, such as the bluster of Festus Derriman, the pseudo-Shakespearian clown.

Yet, when all pleasures have been acknowledged and virtues registered, too much can be made of this novel, as indeed too much has been, both by the beef-and-ale critics of an earlier generation and those of the present, like the *Scrutiny* group, who do not really like Hardy's major fiction. The rustics, and especially the lumbering Festus, become predictably familiar: yes, one feels, Hardy can do that vaudeville again. And as for the leading figures, they are neither picturesque nor bold enough to succeed simply as portraits of surface.

The book suffers, unavoidably, from certain changes in the history of taste. Hardy allows himself an even-paced treatment, and his characters a luxuriance of speech, that by now is likely to seem unwarranted.[1] One stretches for comparisons with second-rank eighteenth century fiction, Fanny Burney or some of Smollett, where there is also an untested assumption that the mere recapture of local detail and the mere graphing of a plot will suffice to hold interest. Such writing is flawed by a naive faith in the intrinsic value of verisimilitude, the charms of representativeness and adept color—or so it is likely to seem from the distance

1. Arnold Bennett, reading *The Trumpet Major* in 1887, already noted that Hardy employed "an excessively slow method of narration" and that the humor was "obvious and Dickens-like." Yet he added that "somehow his persons have individuality."

of the mid-twentieth century. *The Trumpet Major* can be read at leisure and forgotten with ease.

False starts, digressions and the overreaching of ambition are inevitable in the experience of most writers, but in any final reckoning what matters about the work of Hardy during his first decade as a novelist is not the waste but the solid achievement: *Under the Greenwood Tree, Far from the Madding Crowd*, and *The Return of the Native*. And slowly Hardy was working out his own esthetic of incongruity, which in 1881 he expressed with considerable force:

> The real if unavowed purpose of fiction is to give pleasure by gratifying the love of the uncommon in human experience, mental or corporeal. This is done all the more perfectly in proportion as the reader is illuded to believe the personages true and real like himself. Solely to this latter end a work of fiction should be a precise transcript of ordinary life: but the uncommon would be absent and the interest lost. Hence the writer's problem is, how to strike the balance between the uncommon and the ordinary so as on the one hand to give interest, on the other to give reality. In working out this problem, human nature must never be made abnormal, which is introducing incredibility. The uncommonness must be in the events, not in the characters; and all the writer's art lies in shaping the uncommonness while disguising its unlikelihood, if it be unlikely.

In the years since these lines were written, the vocabulary of literary criticism has changed considerably and perhaps become more sophisticated; but what should strike anyone not victimized by the provinciality of the up-to-date is how strongly the tacit premises of Hardy's thought have persisted into our own time.

The World of Wessex

UNDER THE GREENWOOD TREE, the first of the Wessex novels, is a
fragile evocation of a self-contained country world that in Hardy's
later fiction will come to seem distant and unavailable, a social
memory by which to judge the troubled present. Most of the
major fictional series of the nineteenth and twentieth centuries,
certainly those of Balzac, Hardy and Faulkner, require some
image of a better or at least simpler past as a stimulus for their
criticism of the dominant culture. That image, in Hardy's fiction,
is first provided by *Under the Greenwood Tree,* a pastoral or
prose idyll of English country life in the 1830s, before the intru-
sion of industrialism and modern sentiments.

Though light in tone, the book has a scatter of somewhat realistic detail: the characters work, have a modest share of troubles
and sometimes are rather stupid. Wessex provides Hardy with a
tentative or usable nostalgia, but he seldom approaches it without a complicating irony. Modern readers may have some trouble
in registering this tone, for while we have been trained to an
almost nagging insistence upon irony, our criticism says little
about the ranges of voice that irony can accommodate. Hardy's
irony is mild and affectionate, and what allows him to maintain

it toward the very world eliciting his nostalgia is that this world is utterly his own.

Pastoral has usually been the product of a high culture turning away from its surfeit of experience and, through a posture of simplicity, seeking to regain essential truths. But Hardy's pastoral impulse is quite different: it does not involve a yoking together of literary sophistication and a stylized defense of peasant values. While neither an aristocratic poet stooping to a moment of purity nor an actual shepherd recalling the events of his past, Hardy is, if anything, somewhat closer to the shepherd than to the aristocratic poet; at the very least, he has known shepherds. Hardy's pastoral fiction comes out of a collective experience that is still alive and vivid in his mind, still warm with the breath of the recent past. And one result is that, by and large, he can escape the self-consciousness that seems characteristic of the pastoral mode and allow himself an easy, fraternal irony.

The verse of William Barnes is a tactful pressure on the Hardy who composed *Under the Greenwood Tree,* but readers unfamiliar with Barnes may find themselves looking for comparisons with George Eliot's early fiction or even Mrs. Gaskell's *Cranford.* Simply as a picture of a fading style of life, Hardy's book is superior to both: a masterpiece in miniature. This is Hardy in his happiest, if not greatest, voice, the Hardy who writes with complete assurance about people and places he knows completely, and who writes unburdened by the obligation to be prophetic or morose. Not very concerned here with the secrets or depths of character—not very concerned with the secrets or depths of anything—he is content to record the appearances of the natural world and the surfaces of human foible. *Under the Greenwood Tree* is a book to savor, not dissect. Sly humor in incident, mild delicacies of observation, a faint undertow of narrative poignancy and a tacit assurance that no tragedy will be sprung, no terrors evoked—the note is assuredly minor, and thereby likely to be missed by the kind of twentieth century reader whose ear has been fixed upon magnitudes of volume and intensities of mood.

The first six or seven chapters are the best. It is Christmas Eve, and the Mellstock choir, which in the old-fashioned English way contains violins and wind instruments, is preparing to tramp through the parish singing hymns and carols. Warm-spirited, and soon to be warmed by spirits, the choir goes through the familiar rounds—its pleasures derive from an appraised repetition, year after year—with only an occasional minor annoyance to break the tone of friendliness. The next day, the choir ends at the local "trantor's" (or carrier's) house, where there is abundant drinking, food and dancing.

Hardy's knowledge of every flourish of speech and nuance of custom derives from the fact that he is calling directly upon recollections of his youth. But more: it is a knowledge resting upon an experience that has been sustained at a level deeper than words, beyond the reach of ideas. Everything in these opening chapters unfolds with a marvelous poise, and not merely those aspects that are idyllic, such as the friendly relations among the men of the choir, but also those that lean a little toward domestic realism, such as Hardy's observation that the elder Deweys, even while happily caught up in the Christmas ceremonies, continue their long-standing habit of not speaking to one another. Hardy's characteristic fault of trying to impose an excessive burden of significance upon frail materials is quite absent. Perhaps that is why the book seems only a minor masterpiece.

It is a novel that draws its strength from the life of a community still quite sure of itself, still largely untroubled by intrusions of restlessness, and still able to gain a degree of satisfaction, if not an intense spiritual recovery, from a steady adherence to Christmas rites. Not much religion survives in Wessex, but many values are visible which have their source in a long-flourishing and complex religious culture: a tempered humaneness, an easy flow of sociability, a contentment with economic arrangements, all signs not of primitive or untutored virtue but of the molding presence of a deeply set tradition. What these early chapters display is the charm and restraint of a civilization not at its highest level but still greatly to be respected. An enormous quantity of human history has had to pass across the landscape of Wessex before the simple yet cultivated ways of the Mellstock choir could be maintained. It has taken a lot of tumult to bring a little quiet.

The men of the choir are not sharply individualized; it is precisely the art of the book that they not be. For the pleasure that such writing can yield is a pleasure transcending those notions of difficulty and complexity we allow to modern literature. But skimpily differentiated, the figures in *Under the Greenwood Tree* can neither excite nor alarm us, bore nor repel us, involve us with hidden griefs nor disgust us with brutish violence. No more of them is shown, no more exists, than Hardy's chosen mode requires. They play their parts and play them well. They do not compete for attention or think to steal the show. They are just different enough from one another to form a coherent group. There is Robert Penny, bootmaker, "considered to be a scholar, and always spoke up to that level"; Michael Mail, a trifle melancholy, "who walked as if engaged in studying some subject connected with the surface of the road"; Elias Spinks, who "walked perpendicularly and dramatically"; and—here Hardy becomes tiresome—Thomas Leaf, a weak-minded youth, nervous and pliable, quite ready to join in a discussion of his own mental feebleness, as if it were a force apart from himself.

The talk of these men is pithy and amusing. They discuss the difficulties of singing Number Seventy-eight in the Christmas-carol book:

> "Better try over number seventy-eight before we start, I suppose?" said William, pointing to a heap of old Christmas-carol books on a side table.
> "Wi' all my heart," said the choir generally.
> "Number seventy-eight was always a teaser—always. I can mind him ever since I was growing up a hard boy-chap."
> "But he's a good tune, and worth a mint o' practise," said Michael.
> "He is; though I've been mad enough wi' that tune at times to seize en and tear en all to linnit. Ay, he's a splendid carrel—there's no denying that."
> "The first line is well enough," said Mr. Spinks; "but when you come to 'O, thou man,' you make a mess o't."

They recall their old parson who had given them a free hand in the musical life of the parish:

> "And he was a very honorable good man in not wanting any o' us to come and hear him if we were all on-end for a jaunt or spree, or to bring the babies to be christened if they were inclined to squalling. There's virtue in a man's not putting a parish to spiritual trouble."

The elder Dewey reflects upon the individuality of musical instruments:

"Your brass-man is a rafting dog—well and good; your reed-man is a dab at stirring ye—well and good; your drum-man is a rare bowel-shaker—good again. But I don't care who hears me say it, nothing will spak to your heart wi' the sweetness o' the man of strings!"

Accompanying these rustics through the Christmas ceremonies, Hardy writes with a purity he will never quite reach again. Listen to the opening paragraph, with its precise location of the story in the natural world, a setting animated with the noises of life and itself seeming to converse with its human settlers:

To dwellers in a wood almost every species of tree has its voice as well as its feature. At the passing of the breeze the fir-trees sob and moan no less distinctly than they rock; the holly whistles as it battles with itself; the ash hisses amid its quiverings; the beech rustles while its flat boughs rise and fall. And winter, which modifies the note of such trees as shed their leaves, does not destroy its individuality.

If there is to be a story at all, this portraiture must be complicated with a problem of sorts. It comes in the amiable figure of the Reverend Maybold, who would replace the old choir-band with a modern organ and take for his own the local schoolteacher, Fancy Day. There is a splendid scene in which the choir confronts and suffers rout at the hands of Maybold, a scene in which the climactic speech of Reuben Dewey reflects a turning in the life of Wessex. Perhaps this speech comes a shade too close to eloquence. Yet if we are not too severe in our expectations of realism, it conveys a considerable poignancy:

"Well then, Mr. Mayble, since death's to be, we'll die like men any day you names (excusing my common ways)."
Mr. Maybold bowed his head.
"All we thought was, that for us old ancient singers to be choked off quiet at no time in particular, as now, in the Sundays after Easter, would seem rather mean in the eyes of other parishes, sir. But if we fell glorious with a bit of flourish at Christmas, we should have a respectable end, and not dwindle away at some nameless paltry second-Sunday-after or Sunday-next-before something, that's got no name of his own."

As Hardy remarks in his Preface, the withdrawal of the ordinary parishioners from the musical life of the community, which for them is almost the whole of religious life, signifies that "an important union of interests has disappeared." The phrasing is tactful, but the intent grave. Reuben Dewey's speech marks the beginning of a social disintegration, a loss in self-sufficiency and self-regard. This theme will reach a somber conclusion in Jude Fawley's abandonment of country life, but in *Under the Greenwood Tree* it is lightly touched upon and there remains plenty of local strength and confidence. Hardy remarks about Robert Penny's establishment that

> No sign was over his door; in fact—as with old banks and mercantile houses—advertising in any shape was scorned, and it would have been felt as beneath his dignity to paint up, for the benefit of strangers, the name of an establishment whose trade came solely by connection based on personal respect.

The Hardy rustics are a complicated lot, and quite different from book to book. Here, in the first of the Wessex novels, they seldom appear as the Shakespearian clowns and accessories one finds in the middle novels, nor the somewhat seedy knockabouts of the late ones. Stylized in figure and speech, they have as their essential purpose that they be taken as a miniature community representing ways of life that recede far into the past. What matters most is their collective personality, their composition as a group.

Not that Hardy quite escapes some of the difficulties that will later beset him in depicting his rustics. There is a conflict, though hardly yet an overwhelming one, between his liking for them as figures of a cherished past and his temptation to condescend toward them as agents of "comic relief." Hardy himself seems to have been aware of the difficulty, having remarked at a later time that he regretted his treatment of the rustics in *Under the Greenwood Tree* as "penned so lightly, even so farcically and flippantly at times." The point has been made more stringently by an English critic of the *Scrutiny* group, Frank Chapman, who finds the book marred by an "irritatingly facetious tone . . . Hardy cannot stop patronizing his rustics, and there is an unpleasant effect of performing animals going through their tricks." Now it may be presumptuous for an American to speak with any assurance on this matter, since it clearly involves nuances of tact and tradition which depend upon local knowledge. Nevertheless, I venture the opinion that passages in Hardy which may seem patronizing to a modern reader might have had a radically different impact upon those of his contemporaries who knew and were at ease with the world he portrayed. For a poet like Barnes or a novelist like Hardy it was possible to smile at and even make fun of a community like Wessex: it would still remain theirs, beyond doubt or disloyalty. That Chapman hears a "facetious tone" may reflect not so much Hardy's condescension as a modern intellectual's self-consciousness and good will, with the self-consciousness an unavoidable consequence of the good will. Yet it is only fair to add that even if this defense of Hardy be accepted, it does not justify his harping upon poor Leaf's simplemindedness, a literary mannerism later repeated with the vaudeville timidities of Joseph Poorgrass in *Far from the Madding Crowd*. Like too many nineteenth century English writers, which may really be a way of saying like Charles Dickens, Hardy assumed that if it was amusing to notice the idiosyncrasies of a character, it would be all the more amusing to notice them over and over again.

Once the Mellstock choir has been defeated, the book splits in half and there follows, as a complication of plot, a mild romance which bears some elements of social snobbism. In Fancy Day, Hardy even anticipates a trifle his later concern with feminine perversity. All of this has its charm, but mostly a charm that is stock. Hardy does tie the two parts of the book together: Fancy Day, though beginning to suppose herself a bit superior to the Mellstock folk, is still ready to marry the healthy young Dewey, rather than the cultivated outsider Maybold, and thereby, it can be said, the rural community shows its continuing resilience and cohesiveness. The earlier defeat of the choir, it now turns out, is not yet crucial. But to read the final chapters in this way is to reflect upon their theme rather than attend to their life, and in regard to a novel where the surface is so finely brushed and the performance so finely charming, that would be an unfortunate emphasis. The dancing and eating at the wedding of the two young people—whose romance Hardy has kept at an appropriate masque-like distance—bring the men of the Mellstock choir back to front center. There is pleasure in this denouement, as there has been throughout, yet one cannot help wishing, greedily, that Hardy had been able to keep to that vein of his genius which in this book is by far the purest.

If *Under the Greenwood Tree* is a triumph in miniature, *Far from the Madding Crowd* releases a range of potentially major talents. *Far from the Madding Crowd* has never quite received its due from Hardy's critics, even those inclined to give him un-qualified praise; only Virginia Woolf has seen the book for what it really is, a spectacle of country life brimming with an energy and charm such as we do not customarily associate with Hardy. The point is not that his critics fail to grade properly a novel which by no stretch of affection could be called major; the point is that they fail to indicate how lively and various a work it is.

It is not a book to stir the deeper passions, like *Tess,* nor to assault one with grating intensities, like *Jude;* it remains mostly on the plane of external conduct and brute action; and it can be fully enjoyed only by those readers sophisticated enough to con-tent themselves for a time with the pleasures of surface repre-sentation. But *Far from the Madding Crowd* is also the first of the Wessex novels to bring into play Hardy's greatest gift as a writer of fiction—his gift for those compressed incidents or mini-ature dramas, sometimes spoken and sometimes mere dumb show, which in a page or two illuminate whole stretches of experience. Later, Hardy would speak of these as "moments of vision."

Primarily this is a work of pictures highly colored, roles grandly accepted, gestures boldly made, actions quickly taken. The values of the book emerge not from the moral reflections or psychic dis-coveries of the characters, but from the controlled patterns of the action itself. There is barely visible in these pages the novelist of lassitude and despair we will encounter in the later books. Hardy is caught up with a community sufficiently self-absorbed to be-lieve that within its boundaries everything is to be found that need concern men.

What moves and controls the book is a steady preoccupation with the problem of social discipline: discipline as it is gained through the release and containment of the passions, with both release and containment necessary for psychic growth; discipline as a strength which comes from accepting the fevers of youth, sub-mitting to them, and then slowly, at recognizable cost, struggling to contain them. In Hardy's later novels this kind of discipline usually comes to seem inaccessible, sometimes because his pro-tagonists are too thoroughly in the grip of a rigid prometheanism, sometimes because they have become so deracinated they no longer have any social norms by which to guide their conduct, and sometimes because their society has become so sterile it does not allow them constructive work or moral fulfillment. But here, in the Wessex of this early novel, there is still a flourishing rural community which is vigorous, rooted and productive. The maturity of the central characters is achieved through learning to live with—which is also to say, learning to modify—the accepted norms. Reaching a satisfactory balance between individual passions and social responsibilities, Bathsheba Everdene and Gabriel Oak exemplify the process by which the values of civilization are assimilated into character. The sense of life revealed in these pages is thoroughly conservative in its moral and psychic tone. (Hardy would reverse the usual progression of literary men from youthful rebellion to middle-aged adjustment; he began his career as a novelist with a strong attachment to traditionalism and ended as the spokesman for a tormented iconoclasm.)

The discipline won by Bathsheba signifies a capacity to adjust her strong sexual vanity to the requirements of social existence, and in this novel those requirements are not called into question. As Bathsheba gains in discipline, we do not feel that Hardy is twisting his story or his characters to the mold of some preconception. Indeed, the fact that the novel stays close to the conventions of melodrama makes us less concerned with problems of credibility than we are likely to be in reading his later work. Bathsheba and Gabriel pay heavily, marrying not as shiny adolescents but as scarred adults, and if the novel celebrates maturity, there is also a saving touch of ruefulness in the celebration.

What helps to make the theme of discipline dramatically concrete and to situate it in the experience of the characters is Hardy's stress upon the importance of work in the rural community. Not many nineteenth century English novels so thoroughly define their characters through the work they do or fail to do. Bathsheba, in all her emotional phases, is steadily responsible to her farm and the men who work on it: that proves to be her salvation. Troy neglects his fields as he neglects his wife: it is a crime. Boldwood neglects his fields as he neglects his dignity: it is an illness. Oak speaks through his hands, which are trained to do the work that must be done, regardless of weather, temptation or disappointment. Work makes Oak the center of stability that he is, it gives him an objective reality more significant than his narrow repertoire of feelings.

The theme of discipline is especially right for Wessex, where survival as an independent farmer requires steadiness of habit and application. Though at first it might seem a little somber, this theme can be a stirring one, since until the very end of the book Hardy allows for—and to set off the necessary display of contrasts, requires—a full complement of recklessness among the characters. In its neatly symmetrical structure, by means of which Bathsheba tests, rejects and chooses her lovers, the novel points toward the lesson of control; but meanwhile, it is a vibrant and even exuberant narrative because the action is crowded with that range of excesses which Hardy sees as intrinsic to human nature. There is the excess of Bathsheba's feminine willfulness, the excess of Oak's unmanly patience, the excess of Boldwood's sickened love, the excess of Troy's vanity. The whole atmosphere of the book is marked by excess: a macabre death for Gabriel's sheep, a brilliant rainstorm threatening Bathsheba's farm, a drunken revel of farmhands undone by Troy's liquor, a garish coffin scene and a melodramatic killing of Bathsheba's husband, Sergeant Troy, by the maddened rival, Boldwood. In these strong pages, nature is anything but mild and agreeable; it seems to be driven by the same energies and torn by the same passions that drive and tear the characters. There is a relationship, extremely hard to fix in language, between the characters and the natural setting, a partial sharing in rhythm and motion, upsurge and rest. Hardy, as D. H. Lawrence has remarked, shares a quality "with the great writers, Shakespeare or Sophocles or Tolstoy, this setting behind the small action of his protagonists the terrific action of un-fathomed nature; setting a smaller system of morality, the one grasped and formulated by the human consciousness within the vast, uncomprehended and incomprehensible morality of nature and of life itself . . ."

The discipline Bathsheba and Gabriel reach, through their separations and finally their union, is treated by Hardy as an element in the recurrent struggle between nature and culture, unfocused human desire and its tamed social release. Hardy is especially good at evoking the rhythmical character of this experience, the sense that the suffering and chastening which Gabriel and Bathsheba undergo are part of a common fate, forever to be repeated by each generation. Over and over again, a civilization is assaulted by those who are just on the verge of entering it; a conflict follows; and in the end, the civilization renews its forms, but only by absorbing the energies of the young. Gabriel and Bathsheba, painfully educated to the discipline of civilization, learn finally to discover their true feelings, feelings that would remain largely inaccessible to them except for the severities of discipline. But perhaps all this can be said in a less solemn way. Gabriel and Bathsheba, drawn together by the need to straighten out the management of her farm, discover their social appropriateness for one another—and *thereby* their feelings about one another. Slyly diverging from the romantic expectations he has himself created, Hardy savors the irony of this reversal, but he does not allow it to lessen his appreciation of the solid good sense upon which his hero and heroine will now rebuild their lives.

Bathsheba, by far the most striking figure in the novel, is presented almost entirely from the "outside": she is not, after all, a likely candidate for psychological probing. But if external, her portrait is also notable for its strength. She is the most plastic figure in the book, changing markedly in response to the men who surround her. They are fixed, she is volatile. Hardy sees her first as a vain and high-spirited girl eager for conquest and thoughtless of the price, but later as a young woman who must undertake serious responsibilities which force her to a greater social confidence but also to a depressed realization that what she can do or be is limited by the fact that she is a woman. The coquette must assume a commanding role, and the sudden change of circumstances sets off a finely presented flow of emotional and moral consequences. She thereby becomes an interesting woman.

Not only is Bathsheba meant, as Henry James remarked in his chilly notice of the book, to give "a very intimate sense of a young lady's *womanishness*" (a quality not calculated to put James at his ease). She is also thrust into the ambiguous position of a woman who must assume the social burdens of a man even as she feels herself entering the full bloom of her womanliness. At first this stirs her to vanity and malice, especially in regard to Boldwood, but soon it makes her reflect upon the irksomeness of her position and recognize that she cares more about her sex than her status. She is driven, both by her character and opportunities, to keep testing the limits of her power, the limits of her vanity. Though not bold in ideas, she has little choice but to experiment with her life, to see how far she can or should go in remaining at one and the same time a quite conventional young woman, the head of a rural establishment, and a pretty young thing eager for adoration. Unavoidably, through breakdowns in her authority and affection, she runs into trouble.

Our first sight of Bathsheba comes during one of those lovely vignettes Hardy is so skillful at drawing: a green but pretty girl, she is admiring herself in a mirror as, observed unawares by Gabriel, she rides on top of a pile of furniture heaped on a cart. Toward the end, we see her as a bewildered wife, neither secure in traditional dependence nor able to attain an unconventional self-sufficiency. Chastened and even dulled by her troubles, Bathsheba comes finally to accept the usual feminine role, for we know that Gabriel Oak will run the farm, even if we are not wholly sure as to who will run Gabriel. Yet to accept this feminine role, she must first assert herself, with a touch of her old sauciness, just enough to provoke Gabriel into the manliness he never quite manages. The incident is neatly done, for Hardy is always good at love-play:

> Gabriel looked her long in the face, but the firelight being faint there was not much to be seen. "Bathsheba," he said, tenderly and in surprise, and coming closer: "If I only knew one thing—whether you would allow me to love you and win you, marry you after all—if I only knew that!"
> "But you never will know," she murmured.
> "Why?"
> "Because you never ask."

The novel ends in harmony, but the price of that harmony is high. Boldwood becomes a neurasthenic, unmanned by his desire, while Troy disintegrates, wholly the creature of his thoughtlessness and guilt, his wish to have all the good things of this world at once. There is a realistic balance in the rounding-out of the book, with the realism of a writer attached to sound traditions of the past but not deluded as to the damage even they can do. But except in those intermittent passages where Hardy tries to be epigrammatically clever and succeeds only in irritating, the book does not come down with a heavy hand upon its meanings and implications. At almost every point there is enough going on, enough vivacity of local detail, to hold one's primary attention.

For what strikes the eye and ear, first and last, is the color of the depicted scenes, the sheer narrative energy, the way intention becomes absorbed into action. Some of the best, and best-known, sections of *Far from the Madding Crowd* are quite detachable as set-pieces: flights of bravura, spectacular and self-contained. Troy demonstrating his fencing techniques to the bedazzled Bathsheba, a charmingly humorous acting-out of sexual thrust; Gabriel saving the corn in the dark of a stormy night by "feeling with his hands" while Troy and the men lie dead drunk; even the somewhat overwrought coffin scene—these are instances of the youthful Hardy's gift for the high and vivid prose of melodrama.

Even as the book keeps pointing to the values of sobriety and control, its action moves along the path of melodrama, a term used here not for dismissal but for descriptive placement. Melodrama is a strategy for compressing action in a setting where moral significance is securely grasped. Thriving when doubt is banished or, better yet, unknown, it provides equivalents in violent gesture for the psychology of figures who are too simple or monolithic to require a closely depicted "inner" life yet are full of admirable energy, spirit and sometimes health. Melodrama is a contracted and thereby somewhat diminished morality.

In any case, melodrama works perfectly well in *Far from the Madding Crowd*. We are troubled neither by those heavy clusters of coincidence which gather in the later novels, nor by the pall of fatality which settles upon them. The characters still retain a margin of freedom, by means of which to chasten if not totally contain their destructive passions. Melodrama lessens our expectations in regard to verisimilitude and credibility. That in the end Boldwood should kill Troy, or that Troy should kiss the servant girl he had abandoned while she lies dead in her coffin with their dead child beside her and Bathsheba watches unobserved—none of this greatly disturbs us. For we know that what matters in this kind of book is not a fine tissue of consciousness but the fierce motion of characters hurtling to their destinies, totally absorbed in their own little corner of the world, as if indeed that *were* the world.

The Return of the Native is the first book in which Hardy reaches toward grandiose "literary" effects and announces those grim preoccupations with fatality that will become associated with his name. Though he continues to serve as chronicler of Wessex and to employ, with a new and more artful self-consciousness, his repertoire of folk motifs, Hardy now brings to bear upon his little world an array of intellectual and historical pressures that were not to be seen in his earlier books. The fixed country setting is shaken by voices of discontent, the bonds of social solidarity begin to loosen, the characters are overcome by feelings of boredom and estrangement, and a new kind of sexuality, neurotically willful but also perversely enticing, makes its appearance. A thick cloud—the cloud of a modern, inherently problematic consciousness—falls across the horizon of Wessex, and neither virtue nor prayer, will nor magic can remove it.

In almost every critical study of Hardy's work written before the Second World War, as in almost every history of the English novel, the accepted valuation of *The Return of the Native* is that here, beyond doubt, is his first major novel. Decorated with imprecisions about the symbolic resonance of Egdon Heath and the philosophic depths of Hardy's pessimism, this is a judgment now hard to accept. It is hard to accept because the book so clearly falls short of classical rank or resolution, so clearly is a work of stammering awkwardness, unused possibilities and naive bravura. Yet the book does survive, not merely as a classroom favorite enabling one's entry into the adult world, but also as a work that, reread in later years, can still seem impressive in a strange and gaunt way.

Nineteenth century England has given us a number of such books (*Silas Marner, David Copperfield*) which yield pleasure and reach toward buried pockets of emotion, yet cannot quite be regarded as mature works of art in the way that *Middlemarch* or *Nostromo* or *The Bostonians* can. We may try to get round this problem by calling novels like *Silas Marner* and *The Return of the Native* "popular classics," but this is merely to provide a label where analysis is wanted. Such works—it can at least be noted—present no great difficulties to the understanding, no elaborate problems of interpretation, indeed, nothing but the task of literary judgment. What do we really feel, what is our true response, in reading *The Return of the Native*? I doubt that there is a single or simple answer, except perhaps for the wish to reclaim a book which Hardy's earlier admirers never dreamed would require anything but admiration.

The flaws are numerous and striking. One is disconcerted, first of all, by the pretentiousness of Hardy's style, his need, so painfully characteristic of the autodidact, to spread forth a glitter of artistic and literary references (as in his remark that Eustacia's "lips formed, with almost geometric precision, the curve so well known in the arts as the cima-recta, or ogee." Ogee indeed!) If there is one important Hardy novel that justifies the cruelty of T. S. Eliot's judgment that his style touched "sublimity without ever having passed through the stage of being good," it is *The Return of the Native*. Yet together with pasteboard flashiness there is, repeatedly, a passage of sublimity. The sounds of the heath, writes Hardy, formed a distinctive note, "what may be called" its "linguistic peculiarity":

> Throughout the blowing of these plaintive November winds that note bore a great resemblance to the ruins of human song which remain to the throat of four-score and ten. It was a worn whisper, dry and papery, and it brushed so distinctly across the ear that, by the accustomed, the material minutiae in which it originated could be realized as by touch.

It soon becomes evident that if the book is to yield any pleasure one must simply accept, as a recurrent irritation, Hardy's straining toward a brilliant stylized prose quite beyond his capacity and at odds with his most authentic gifts. But even at its worst, this impulse toward set-piece bravado is little more than an irritation: Hardy's failures, like his achievements, cannot be grasped by citing a few sentences.

To the subject of *The Return of the Native*, Hardy brings a somewhat fitful energy, so that the book seems ripely fulfilled in some parts and meagerly sketched in others. There are scenes in which the writing blazes with dramatic force and a marvelously frank speech (almost always when Mrs. Yeobright's dry anger flames into argument with the younger people). There are scenes in which the writing declines into a curious somnolence, as if it came from a novelist who sleep-writes the way some people sleepwalk. Except for *Tess of the D'Urbervilles*, this trouble will recur in all of Hardy's books, with rich detail and perfunctory synopsis repeatedly jostling each other. And one consequence, in *The Return of the Native*, is that crucial elements of intent and motive—what precisely is the cause of the estrangement between Clym and Eustacia?—seem to have been overlooked. To read the book is somewhat like watching a play for which the lighting works erratically, at one moment too glaring and another too weak.

Behind these troubles there is, one suspects, a confusion of literary purpose. The novel as blocked out—the novel as a scheme of situations and meanings—requires an action largely realistic, since it focuses upon a conflict of personal styles which, to gain their full value, must be presented through an opposition of social allegiances. What seems—I say "seems" because Hardy does not provide sufficient dramatic evidence—to be involved in the marital struggle between Clym and Eustacia is the problem of how men should live, by what standards, toward what ends. This kind of struggle, to be defined with maximum clarity, has to be located in a structured historical circumstance and organized about a specific social difficulty. Now Hardy seems very much aware of what that difficulty might be (as in his description of Clym as a man in whom "thought is a disease of the flesh"), but what he does not have available is a plot sufficiently complex and sustained to carry his awareness to its limits. The plot does not absorb and employ enough of Hardy's materials, too much is left hanging in mere remarks and fragments of incident; and the result is that one is constantly forced to notice the discrepancy between what happens and what the happenings are supposed to signify. Since the plot is, so to speak, too weak for the subject, there is no choice but to make a somewhat embarrassing reduction in one's mind as to the scope of the book. One thinks of it less and less as a novel charged with ideas about social restlessness and disorganization, more and more as a romance confined to a triangle of passionate misunderstandings.

To fill out his plot, Hardy falls back upon the rustics. By now these charming puppets have been so well trained, they can go through their act whenever Hardy curls a finger. But since he is not content to keep them as atmospheric diversion and must entangle them in his plot, Hardy burdens the rustics with responsibilities beyond their capacity to bear. Crucial turnings in the plot—for example, the whole painful misunderstanding that cuts off Mrs. Yeobright from the son she hoped to assuage—depend upon the rustics, as a result of which these figures are now transformed into agents of fate and chance. But because of what they are intrinsically—creatures, Albert Guerard notes, originally conceived as "immune to suffering and change"—they have a way of deflecting attention from the severity of the cosmic order and toward the inadequacy of the novelist's imagination. It is as if the low-comedy characters of *A Midsummer Night's Dream* were suddenly thrust into the milieu of *Madame Bovary*.

The best things in the novel are not sustained developments of realistic action and social detail, nor the overpraised descriptions of the heath, which seems closer to theater than to nature; they are incidents bordering on the grotesque. In most of his important novels Hardy was a writer struggling toward expressionist and symbolist fiction at a time when the only tradition immediately available to him was the conventional realism of the nineteenth century. In his later books he papered over these difficulties, and once or twice, certainly in *Tess,* found an action that helped release his deepest impulses as a writer. But I doubt that he ever quite solved the problem, except insofar as he abandoned prose fiction altogether and turned to verse, where he did not have to keep grappling with difficulties of plot and could content himself with the glancing effects of the vignette.

The vignettes of which I speak are often marvelous, coming as brief moments of illumination, usually when either Eustacia or Mrs. Yeobright ensnares a character in her passions. The book has another kind of power: long after one has brushed aside the passages of mannered or dead prose, one keeps in mind Hardy's central fable, a design of fatality resting on a triangle of mother, son, wife. I wish to distinguish here between plot, which is the form or curve of the action, and fable, which is the bare situation or dynamic of the characters. Most of the time, in *The Re-*

turn of the Native, plot is inadequate to fable. But the fable itself survives as a pure outline of human possibility, the conception behind the confusion.

Reading the novel one finds oneself thinking now and again: *here is a man who knows, who has seen and felt.* Many of the usual concerns of the nineteenth century novel—articulated conflicts of class, differentiations of manners, the workings of society as a complex but self-contained organism—are barely evident in Hardy's fiction. The ethical dilemmas that absorb George Eliot, the nuances of conduct that trouble Henry James, the abysses of nihilism that haunt Joseph Conrad are largely beyond Hardy's reach. Compared to such writers he seems simple, crude, rough; but also full of an instinctive wisdom, an enormous weight of experience and reflection.

Hardy had an almost preternatural grasp of the dominant human passions, those which rip and tear our lives. He draws these passions with bold, unmodulated strokes—Mrs. Yeobright raging against her daughter-in-law, Clym mourning the death of his mother. The characterization is block-like, unshaded, monochromatic. Hardy reaches intuitively toward the few basic facts of human psychology and does not trouble to modulate or muddy them with psychological analysis. Usually his figures are in the grip of a single desire: Eustacia to realize romantic fantasies about herself, Clym to graft upon his life some significant purpose, Mrs. Yeobright to cling to the prerogatives of motherhood. What goes on within the minds of these figures we seldom know, nor need to. Our attention is directed not to their inner selves but to the stylized relationships among them, and the psychology of it all emerges not through a worrying of private scruples but through an almost ritualistic pattern of yearning, risk, nemesis and fate. The characters of *The Return of the Native* are not to be measured by the familiar standards of realistic probability: that is a test not many of them would pass. They are too large in scale, too singular in purpose to fit comfortably into the usual social novel. Like figures in traditional romance or ballad, they are embodiments of a ruling passion, or like figures in modernist fiction, they are agents of a tyrannical obsession. They live out their destinies, they die.

These people of Wessex, writes D. H. Lawrence,

are always bursting suddenly out of bud and taking a wild flight into flower, always shooting suddenly out of a tight convention, a tight hide-bound cabbage state into something quite madly personal . . . it is all explosive . . . This is the tragedy of Hardy, always the same: the tragedy of those who, more or less pioneers, have died in the wilderness, whither they had escaped for free action, after having left the walled security, and the comparative imprisonment, of the established convention. This is the theme of novel after novel: remain quite within the convention, and you are good, safe and happy in the long run, though you never have the vivid pang of sympathy on your side; or, on the other hand, be passionate, individual, wilful, you will find the security of the convention a walled prison, you will escape, and you will die, either of your own lack of strength to bear the isolation and the exposure, or by direct revenge from the community, or both.

Yet if the central matter of *The Return of the Native* is a conflict between figures of convention and figures of rebellion, it can also be regarded as a struggle for the soul of a man who is not strong enough to shape his destiny or prevent his women from misshaping it. This struggle takes place between Eustacia, the smoldering country Delilah, and Mrs. Yeobright, a grim and perceptive woman, but in her willfulness not perceptive enough. Representing the rival claims of sensuality and constraint, these two women hover over Clym and allow him no peace. Gradually the thin substance of his manliness gets worn down. Clym's partial blindness is brought on by himself, an instance of that self-destructiveness which courses through the major characters and is regarded by Hardy as inseparable from the fevers of Romanticism. But the decay of Clym's sight also suggests a diminished virility. Eustacia need not shear the locks of this fretful husband, who can at best be stubborn when his need is to be strong; it is quite enough that he declines into a leaden figure doing his mindless chores and withdrawing into heavy sexless sleep.

To have conceived Clym Yeobright, one of the earliest characters in English literature dominated by modern deracination and a hunger for some nameless purpose, was surely a triumph. Had Hardy known what to do with Clym in the actual course of the novel, his triumph would have been considerably greater. It is a common response and, I think, a correct one to see Clym as far too dim and recessive for the role Hardy assigns him. In first catching sight of what Clym means, Hardy could not yet see him clearly or fully enough to work him into a living action. Hardy's remarks about Clym are very acute, far more than anything he shows Clym himself to be doing or thinking. Often we have to take Hardy's word for it—since he does not adequately show us—that Clym is the kind of man who could win a girl as passionate and willful as Eustacia. The point is not that we fail to see why Eustacia should be drawn to a young man of some cultivation, just back from Paris and with a decidedly superior personal style. Here Hardy's psychology is very sharp, since it is precisely the destructiveness, and self-destructiveness, of a Eustacia that she should dream of satisfying her fantasies of worldly brilliance through a connection with a man of intellectual seriousness. There is a certain, though limited, comparison to be made with the marriage of· Lydgate and Rosamund in *Middlemarch*, where a young girl's desire for worldly status also attaches itself to a man who begins without worldly ambition. But the concreteness of observed detail George Eliot could bring to her portrait of Lydgate, the care and patience with which she traced his gradual enslavement in domestic philistinism, are precisely what Hardy cannot bring to his rendering of Clym. We respond to Clym's dilemma more than to Clym; we see him as a possibility, a fictional forerunner more than a completed figure—though there are moments when he *is* strongly present, as in the scene where he sleeps heavily after his work at the furze-cutting, a man sliding into apathy. In the main, however, Clym is an idea, evidence of Hardy's stabbing insight, not a character grasped and realized.

Eustacia, by contrast, rises above the novel like a young goddess of sensuality, also like a young girl of petulant vanity. A bit larger than life, she is partly decked out in *papier-mâché*, and the falseness of it is utterly right. She knows the power of her beauty, but lacks any vision that might enable her to put it to more than trivial use. She quivers with the force of her sexuality, but what she wants most is a carriage in Paris. She has a fine mind, but wastes it on Wildeve, telescopes and daydreams. She harbors fantasies of a great and unconventional triumph, but the stuff from which she compounds these fantasies is utterly commonplace. "She had advanced," writes Hardy with quiet exactness, "to the secret recesses of sensuousness, yet had hardly crossed the threshold of the conventional." A "Queen of the Night" in the somewhat lurid seventh chapter, she is also a poor befuddled young thing, trying painfully to impress the young gentleman from Paris. ("What depressed you?" asks Clym in their first conversation; "Life," replies Eustacia.) Her portrait is done in colors of grandeur, yet with at least a few specks of irony.

Clym cannot cope with her, either as a character in the story or as a force counterposed to him in the dialectic of the book. Only Mrs. Yeobright can, and we are grateful for the old lady, without whom there would be no astringency and little conflict. In my own experience of the novel Mrs. Yeobright keeps growing in force, this gritty puritan woman who alternates between passionate outbursts of self-assertion and sudden lapses into country stoicism. Surely Mrs. Yeobright served D. H. Lawrence as a model for the still more powerful Mrs. Morel in *Sons and Lovers*. In both of these mothers the thrust of will, the resources of age and the tyranny of experience frighten away the eager young girls loved by their sons. Fully achieved, Mrs. Yeobright comes out of Hardy's knowledge of Wessex particulars, but with a resonance more nearly universal.

These three figures meet in a struggle of wills, each pitting his or her stubbornness against the other, and the battle that follows, impressive as it is, really has little to do with the themes that have been adumbrated at the outset. Not Clym and the diseases of modernity, but the timeless rage of the clash between generations, the old clinging and the young grasping, provides the drama of the book.

It is in this perspective that we must see the problem of chance and coincidence, so troubling to Hardy's critics and sometimes even to his readers. No amount of critical ratiocination can— and more important, none should—dissolve this problem, for if we experience it as a difficulty in the reading of Hardy's novels, we must accept it as a problem in thinking about them. Yet there may be ways of controlling the difficulty. Chance and coincidence are used repeatedly in *The Return of the Native*, and readers untrained to a large allowance of probability in fiction are likely to be troubled. But we must learn to bring expectations to the reading of Hardy different from those we bring to George Eliot or Jane Austen or Stendhal, for books like *The*

Return of the Native deal less with the logic of the probable than the power of the implausible as it is made, now and again, to seem inevitable. Hardy believed in chance and coincidence, both as manifestations of fate and as signs revealing the dynamics of character. When Wildeve fails to get the marriage certificate, Mrs. Yeobright remarks, "Such things don't happen for nothing." She is right. Hardy is trying to say through the workings of chance what later writers will try to say through the vocabulary of the unconscious. The same holds true for Mrs. Yeobright's decision not to give the money to Wildeve but to entrust it to an unreliable yokel. It is apparently a chance act precipitating a series of disasters, but also another instance of Mrs. Yeobright's damaging pride and aggressiveness. Most of the chance events in the novel can be explained in such terms, which is not to suggest that all of them can thereby be justified or accepted.

Hardy is seldom a moralist. He watches over the men and women of Wessex with an almost maternal sympathy, as if he were a voice from the depths of time rehearsing the endless alternation of effort and collapse, desire and denial, rebellion and defeat. In the light of eternity, the impulse to moral judgment seems not very important. What matters in Hardy's world is the large and recurrent rhythms of life, the rhythms of happiness and suffering—and then, the small immediate incidents into which these are dramatically compressed. I think of the moment when Eustacia, as the result of a quarrel, prepares to leave Clym:

> At last all her things were on. Her little hands quivered so violently as she held them to her chin to fasten her bonnet that she could not tie the strings, and after a few moments she relinquished the attempt. Seeing this he moved forward and said, "Let me tie them."

In that one fragment, as it displays the force of habit in marriage at the very moment of its dissolution, Hardy caught the essence of human pain. Only a great novelist can fully apprehend such a moment, and only a great novelist can make it seem emblematic of our life.

IV

Comic Fiction, Middle Age,
Short Stories

DURING HIS TWENTY-FIVE YEARS AS A NOVELIST Hardy tried his
hand at almost every kind of fiction, and the kind he managed
least well, it is usually agreed, was comedy. There are very fine
stretches of comic byplay and diversion in his major books, almost always focused on the antics of "low" characters and reflecting Hardy's pleasure in rural amusements; but whenever he
tried to do a book primarily in the comic vein he faltered. The
common explanation for this failure has been either that Hardy
was too deep and dark a thinker to indulge in frivolities or that
he lacked the lightness of touch comedy requires.

Neither explanation is wholly true. When it suited his purpose Hardy could brush aside his philosophical interests, and
in sections of novels like *Under the Greenwood Tree* and *Far
from the Madding Crowd* the comic impulse is strongly at work.
In the stylized presentation of his rustics, who form a kind of
repertory troupe steadily reappearing in the Hardy theater, he
could be charming and playful. One may know, while reading
these sections, that a familiar routine is about to start, but frequently enough, and especially in the twists and turns of speech,
Hardy manages it with expert control. There is pleasure of a

kind in watching a man do well what we know he can do superbly.

Why then did Hardy fail in those novels, published in the late 1870s and early 1880s, where comedy is meant to be dominant, either in the depiction of sophisticated society or the play of social incongruity? My surmise would be that he did not take the idea of comedy with enough seriousness, perhaps because he regarded it merely as popular entertainment not requiring the care he would give to his serious work. He failed to see that in fiction the comic mode has its own integrity—its own requirements and limitations—which cannot be violated without loss. He failed to realize that while the norms of probability might be relaxed in a comic novel, they could not simply be disregarded. He failed to understand that a comic scene might lose its charm or satiric edge if used simply as an interlude between stock adventures. He failed to recognize that characterization in comic fiction, though it need not be as intense or shaded as in realistic fiction, still demanded certain patterns of consistency and credibility. He failed to study the world of urban sophistication with the care that his use of it required. And perhaps most damaging of all, he suffered in his comic fiction from the difficulty of finding plots that could sustain the imaginative impulses he had set in motion through character, incident and setting.

Yet Hardy had a considerable talent for comedy—and not merely for the monkeyshines of country lowlife, but also for worldly farce and light portraiture of manners. He was especially good at the kind of summery comic fiction in which young people meet in the country and then, because of disparities in status and intellectual development, entangle themselves in half-ridiculous, half-painful complications. This view of Hardy's talent is one that can reasonably be entertained only by the small number of persons who have read through his minor fiction, since only they will know that together with the limpness, the padding and the sheer silliness, there are sections both clever and amusing.

A Laodicean (1881) starts attractively. Paula Power is a young woman who, in the argot of the 1960s, does not easily "lose her cool." Crisp and alert, rich and pretty, she has many interests but no visible passions. She cannot make up her mind between the Baptist faith of her father and the humanist skepticism floating in the background. She is torn in her tastes between fondness for the medieval castle her father has bought her and the modernity symbolized by her private telegraph arrangement. She is inclined to provoking delay in her romantic life, just enough to test her powers though not so much as to cause excessive torment. For several chapters, she is interesting.

Her young man, George Somerset, is an architect, firmly drawn and credible in a way Hardy's intellectuals seldom are. The opening scene presents Somerset watching Paula refuse at the last moment the baptism she is scheduled to undergo; and it is beautifully done, in the light pencil-sketching that is one of the charms in Hardy's minor fiction. Somerset's curiosity is piqued by the young woman to the point where he maneuvers to make her acquaintance, gains a commission to remodel her castle (even, out of a blend of affection and discretion, agreeing to her scheme for a "Greek court") and finally wins her lukewarm love. The thrust and parry of the lovers is handled by Hardy with a coolness to match the heroine's; all is clarity of touch and line.

At this point, so full of promise, the book completely collapses. Hardy's biographers offer the explanation that while composing chapters for the serial version he fell seriously ill with an internal hemorrhage and had to finish the book by dictating whatever came into his mind. The result was a brew containing a semi-mephistophelean villain, a second villain who proves to be a radical bomb-thrower wanted by the police, and a tiresome tour across Europe. Now it would be foolish to deny that Hardy's illness disabled him, but it is also worth noting that the trash he fell back upon was precisely of the kind he had used in earlier novels like *Desperate Remedies* and *The Hand of Ethelberta*. Lost sight of, meanwhile, were the possibilities embodied in Paula Power, who declines from an intriguing laodicean to a stuffy Victorian.

The book sold poorly and caused Hardy both pain and embarrassment. He was caught out in a minor plagiarism, a two-hundred word passage of no consequence, which busybodies on both sides of the Atlantic worked up into a journalistic fuss; and in February 1882 *Harper's Magazine*, which had paid well for the serial rights, took the step of criticizing *A Laodicean* as "languid . . . tame and colorless . . . hackneyed." Partly true, of course; but still a coarse violation of editorial courtesy.

There were times when Hardy would write letters to editors defending or explaining his intentions, but on occasions such as these he wisely kept quiet, aware that against gratuitous malice he had no defense. Meanwhile the recovery from his illness was slow and painful, requiring that for months he lie in bed with his feet higher than his head. He worried about money, for the style in which the Hardys now lived, with frequent trips to London and the Continent, required that he keep turning out serials. He worried about his health, fearful as to what might happen to his wife in case he died. He worried about his work, all too sensitive to the attacks he had recently suffered for his inferior books. He realized that no matter how difficult his relations with his wife had become, she still remained, even in her silence and aloofness, the human being closest to him, faithful in attendance during his troubles. And he tried to console himself with the reflection that "there is mercy in troubles coming in battalions —they neutralize each other." Some were unique to his temperament or calling; but some, he had ruefully to acknowledge, were simply the consequence of middle age.

These difficulties were transient, felt acutely enough by the man who had to live through them, but not serious impediments to his career. Soon he would recover his health, and by the mid-1880s there would begin the most fruitful decade of his life as a novelist. For apart from his personal feelings, which he kept pretty much to himself and his notebooks, Hardy had reason for satisfaction. He was elected to the Rabelais Club in London, a distinguished literary society. He met Browning, Arnold and Tennyson. He enjoyed his visits to the Continent. He attended a dramatic performance based on *Far from the Madding Crowd.* He had the pleasure of reading two warm critical appreciations of his work, one by a then-unknown young man named Havelock Ellis, which appeared in the *Westminster Review* in 1883, and the other by the poet Coventry Patmore, which came out three years later. With these essays there began a line of criticism which, despite the rantings of priggish reviewers, took Hardy with the utmost seriousness and would reach a peak of distinction in 1895 when Lionel Johnson brought out his study of Hardy's fiction.

Once recovered from his illness, Hardy settled for good and all in the Dorset countryside. Whatever feelings of chagrin his wife may have felt, she acquiesced in this choice, apparently recognizing that for reasons of both health and work Hardy needed to spend a large portion of his time in the country. In 1883 he set to work designing and building the house in which he would live the remainder of his life, "Max Gate," named after an old site and located about a mile out of Dorchester. Unhappily, it turned out to be a rather dismal villa. "I was resolved," said Hardy, perhaps by way of explanation, "not to ruin myself in building a great house, as so many other literary men have done." At about this time he also began to indulge his interest in Dorset history and archaeology; when some Roman relics were discovered during the construction of "Max Gate," Hardy wrote up an account for the Dorset Field Club. And in 1883 he published a superb essay, "The Dorsetshire Labourer."

Important both for its own sake and for the light it casts on the Wessex novels, "The Dorsetshire Labourer" begins with a sharp defense of "Hodge," the stereotyped figure of rural sloth by means of which middle-class English culture kept itself from apprehending the humanity of the men who worked in the fields. Hardy then proceeds to describe what is socially distinctive in their lives, noting with special care the effects of the gradual modernization of the rural world. He paints a strong sketch of "a wet hiring-fair at Candlemas" at which the workers search for new employment and a bewildered shepherd, too old for work, stands alone.

Under the pressures of industry and commerce, country life is shedding some of its distinctiveness and the agricultural workers are losing

> their peculiarities as a class . . . hence the humorous simplicity which formerly characterized the men and the unsophisticated modesty of the women are rapidly disappearing or lessening, under the constant attrition of lives mildly approximating to those of workers in a manufacturing town.

But Hardy does not stoop to sentimentality. As he remarks in a fine passage, the country women:

are losing their individuality, but they are widening the range of their ideas, and gaining in freedom. It is too much to expect them to remain stagnant and old-fashioned for the pleasure of romantic spectators.

In the early 1880s Hardy made still another stab at writing a romantic comedy. *Two on a Tower* (1882) is surely the best among his minor novels, and parts of it are decidedly better than minor, yet apart from some keen paragraphs by Albert Guerard, the book has not been adequately judged by Hardy's critics.

Two on a Tower suffers the handicap of being ill-described by Hardy himself, who speaks of it in his preface as "the emotional history of two infinitesmal lives [set] against the stupendous background of the stellar universe." And so it seems, at the beginning. Swithin St. Cleeve, a young man of mixed social origins, lives totally absorbed in the study of astronomy; he is innocent, pure-spirited, bright—and remarkably good-looking. Nearby looms the manor of Lady Viviette Constantine, who has been abandoned by a despicable husband and can find no release for her sympathies or energies. Having reached the ripe age of twenty-nine she is in full emotional and sexual bloom, but "languishing for want of something to do, cherish, or suffer for." Lady Constantine helps the poor youth acquire astronomical equipment, and soon the inevitable romance begins. St. Cleeve, absorbed in the stars and his dreams of professional glory, hardly knows what is happening; Lady Constantine knows only too well.

Hardy's portentous description, it soon becomes clear, is quite beside the point. Not the insignificance of human desire against the backdrop of a neutral universe, but as Guerard says, "the conflict of mature and youthful temperament" forms the center of interest. Life is at the full in the woman, not yet so in the youth; the result must be disharmony. The subject, adds Guerard, "is abandoned almost as soon as it is masterfully established, at the moment when Lady Constantine and St. Cleeve recognize they love each other even more than the stars . . . Lady Constantine's first husband has long since disappeared and is presumably dead. The lovers are free to marry; the introduction to the book is complete." Yes; and the irony is sharpened by the fact that it is the mature woman who stands for impulsiveness while the youth is reticent and vain. The result is a comedy of the incongruous, in which a passionate woman, against her better intentions and sincere solicitude, sweeps up a young man who cannot possibly care for her as much as she for him.

Lady Constantine is one of Hardy's finest ventures in feminine psychology: warm, volatile, proud, ripe, frustrated, yielding herself at one moment with a reckless, an almost maternal generosity and then withdrawing out of hurt pride and awakened conscience. In the first hundred or so pages, and then in the concluding chapter, she is drawn with great plasticity, as she struggles both to realize and to thwart her desires; and though Hardy makes quite clear the tragic potential of such a woman, he rightly maintains a tough-spirited comic perspective.

What happens after the first hundred pages is that Hardy, to quote from Guerard once more, "abandoned an unfamiliar and stimulating manner at the very moment this manner became most difficult. . . . The comedy would require, of course, that its victims remain side by side, as they had been on their observation tower." Side by side, so that the damage of their infatuation might work itself out. But Hardy falls back, instead, on mechanical plot complications, not as ineptly as in *A Laodicean* but bad enough. Lady Constantine and St. Cleeve are separated, she to marry an urbane bishop and he to go off to an observatory in South Africa. In the final chapter, but not until then, there is a partial recovery. St. Cleeve returns to find Lady Constantine a widow, but looking at her now, he sees "another woman . . . and not the original Viviette. Her cheeks had lost forever that firm contour which had been drawn by the vigorous hand of youth, and the masses of hair that were once darkness visible had become touched here and there by a faint grey haze, like the Via Lactea in a midnight sky." St. Cleeve's face betrays him; his affections have cooled. Lady Constantine "saw it all, and knew that Time had at last brought about his revenges."

Two on a Tower, or at least parts of it, can still yield pleasure, for Hardy wrote better than he knew, concentrating on those incongruities in human experience which no amount of good will can remove and employing that cool, hard comic tone which would later reach a kind of perfection in E. M. Forster's novels.

Whatever demon of solemnity it was that kept Hardy from fully realizing his comic gifts cost him most dearly in this book, for in no other did those gifts come so close to fulfillment.

The Hardy of these years, a man in his early and mid-forties who has behind him three works of considerable dictinction and will soon be entering a creative breakthrough, seems a figure curiously hard to reach. He is not inaccessible, only elusive. One can be intensely aware of the aura, the sense of compassionate goodness, that emanates from Hardy's pages, and one may know a reasonable number of facts about his life. As a public figure, however, he barely exists—and perhaps it is just as well. For Hardy was one of those writers who abhor the thought of making their own lives into an allegory of their vision or a gloss upon their work. The reticence which everyone noticed upon meeting him was not merely shyness, nor merely the result of a wish to keep free from the murky entanglements of publicity. It was a reticence that went deep into his psychic composition and had a strange reflection in the fact that he always disliked being touched by other persons—apparently he was thin-skinned in more ways than one.

Hardy's private life was his own, and lived out by him with silent absorption; he took his experience to the full. But there is a sense in which he can be said to have been devoid of a public personality. He had no interest in "creating" himself as a legend or myth; he did not care for interviews or mobs; he wished to leave no area for observation between his private life and the writing he offered in public. *He drained himself into his work.* Only there does he, and only there need he, exist; so that nothing or very little apart from the work was left for public inspection or tampering. Persons both famous and ob- scure who visited Hardy have all testified to his considerateness, but also a certain abstractness, what seems a gentle distance from his own life. That he ever showed or revealed much of himself is to be doubted. And perhaps the point to be stressed —I mean it as a kind of praise—is that Hardy had nothing to show or reveal, no public face in the style of Byron or Dickens or Hemingway. He reminds one a little of Faulkner who, except perhaps to his intimates, also had nothing to offer but his work.

This screen of reticence seems to me admirable, and in our publicity-drugged age, especially worthy of emulation.

One thing, however, is clear: how mistaken were those who took Hardy to be a naif, on the naive premise that because he wrote about simple country people (or, as the patronizing and inaccurate expression has it, about "peasants") he must himself have been one. Henry James sneered at "the good little Thomas Hardy" and Somerset Maugham would remember Hardy as "a little man with an earthy face. In his evening clothes, with his boiled shirt and high collar he had still a strange look of the soil." Later, T. S. Eliot would elevate patronage into ideology.

Now it is one thing to conclude that Hardy did not have an original or first-rate mind as an aspiring philosopher; quite another to indulge in the kind of condescension that betrays the pressures of English class snobbism. Hardy was not a yeoman turned genius, not a peasant, not a primitive. He was a man who had grown up in the country and, from a perspective of some distance and considerable ambivalence, wrote about its life. He was an immensely earnest man who read widely and steadily, in fact, a good deal more than most English novelists before or after him. He tried to grapple with the problems of his day. He took to heart the responsibility of educating himself in the classics of the past. And despite the strain of self-depreciation he sometimes adopted—clearly as a defensive maneuver—when talking about his own fiction, he devoted himself to literature with absolute seriousness.

His productivity as a writer during the 1880s and 1890s was remarkable, not merely in a steady stream of novels, some verse and occasional essays, but also in a good many short stories. In 1888 he published *Wessex Tales*; in 1891 *A Group of Noble Dames*; and in 1894 *Life's Little Ironies*—which together contain most of his better stories. Before turning in the next two chapters to Hardy's major fiction, I propose to stop for a few moments and look at his stories: which will mean breaking the line of chronology but gaining in compactness of discussion.

That Hardy's stories are little read is not a scandal, it is merely a pity. Most of his stories, serviceable products for magazines, are not worth salvaging; seven or eight are very fine; and one,

"The Fiddler of the Reels," can be called great. To write a history of modern fiction or modern poetry without seriously considering Hardy would be unthinkable. To omit his name from a study of the modern short story would be plausible. I would only add to this usual judgment that the best of Hardy's stories can still yield a distinct pleasure. They have little to do with the main line of the modern short story. Hardy cannot be said to have anticipated such masters as Chekhov, Joyce and Hemingway in the short story even to the limited extent that as a novelist he anticipated D. H. Lawrence. There is little in Hardy's stories of Chekhov's psychological plasticity, even less of the impressionistic economy of the *Dubliners,* and nothing whatever of the tight-lipped stylization we associate with Hemingway. As if to sharpen the contrast, Hardy's short fictions might be described as tales, since that is to put them in a mellower light and relate them to a more easy-paced and amiable mode of narrative than we can usually find in the modern short story.

The bulk of his stories were composed during the 1880s and 1890s, the period of Hardy's most prolific and accomplished work as a novelist. He seems to have regarded the writing of stories as mere journeyman's work by which to earn a living, and to have dashed them off with the casualness of purpose and desire to please a large audience which he claimed to be characteristic—though we have reason to be skeptical—of the way he wrote his novels. Yet anyone who has become familiar with the timbre of Hardy's voice, both in an early work like *Under the Greenwood Tree* and a late one like *Tess of the D'Urbervilles,* could not fail immediately to recognize a tale like "The Withered Arm" or "The Three Strangers" as uniquely his. Like most short fictions composed by novelists, Hardy's are fragments chipped off his larger work, or developments of major themes in modest scope, or exercises at sketching the figures and locale of his more ambitious books.

If once you have fallen under the spell of the kind of writer who creates his own fictional world and keeps returning to it in book after book—as Faulkner does with Yoknapatawpha, or Balzac with Paris, or Hardy with Wessex—even his minor stories will hold a lively interest. For in them loose narrative ends may be tied together, bits of information casting light on the novels casually provided, and an imaginary place we have come to know once again exhibited. And exhibited more quietly, more reassuringly than in the full-scale narratives. The reader who has suffered vicariously the blows and disasters of Hardy's major novels may find a special charm in turning to "A Few Crusted Characters," an utterly winning survey of Wessex conduct and idiosyncrasy, free from the darkness of spirit that hovers over Hardy's novels and buoyant with the delight of coming back to a familiar world of youth. Does the pleasure in reading a great novelist's minor work rest on a childlike desire for "just a little more"—another glance at Wessex, its places, customs and people? Perhaps so. But which writer would not be delighted to command precisely this "naive" response from his audience?

Now, what crucially distinguishes the stories from the novels is that in the former there is hardly a trace of the "modern" Hardy, the writer who created Jude Fawley and kept fretting himself over "Crass Casualty" and "Immanent Will." You could barely know from these stories that Hardy had ever been captivated by the theories of Herbert Spencer, John Stuart Mill and Thomas Huxley; you could never suppose he would keep struggling with the pessimistic visions of von Hartmann and Schopenhauer. In the stories Hardy allows himself to feel more pleasure for the ordinary course of life than he does in the major novels, and perhaps more pleasure than, strictly speaking, his philosophy allows. He relaxes into nostalgia and anecdote; the pastoral impulse flows with a purity he could seldom preserve in his more ambitious novels. There is little in these stories of that thwarted, painful and exhausting struggle with the dilemmas of estrangement which distinguishes *Jude the Obscure*; but then neither are there the cumbered prose, the tiresome philosophizing and the inert submission before intellectual fashion that mar even the best of his novels.

In atmosphere, though not narrative tone, Hardy's stories recall the pastoral fiction of George Eliot. Perhaps the greatest success of this kind among Hardy's shorter pieces is the string of anecdotes, set-pieces and miniature portraits called "A Few Crusted Characters." Most of his critics, eager for philosophical big game, have ignored this work, but to me it seems a minor masterpiece full of that good humor and acceptance of common life which one associates, if not with the English countryside itself, then with a certain tradition in writing about it. A cultivated man returns to his native village after a long absence; allows himself to sink into the pleasures of recollection while taking the carrier's van from the marketplace and querying the other passengers about the friends of his youth; and then, as the narrative glides from speaker to speaker, he is gradually brought to an enlarged awareness of his past. Except for a sketch of obsessional vengeance, the whole thing is light and untroubled, certainly untroubled by those philosophic notions that burden Hardy's major work. The story-in-the-round structure is familiar enough, but Hardy's ease in rendering country manners and byplays of humor is a rare thing, possible only to a great writer relaxing with a small effort. Such mild sketching of English country life—whether by Hardy, George Eliot or Mrs. Gaskell—is not much admired in our theoretic age, but in the long run it may require more literary tact to enjoy fiction of this kind than to play with the symbols of *Moby Dick*.

I have already mentioned the distinction sometimes made between stories and tales: it is a distinction all but lost in our usual literary discourse. And that is a pity, since the demarcation of *genres* helps us to grasp the variety of ends separating kinds of composition and thereby to bring pertinent expectations to the reading of literature. Between story and tale there is, of course, no insuperable barrier, yet for a moment I propose to write as if there were, overstating the case in order to see what might be distinctive in Hardy's short fictions.

The tale is usually told, or retold, by a speaker addressing an audience that forms a natural or social community. Hardy modifies this method by employing an omniscient narrator, but one whose voice soon reveals itself to be that of a traditional teller of tales. It is a voice leisurely in rhythm, with flourishes of comment and digression, as if quite confident that the audience will enjoy not merely the matter of the narrative but also its incidental flourishes and charms. Suspense remains a primary objective, but a suspense depending on the tactics of a dominant speaker and curiously different in kind from that which is possible to an impersonal drama. By contrast to all this, the story aims at a self-sufficiency of context; it usually consists of an action directly rendered, a complete and unglossed impression; and it tends to employ prose toward the effect of transparency.

Between tale and story there is a sharp difference in pacing, what might be called their respective versions of "the time sense." The tale stops, starts up again and wanders, seemingly uncon-cerned with effects of accumulation or foreshortening: as if the clock were no enemy nor the impatience of an audience a constant pressure. One thinks of a tale as spoken before a fire in a pleasant country house and of a story as read on the subway to work.

The tale seeks to evoke in listeners a feeling of wonder, some-times awe, before the strange and the marvelous; the story tends to be more dependent on the conventions of realism. Unburdened by notions about the impersonality of art, the tale may end in explicit moral or philosophical reflection, perhaps in a hushed agreement as to the inscrutability of the mysterious; the story, however, ends in a climax of revelation or a turning of irony, which is also a kind of revelation. The tale compresses a lengthy or complicated action into a brief span; the story exhibits in dramatic fullness a brief action.

These distinctions are of course schematic. To be of any use they must be. Instances can be found, as in Hawthorne, where it seems almost impossible to say whether a given fiction should be called a story or a tale. Then, of course, it does not matter. But to think of "The Three Strangers" or "The Withered Arm" as closer to the tale than the story is to recognize what makes Hardy's short fictions distinctive. That done, we have no choice but to fall back upon the imprecision of ordinary usage and continue to call them . . . Hardy's stories.

Sometimes these stories show a certain kinship—say, that of a second cousin—to the traditional English ballad. Hardy himself was aware of this, and rather proud of the traditional sources and characteristics of his storytelling:

> We tale-tellers are all Ancient Mariners, and none of us is warranted in stopping Wedding Guests unless he has something more unusual to relate than the ordinary experience of every average man or woman.

About this aspect of Hardy's work an English critic, Douglas Brown, writes illuminatingly:

One by one the striking things about Hardy's art as a story-teller fall naturally into place as functions of balladry. There is the reliance, especially at the outset, upon the sharp definition of scene and background. There is the easy alliance of the grotesque and disproportionate with the substantial and natural, and the unselfconscious boldness with which they are offered. There are the slighter rhythms and movements of the story suggesting that the sung stanza is never far behind. There are the neat, rounded and intertwining groups of events, the simple and decisive balancing of characters. There is the vivid sense of the meaning of scenery, the human and the natural involving one another. There is the narrative method whereby encounter (whether of person with person, or person with Fate) is the life of the tale.

As in ballads, lovers are crossed and hopes destroyed, sometimes through impersonal agencies of fate or chance, sometimes through the inner unfolding of character. In the country world of Wessex, what may seem to us extraordinary is looked upon, with a credulous fatalism, as quite ordinary. It is here to be expected that a woman wronged, as in "The Withered Arm," will cast a spell upon her fortunate rival and cause her to suffer physical waste. Read with the expectations of conventional realism, this story groans with improbability, yet as often happens in Hardy, it can be valued as a curious mixture of traditional folk belief and modern hypothesis, assumptions drawn from before and after the Enlightenment. If one cares or needs to—though I do not know why anyone should—it is easy enough to "translate" the events of this grotesque tale into an acceptable instance of character psychology, but the result of such gratuitous sophistication can only be a literary loss, a distraction from Hardy's boldness of narrative.

In some of his stories, the grotesque and demonic are entirely absent, and what claims our attention is a familiar landscape faithfully drawn, solidly sketched figures in their appropriate place, a setting of work, pleasure and trouble. In "The Distracted Preacher" the stress is comic, a sly thrust at Victorian convention in the person of the Reverend Stockdale, who meets an attractive young widow in a coastal town where, to his dismay but her profit, she is cheerfully engaged in smuggling. The story not only permits Hardy to skim a favorite theme—the overflow of youthful energy past the perimeters of moralism—but also to indulge in zestful descriptions of the smugglers teasing and tricking customs

men. Hardy controls the scene expertly, and except for a concluding lapse into virtue, presumably forced upon him by the needs
of magazine publication, he makes no excessive demands upon
this material. He does not hover and ruminate, squeeze and prod,
as even in his best novels he is inclined to do. He accepts, records,
enjoys.

In other stories a similar grasp of local detail is used to support
some of Hardy's usual concerns: betrayal, dismay, moral confusion, crossed fates. "The Waiting Supper" is a fine tale about the
interplay of personal vanity and social ambition: two lovers are
separated through class prejudice, the girl marries a man of
higher status only to suffer quick desertion, and years later her
spurned lover, now wealthy, returns to woo her. But how different
from, how much less exalted and more sadly probable than
Wuthering Heights! For the reunited lovers do not know whether
the missing husband is still alive; and only late, too late, as they
drift into old age, neither quite together nor quite apart, do they
learn that the husband is indeed dead. The aging lover continues
to propose marriage at intervals, but time has grayed their passion: "Occasionally he ventured to urge her to reconsider the case,
though he spoke not with the fervour of earlier years."

The writing in these stories is happiest when Hardy is most at
ease in his country world. Then the prose is pure and unstrained;
there is no grasping after unearned intensities; the very rhythms
suggest psychic comfort. Rarely approaching the sublimity that
Hardy can now and again reach in his novels, the best of his
stories are also free of the turgidity to which the novels frequently
succumb. How nicely and delicately he can sketch a rural scene:

> The level rainstorm smote walls, slopes, and hedges . . . Such sheep
> and outdoor animals as had no shelter stood with their buttocks to
> the winds; while the tails of little birds trying to roost on some
> scraggy thorn were blown inside-out like umbrellas. The gable-end
> of the cottage was stained with wet, and the eavesdroppings flapped
> against the wall.

Hardy loved the contentment of this world, its freedom from
unsettling ambitions and distraught egos:

> Absolute confidence in each other's good opinion begat perfect ease,
> while the finishing stroke of manner, amounting to a truly princely
> serenity, was lent to the majority by the absence of any expression

or trait denoting that they wished to get on in the world, enlarge their minds, or do any eclipsing thing whatever. . . .

There remains "The Fiddler of the Reels," one of the great, if barely known, stories in the English language. Wessex is the familiar locale, and equally familiar are the disruption and excitement that follow upon a stranger's arrival. But this time Hardy strikes into depths of obsession that he never approaches in his other short fictions.

Into the placid village of Stickleford comes a handsome stranger, "from nobody knew where." Wat or "Mop" Ollamoor, "musician, dandy and company-man," plays the violin with ravishing beauty, his "chromatic subtleties" lending him a demonic power over listeners, "especially young women of fragile and responsive organization." One such young woman, Car'line Aspent, abandons her village sweetheart because she has become hopelessly enchanted by the sounds of Mop's fiddle. A few years later, abandoned in turn by Mop, she arranges a marriage with her former sweetheart, now soberly employed in London, and brings with her to the city, as a dowry of sorts, the child she has had by the wizard-musician. All seems quiet and stable—until Car'line chances upon Mop fiddling in a country inn:

> A tremor quickened itself to life in her, and her hand so shook that she could hardly set down her glass. It was not the dance nor the dancers, but the notes of that old violin which thrilled the London wife, these having still all the witchery that she had so well known of yore, and under which she had used to lose her power of independent will. How it all came back! There was the fiddling figure against the wall; the large, oily, mop-like head of him, and beneath the mop the face with closed eyes.

The dancing grows wilder and Car'line yields herself to a solitary paroxysm, "defiantly as she thought, but in truth slavishly and abjectly, subject to every wave of the melody. . . ." When she finally collapses, Mop seizes their little girl and races off; the concluding note is that Car'line, still safe with her worthy husband, seems not too unhappy that something of hers remains with Mop.

It is a country tale, but told with severity and sophistication. The rhythms speed up, the language swells, a note of tentative abandon is struck. Not even in the quiet of Wessex can there be assurance that a life will not be disordered or exalted by some intruding power, some obsession bearing possibilities of the un-known. Mop himself is kept at a distance, ominous but unex-plained: a demon-lover of country taverns, for whom music and sexuality flow together and the lure of abandon speeds through the scrape of a bow.

V

The Struggles of Men

To SHAKE LOOSE FROM ONE'S WIFE; to discard that drooping rag of a woman, with her mute complaints and maddening passivity; to escape not by a slinking abandonment but through the public sale of her body to a stranger, as horses are sold at a fair; and thus to wrest, through sheer amoral willfulness, a second chance out of life—it is with this stroke, so insidiously attractive to male fantasy, that *The Mayor of Casterbridge* begins. In the entire history of European fiction there are few more brilliant openings.

When some of the reviewers complained that Michael Henchard's sale of his wife is incredible, Hardy hastened to defend himself with his customary appeal to history. Cases of wife-selling, he noted, had been frequent in rural England and were still to be heard of during the mid-nineteenth century. Today this argument seems naive: we recognize that the historically possible or even the historically actual is not a sufficient basis for the imaginatively plausible. Still, Hardy's defense is not quite so irrelevant as recent criticism has made out, for in ways more complicated than Hardy could say, history does form a matrix of the literary imagination. Had he lived a few decades later than he did, Hardy might have argued that the opening scene of the novel, partly because it does rest on a firm historical foundation, embodies a mythic kind of truth. Speaking to the depths of common fantasy, it summons blocked desires and transforms us into secret sharers. No matter what judgments one may make of Henchard's conduct, it is hard, after the first chapter, simply to abandon him; for through his boldness we have been drawn into complicity with the forbidden.

The detached composure with which this first chapter is written Hardy would seldom equal again. Nothing is rushed, nothing overstated. There is almost no effort to fill out the characters of Henchard and Susan, since for the moment they matter as representative figures in outline, a farm laborer and his wife plodding along a country road in search of work. Nor is there any effort to set off a quick emotional vibration. What Henchard feels we barely know, and Susan, carrying her baby and trying—the phrase is subtly evocative—to keep "as close to his side as possible without actual contact," remains impassive in her distress. Hardy's intention here is not to penetrate the deeper feelings of his characters, but to set up a bare situation that will serve as the premise of their fate. This is a novel in which plot—the shaping of an action toward a disciplined implication—is to be central. And accordingly, the prose displays few signs of portentousness, strain or ornament. At least in this book, Hardy trusts the tale.

We encounter at the very outset Hardy's characteristic mixture of realism and grotesque, with the realism in the characterization and the grotesque in the event. The place is the familiar countryside of Wessex, and the figures are the familiar agents of its traditional life; but the action seems startling, extreme, and with an aura of the legendary. Details of conduct establish a context of verisimilitude: a farm laborer with the "measured" and "springless" walk of "the skilled countryman as distinct from the desultory shamble of the general laborer"; and then the two of them, husband and wife, sullen in their "atmosphere of stale familiarity." Each feels trapped, neither quite knows why. Through a few broad descriptive strokes, these barely articulate people are sketched in. Henchard and his wife are approaching the town of Weydon-Priors, in Upper Wessex, and it is a fair day. First the stress is placed upon the economics of trading and hiring, but then, a few paragraphs later, Hardy turns to the fair as a communal activity, with its slackening of moral standards and its echoes of old custom. "A haggish creature," the furmity woman sits in her tent and mixes her brew—she looks like one of the witches in *Macbeth* and is clearly meant to be more than realistic in reverberation. Henchard, grown "brilliantly quarrelsome" on drink, sells his wife for five pounds. That he does this through a travesty of an auction heightens the terribleness of his deed. For, with the spitefulness to which guilt can drive a man, he forces himself to prolong and brutally measure out what had begun as a whim.

The terms of the drama are now set: a violation of human dignity, by which an intimate relationship is made subject to the cash nexus. Yet it should be stressed that Henchard does this not out of greed but because he is supremely dissatisfied with the drabness of life and driven toward a gesture that will proclaim his defiance and disgust. What Henchard does now will later become a curse settling upon his life—Hardy might, with Hawthorne, have said, there will be blood to drink! The intended stroke of liberation proves to be a seal of enslavement; the seller, sold. And much of what follows in the novel consists of a series of variations upon Henchard's initial crime, with each variation crowding him further into aloneness. As a realistic portrait of social life, *The Mayor of Casterbridge* is by no means always credible or well drawn; but as a chain of consequences in which Henchard is trapped and from which he keeps struggling to break loose, it is severely appropriate. Here, as often in Hardy, versimilitude is subordinated to internal pressures of theme and vision. To the ordinary program of literary realism Hardy cannot long be faithful.

At the same time, the sale of Henchard's wife constitutes a kind of fortunate fall. From this deed there follows whatever suffering and consciousness Henchard can reach—and it is one of Hardy's most remarkable achievements that, through incident and gesture, we are steadily made aware of how deeply Henchard suffers at being unable to declare in language the consciousness he has won. A major reason for Henchard's recurrent fits of temper is a rage over the inadequacy of his own tongue.

In the opening chapter, then, the dynamics of Henchard's psychology are set into motion. He is a man with energy in excess of his capacity for release. He is a blundering overreacher confined to a petty locale, so that he must try to impart some grandeur to a life of smallness even while dimly sensing the futility of his effort. He thrashes out at whatever comes within reach, sometimes with open hostility, sometimes with clumsy affection—but soon enough, with exhausted regret and self-contempt. He can neither contain his aggressions nor keep them going in cold blood. Everything he does comes from inner heat and ends with the clammy despair of contrition. He cannot draw a clear boundary between self and other, what is his and what is not. Having sold his wife, he is foolishly indignant that she keeps their child: "She'd no business to take the maid—'tis my maid." There is an element in human character which consists of primitive thrusting will and fiercely refuses social adjustment; it is particularly strong in Henchard.

Once he realizes what he has done, Henchard searches for months to find his wife and child, for he is now convinced that he must "put up with the shame as best he could. It was of his own making, and he ought to bear it." There is, as Hardy remarks, "something fetichistic in this man's beliefs." To give this observation its proper weight, a cannier novelist would have postponed it until later in the book, but even here, awkwardly placed, it has a strong impact. For Henchard is one of those unfortunate people whose burden it is that he responds with excessive force to both the demands of ego and the claims of moral commandment. He is "fetichistic" in that he lives by the persuasion that meaning does inhabit the universe, but a meaning that, somehow, maliciously eludes him. Bewildered, he must fall back upon curses, superstition and self-lacerating vows (he swears he will not touch liquor for twenty years).

Meanwhile, another motif is introduced in these early pages. Throughout Hardy's novels there keep appearing figures who need to confront life as if it were a dramatic performance being acted out on a cramped stage. Seldom conscious rebels yet refusing to accept their lot, they choose, at whatever cost, the roles of assertion and power. Is the world indifferent, dry and listless? Then they will impose themselves upon it. Is the universe drained of purpose and faith? All the more reason to impress upon one's time, with a kind of clenched prometheanism, the conquest of personality which a chosen act of drama can signify. The impulse to create a drama of self-assertion is one of the main sources of "character" in Hardy's world, "character" here indicating energy and pride of personal being. (Not accidentally, there is at work in the novels a counter-principle to which Hardy is still more strongly attached: a wisdom of passivity that consists in accepting traditional roles and bearing inherited burdens.) In a world where the trees and the waters no longer speak of meaning or spirit, certain powerful figures can still slash their way to a marred identity. Their probable end is failure and pain, but struggle remains the substance of their experience. "My punishment," says Henchard at the end, "is *not* greater than I can bear."

It is this contrast between a setting of dusty indifference and figures both fierce and zestful in their performance that provides much of the drama in *The Mayor of Casterbridge*. The two are kept in a balance of tension, as if to satisfy Coleridge's description of the poet as one who achieves a "reconciliation of opposite or discordant qualities." Once the cast of the book is brought fully on stage, there follow a number of contests structured as a series of intensifying crises, and through these contests Henchard realizes himself to the full—that is, completes his own destruction.

Strong anticipations of this clash between listlessness and desire, the inert universe and driven men, appear in the first few chapters. The road upon which Henchard walks is "neither straight nor crooked, neither level nor hilly," just another nondescript and wearisome road such as men have climbed for centuries. The only sound breaking the silence is "the voice of a weak bird singing a trite old evening song that might have been heard on the hill at the same hour, with the self-same trills, quavers, and breves at any sunset of that season for centuries untold." And then comes Henchard's gesture of perverse self-definition—the humiliation of the human being closest to him—by means of which he seeks to release his grievance against the universe. Yet, no sooner does he leave the furmity woman's tent than things lapse back into their accustomed listlessness. The rural folk who have watched the sale of Susan now sink into a drunken stupor, and the only creatures witnessing Henchard's departure are a dog and a fly.

The irony here is both austere and wounding. Henchard's defiance of customary standards and the moral law has no importance to anyone but a handful of people; the world, barely noticing, continues with its customary drone. Henchard has strained past decorum and conscience to assert himself, but Hardy, watching, as it were, from a distant height, sees that in any larger scheme of things even the most extreme gesture is trivial and unavailing. Later—it is another superb touch—the furmity woman, who is to be Henchard's Nemesis, will barely be able to remember what happened in her tent. Fate itself seems absentminded.

The prologue is now complete. A period of twenty years is skipped over, years in which Henchard rises to mercantile prosperity and political prominence. This leap in time is strictly justifiable, once we have been persuaded by the opening chapters that, if Henchard can but hold his turbulence in check, he is a man vigorous ..nd hard enough to succeed in the commerce of a country town. The way is thus open for the main action of the novel: Henchard's steady downward course in both personal life and social condition. And what sets this downward course into motion is precisely the complex of character traits that has been at work in his opening appearance. The spring of Henchard's decline is personal in nature—the return of his wife Susan and her daughter Elizabeth-Jane to Casterbridge, which makes impossible any further evasion of his youthful sin. The occasion for Henchard's decline is social in nature—a prolonged and doomed struggle with a new merchant, Donald Farfrae, who brings to Casterbridge methods of economy Henchard can neither understand nor compete with. And the plot of the novel, as it moves from Henchard's vulgar triumph as mayor to his lonely unregenerate death, is structured with the intent of making the consequences of Henchard's past seem organically related to the social struggle occupying the present.

As a maker of plots—I assume for a moment that this aspect of a novel can be conveniently isolated from the total act of composition—Hardy was never brilliantly successful. He came at a difficult moment in the history of English fiction: he could neither fully accept nor quite break away from the conventions of his Victorian predecessors. He felt obliged to use a variant of the overelaborate and synthetic plot that had become fixed in the Victorian novel, the kind of superstructure that, becoming an end in itself, could smother seriousness of thought and make impossible seriousness of characterization. And he kept using the Victorian plot not only because it satisfied the requirements of the serial form in which he first printed his fiction but also for a more important reason: he wanted plot to serve as a sign of philosophic intent and this seduced him into relying too heavily upon mechanical devices. Yet Hardy also came to look upon the Victorian plot as a rigid and repressive convention, from which in his final great novels he would slowly "liberate" himself. What he could not do, however, was either to employ a plot with the confidence of a Fielding that it would release his full vision, or work his way into a modern view of plot, according to which the action must be strictly adjusted to the psychological makeup of the characters. His novels are therefore likely to seem curiously uneven: the men and women he imagines are superbly vital, while the events he assigns to them are frequently beyond their bearing or our belief.

Hardy made excessive demands upon his plots. Just as certain writers of our day suppose that the color of a man's soul can be inferred from the way he holds a cigarette or bends the brim of his hat, so Hardy supposed that the motions of fate—which he declared to be ethically indifferent while often writing as if they were ethically malicious—could be revealed through the manipulation of plot. Whether operating as psychological claim or literary method, such assumptions are naive. They posit equations too neat for our sense of social reality or our sense of literary form.

Hardy hoped to endow the worn devices of Victorian plotting with nothing less than a metaphysical value: the plot of *The Mayor* is meant to serve as a kind of seismograph registering his vision of man's place in the universe. Where plot in Victorian fiction had often become little more than a means of providing a low order of suspense and complication, plot in Hardy's novels is supposed to signify, through its startling convolutions, a view of the human condition. But to succeed in such an aim, Hardy would have had to establish in his fiction an aura of the inevitable —and this was very difficult for a writer whose idea of fatality was itself pretty much of an improvisation. The aura of the inevitable was possible to classical tragedy, in which the gods were clearly apprehended and their desires, if not always their motives, were beyond question. It is also possible, I think, to modern fiction, in which the psychology of the characters controls the action. But it is virtually impossible for a novelist using the Victorian plot or something like it. Because Hardy remained enough of a Christian to believe that purpose courses through the universe but not enough of a Christian to believe that purpose is benevolent or the attribute of a particular Being, he had to make his plots convey the oppressiveness of fatality without positing an agency determining the course of fate. Why he should have boxed himself into this position is intellectually understandable but very hard to justify esthetically. The result was that he often seems to be coercing his plots, jostling them away from their own inner logic. And sometimes, in his passion to bend plot to purpose, he seems to be plotting against his own characters.

The plot of *The Mayor* suffers from most of Hardy's faults: coincidences which cannot be justified even in terms of his darkening view of life, transitions so awkwardly managed they cannot be excused by references to Hardy's kinship with the balladeers, improbabilities that threaten the suspension of disbelief he has himself induced. Yet the plot of *The Mayor* is probably the best that Hardy ever contrived, if only because its numerous flaws pertain to the things happening near and around Henchard but never seriously diminish his power at the center of the book. The thread of credence may be broken by certain turns of the action, such as the reappearance and withdrawal of the sailor who had bought Henchard's wife; such incidents are poorly managed, and it would be foolish to seek excuses, through vague invocations of Hardy's metaphysics, for what is mostly ineptitude and carelessness. But Henchard's own responses at such critical moments—his boiling self-incitements which start with a plunge into brutal aggression or oppressive affection and end with a dull and bewildered regret—are always credible. The accumulation of disasters with which he is afflicted must strike even the most indulgent reader as excessive; but the mixture of heroic force and sickening blindness with which he confronts these disasters is never in doubt. The plot may creak, but Henchard lives. And since he does emerge vivid and intact, it seems reasonable to conclude that the plot serves the rough but essential purpose of charting and enabling the curve of Henchard's fate. The plot fulfills the potential for dramatic gesture—or, if you prefer, self-destruction—which is Henchard's project in life. It does not do this smoothly, or without shocks of disbelief; it does not always persuade us that quite so overwhelming a concentration of troubles is really in the nature of things; but what it does succeed in doing is to persuade us that Henchard's personal struggle —the struggle of a splendid animal trying to escape a trap and thereby entangling itself all the more—is true. By the end of the story, there is nothing further for Henchard to do; he has exhausted himself as a man, he has exhausted himself as a character.

In its opening chapters *The Mayor of Casterbridge* reads like a fable, a story stripped to a line of essential happenings, but once Hardy leaps across two decades and shows Susan and Elizabeth-Jane returning to the town where Henchard is now a prosperous middle-aged merchant, the setting is thickened with social detail. Hardy portrays Casterbridge in its unsettled condition, which is somewhere between a small-scale market economy and the new impersonal commerce.

In these pages Hardy comes as close as he ever can to being a social novelist. It would be idle to look for the subtleties of observation we associate with a book like *Middlemarch,* that marvellous confrontation of social status and spiritual being. What Hardy does offer is an authoritative portrait of a country town as it begins to experience a social change it can neither control nor comprehend. He keeps observing the lag of consciousness behind events, both as a factor in historical development and a common fact of existence. Few people in Casterbridge try to grasp any meaning in their lives, few even suppose there is a need to. Most accept the lumpishness of daily routine. Henchard does not really care to understand what is happening to him; he merely wants, through will and magic, to coerce the direction of his personal fate and the turns of the impersonal market, which in his case are almost indistinguishable.

Slowly the isolation of Casterbridge is coming to an end; that mystery known as the market, beyond scrutiny or challenge, plays on every nerve; and soon machinery will transform and replace labor. Yet it is crucial to Hardy's theme that Casterbridge remains a town dependent on agriculture, "the complement of the rural life around, not its urban opposite."

Signs of class division are frequent, but not yet fixed into a rigid hierarchy. Hardy contrasts the mayor and his half-drunken merchant cronies at the banquet with the poor folk staring through the window; he quietly remarks upon the snobberies to which Susan and Elizabeth-Jane are subject when they come to town; and he soon brings into play the shabby "rustics" of Mixen Lane, who form a kind of *lumpen* mixture during the transition from country to town. Yet all of these people are bound together in a community of sorts—which is not to say that they live in harmonious bliss but that they do experience a sense of relationship with both one another and their common past. When Henchard's doting workman, Abel Whittle, cannot wake up early enough to begin a business journey, Henchard does not discharge him as an "enlightened" employer might. He does something better and worse. He rushes to Whittle's cottage, shakes him out of sleep and marches him through the town without his breeches —in order to teach him a lesson and get him on the job. It is an outrageous thing to do, but it is personal and direct.

Hardy is shrewd at juxtaposing old and new styles of economy:

> Here lived burgesses who daily walked the fallow; shepherds in an intra-mural squeeze. A street of farmers' homesteads—a street ruled by a mayor and corporation, yet echoing with the thump of the flail, the flutter of the winnowing fan, and the purr of milk into the pails . . .

The tone here, as throughout the book, is dispassionate and balanced. Hardy is not so foolish as to yield himself to an unqualified nostalgia for the agricultural past nor so heartless as simply to embrace the ways of the future. The social biases at work in both his earlier and later novels come together in *The Mayor* as an uneasy equilibrium, somewhat like that which forms the character of Henchard.

The portrait steadily built up of Casterbridge is never to be at the center of Hardy's concern, yet is essential to all that follows in the book. For without a full exposure to this social milieu, it would not be possible to register the significance of the struggle between Henchard and his young rival, the Scotchman Farfrae.

First his friend and employee, then his competitor in business and love, and finally his employer and replacement as mayor, Farfrae comes—his name suggests it—as the stranger from afar. At first their conflict is apprehended as a clash of temperaments, a contrast in kinds of character. So the absorbed reader is likely to regard the book, and so the scrutinizing critic ought finally to take it.

Henchard responds to his personal experience passionately, through volcanic upheavals; Farfrae sentimentally, through mild quaverings. Henchard wishes to wrench his environment; Farfrae to glide through it. Henchard can never adjust self to social role; Farfrae keeps self and social role harmonious, as partners in a busy enterprise. Henchard is rock; Farfrae smooth pebble. Their clash cannot be avoided, if only because Henchard keeps assaulting whatever equilibrium of personal and business relations they establish. Repeatedly Henchard provokes Farfrae to contests of manliness and guile, without realizing that the two are by no means the same. And the more Henchard emerges as a personal force, the less he survives as a social power.

Their conflict reflects, but is not reducible to, a shake-up within the dominant social class of Casterbridge, the merchants and traders. Men accustomed to a free-and-easy personal economy, in which arrangements are sealed by a word, will now be replaced by agents of an economy more precise and rational, in which social relationships must be mediated through paper. Henchard is "bad at figures," he keeps his money in an old safe, and

> His accounts were like bramblewood when Mr. Farfrae came. He used to reckon his sacks by chalk strokes all in a row like garden palings, measure his ricks by stretching with his arms, weigh his trusses by a lift, judge his hay by a chaw, and settle the price with a curse.

Henchard runs his affairs by hunches—which works well enough as long as he need only confront problems he can apprehend intuitively, as elements of an economy local and familiar. Toward the men who work for him Henchard is both generous and despotic, close and overbearing. He can be an autocrat, but never a hypocrite. He prepares the way for a triumph of bourgeois economy, but cannot live at ease with the style it brings. And he is not really able to distinguish between business and personal affairs, since for better or worse, he assumes that a man's life should be all of a piece. Will Farfrae be his manager? Then Farfrae must be his friend. And not only must Farfrae help with the books and the grain, he must eat heavy breakfasts with him and listen to the story of his life, as if to slake Henchard's thirst for relationship and impact.

Farfrae, says Hardy at one point, "is the reverse of Henchard." It is an important observation, and important, paradoxically, because of its generality. For what matters in the kind of social displacement Hardy is here portraying, is not so much the character of the newcomer, who must be something of a riddle precisely because he is new, as the ordeal of the old-timer, who forms part of a known and shared experience.

Farfrae bears the fruits of science; he introduces new machines to the farmers; he treats his men with "progressive" blandness, which at this point in history means neither to abuse nor pay them as much as Henchard. With Farfrae there comes to Casterbridge the rule of "functional rationality," what Karl Mannheim describes as "a series of actions . . . organized in such a way that it leads to a previously defined goal, every element in this series of actions receiving a functional position and role." This outlook is expressed by Farfrae with amusing precision when he explains the benefits of the new seed-drill:

> "It will revolutionize sowing hereabouts! No more sowers flinging their seed about broadcast, so that some falls by the wayside and some among thorns . . . Each grain will go straight to its intended place, and nowhere else whatever."

Who, comparing the ways of Henchard and Farfrae, will easily choose between them? Certainly not Hardy. He is too canny, too reflective for an unambiguous stand, and his first loyalty is neither to Henchard nor Farfrae but the larger community of Wessex. Hardy's feelings may go out to Henchard but his mind is partly with Farfrae. He knows that in important respects the Scotchman will help bring a better life to Casterbridge, even if a life less vivid and integral. Yet he also recognizes that the narrowing of opportunity for men like Henchard represents a loss in social strength. In his own intuitive and "poetic" way Hardy works toward an attitude of mature complexity, registering gains and losses, transcending the fixed positions of "progress" and "tradition." Because he is so entirely free of sentimental or ideological preconceptions in *The Mayor,* he achieves not only a more balanced view of the developments in Casterbridge than either Henchard or Farfrae can reach; his voice also emerges as that of a communal protector and spokesman.

Hardy's design requires that, to sharpen the contrast between looming protagonist and the secondary figures, Henchard be scaled as somewhat larger than life: that which is passing away seems larger than that which is yet to come. And in defeat men can grow into eloquence; they rant, they rave; sometimes they even discover their humanity. Farfrae, however, has no reason to cry out. He lives in modest harmony with the prevailing social trends, and need never call upon—need not even discover whether he has any—deeper emotional resources. Farfrae's feelings are always obedient to his will and are not, in any case, of a kind that could seriously interfere with his role as businessman. But Hardy also recognizes tacitly that a disagreeable role in society does not necessarily make for a disagreeable character, and he avoids the error of portraying Farfrae as a slick commercial schemer.

It has been customary among Hardy's critics and, I would guess, frequent among his readers to feel some dissatisfaction with Farfrae. He is said to be a figure too dim, never closely examined, more outline than substance. This kind of complaint rests, I think, upon a misunderstanding of both the book and the character. *The Mayor* is not a psychological novel in the sense that it provides, through a narrator's scrutiny, an intensive probing of psychic life. Henchard's psychology is, of course, extraordinarily interesting, but it is a psychology neither analyzed nor minutely examined: we must infer it from the unfolding of his behavior. Much the same, if on a smaller scale, holds true for Farfrae. And dramatically there is no reason why we should be allowed a fuller scrutiny of Farfrae's inner life. His function in this novel is to serve as "the reverse of Henchard," and if there is something a little shadowy about him, that is partly because he is a stranger bringing untested ways to a tested place.

In any case, Hardy maintains a finely balanced poise—it holds together wariness, irony and some respect—toward Farfrae. Clearly the Scotchman cannot engage Hardy as a Jude or even a

Henchard can, yet he is conceived with clarity of outline and a modest quotient of sympathy. Farfrae wants no revenge upon Henchard and is quite ready to help him once everything has been lost; in fact, Farfrae wants nothing but quiet prosperity, domestic peace and modest preferment. As the victor, he is even ready to be tolerant toward Henchard's outbursts and provocations. That there must also be something intolerable in the tolerance of the victor, Hardy silently recognizes—it is the kind of recognition we expect from him. And it informs some of the most striking incidents in the novel, those showing Henchard, after his downfall, in the grip of a compulsive and self-lacerating pride. They are incidents that stay in one's memory as tokens of Hardy's intuitive craft: when Henchard comes to work as a day laborer for Farfrae, wearing the silk hat that is the single remnant of his lost prosperity; when he encounters Lucetta as the wife of his new employer and elaborately pretends to humble himself before her; and when he thrusts himself forward, as if from an inflamed will, during the visit of "the royal personage."

Shrewd as a Scotchman, Farfrae is sentimental as a Scotchman. At the Three Mariners tavern he delights the Casterbridge folk with his nostalgic song, *"It's hame, and it's hame, hame fane would I be."* Yet this is the same Farfrae whose first appearance in the novel comes as a man who has chosen to leave his old hame, like many Scotchmen of the nineteenth century who had drifted south in search of prosperity. As Hardy remarks in a quietly sardonic sentence, Farfrae is always "giving strong expression to a song of his dear native country that he loved so well as never to have revisited it." That anyone should manage as readily as Farfrae to compartmentalize his experience is a somewhat comic idea: the dry comedy of self-insulation.

Hardy marshals expertly the materials compelling us to see Henchard and Farfrae as representative men, each the agent for an embattled segment within the merchant class of Casterbridge; yet he also writes out of a fine realization that no human figure, unless meant as comic caricature, can be grasped entirely through his social function. Men like Henchard and Farfrae will release impulses and display characteristics that are not strictly harmonious—indeed, are likely to clash—with their social roles. Farfrae is indeed a new man of commerce, but also a stranger, a sentimentalist, a creature of milky mildness. Henchard does come out of the besieged old order, but also carries within himself some of the vices that will characterize the new. Among the most striking pages in *The Mayor* are those in which the private voice of one man is taken as public speech by another—as in the critical incident in which Henchard pleads with Farfrae to return to his sick wife and, because of the battle that has just occurred between the two men, is simply not believed.

I have spoken of Henchard's guilt and of his drive to impose significance upon his life through a dramatic overreaching of the will. Let us, for convenience, call these the personal themes of *The Mayor*. How then—the question must arise—do they relate to the social confrontation between Henchard and Farfrae, so clearly meant to have a large representative weight?

The first impulse of a critic facing this kind of question is usually to look for patterns of neat alignment, so that the different strands of action can be brought together and the novel declared to have a satisfactory structure. I wonder, however, at the value of such a procedure. Is it not a mistake to keep tidying up works of fiction, like compulsive housekeepers after a wild party? Is not one of the pleasures of the novel as a *genre*—and the novel more than any other *genre*—that within a structure of some comeliness and coherence there is likely to be a portion of that contingency, that vital disorder we know to be present in human existence? For a novel to emerge as a work of art, its materials must be shaped, selected, suppressed; for the form thereby achieved to persuade and move us, it must also create an illusion of the rich formlessness of reality.

Now what I have called the personal and the social themes of *The Mayor* do converge toward a significant interlocking. Henchard's personal qualities are distinctively his own, but they take on a resonance that would be quite impossible were they not rooted in a portion of Wessex history. The fortitude of character that renders him so notable a man is not merely an idiosyncratic trait; it has been nurtured and made possible by the society of old Wessex. A figure of potency and assurance in the Wessex that is dying, he is a mere foundering wreck in the Wessex that is coming to birth.

After the first few chapters we see that Hardy is weaving together an entanglement between the personal and public sides of Henchard's experience, the psychic turbulence that erupts within him and the social contests in which he finds himself caught up. This entanglement is tightened at a key point, when the old furmity woman comes before Henchard sitting as magistrate. She serves the plot as a kind of Nemesis, the voice of memory as it dredges up the mayor's shame. Thereby the theme first advanced in the opening chapter is brought to climax: Henchard cannot escape the consequences of his past. But reappearing at the moment she does, the furmity woman also hastens the collapse of Henchard as a social force in the world of Casterbridge.

That this connection is logically unassailable may surely be doubted. There is no necessary or sufficiently coercive reason why the consequences of a personal sin should coincide in time and impact with the climax of a socio-economic failure. Several things, to be sure, are working for Hardy which enable him to paper over the difficulty: first, that behind the two strands of action—Henchard's personal story and his social struggle—there operate the same turbulent elements of his character, so that we may thereby be induced to accept a similarity of effects; second, that we are emotionally persuaded to acquiesce in the notion that troubles run in packs, one kind precipitating another; and third, that by this point in the book Hardy is so involved in overplotting that the relentless accumulation of intrigue distracts us from the weakness of this major turning point in the plot. Yet, even if one makes all these allowances, it cannot be said that Hardy succeeds in establishing the aura of inexorability which both the logic of his story and the conception behind his protagonist require. The fault is a serious one, still another instance of the way Hardy's plots crumble beneath the thematic weight with which he burdens them.

Faults of this kind and magnitude can be found in all of Hardy's fiction, and it would be idle to deny that they are troublesome; yet they are not, either in *The Mayor* or Hardy's other major novels, finally decisive. They count for more in one's reflections upon Hardy's work than in one's actual experience of it. For the strongest impression created by a book like *The Mayor* is

that of a unified tone, an integration of sensibility and effects.
And if we do not claim for the book a tragic stature it neither invites nor requires,[1] the impression of unity is particularly strong.
It is an impression that depends upon specific compositional
achievements.

The Mayor is a novel packed with incident, and if we examine
closely some of the devices Hardy used to keep his serial exciting,
we can charge him with overcrowding. Except, however, in the
first few chapters, none of the incidents is developed at much
length or with much fullness. Hardy continues—rightly enough,
since this is where his greatness lies—to depend upon a series of
intensely wrought and symbolically charged bits of action, scattered through the book and so brief in scope as to prevent us from
thinking of them as dramatic scenes. These bits of action form
the intermittent points of climax, transition and accumulation in
the movement of the plot.

Another reason for the integration of effects is the way Hardy
handles his "rustics." In his earlier novels these figures weave in
and out of the main action, serving mostly as comic relief or minor
conveniences of plot, at best as a low-keyed chorus expressing a
traditional wisdom in response to the deracination or defeat of
the major characters. But in *The Mayor* they form a significant
part of the story. It is they who precipitate the skimmity-ride

1. Apparently out of a wish to honor the novel, critics in recent years have
spoken about *The Mayor* as a tragedy, with consequent comparisons between
Henchard and Oedipus and Lear. I doubt that these help us in responding
to the book Hardy actually wrote.

Certain elements in *The Mayor* do bear a resemblance to a tragic action,
but then so do elements in any serious work of fiction. What seems lacking
in the story and character of Henchard, however, is that "proper magnitude"
of which Aristotle speaks. By this admittedly vague phrase I take Aristotle to
mean a resonance of large philosophic and cultural issues: the destiny of a
race, the fate of a people, the ordeal of a hero who embodies the strivings of
a nation. Impressive as Henchard may be, he cannot be said to embody in
his character or conduct issues of such magnitude. He is too clearly related
to the particularities of a historical moment and a social contest; he is too
clearly a character with only the most limited grasp, or growth, of consciousness; and he does not elicit, in my judgment, that blend of pity and terror
amounting to awe which is characteristic of the tragic hero.

My own sense of Henchard would place him not in the line of tragedy but
in the tradition of romanticism. He strikes me as a descendent of those
stubborn figures in romantic poetry and fiction who refuse to submit to their
own limitations and demand more from the world than it can give them.

which throws Lucetta into a fever and then death. The social transformation Hardy dramatizes through the clash between Henchard and Farfrae is sharply reflected in the life of the "rustics," now ill at ease in the town, beginning to express a measure of social *ressentiment,* and clearly losing their cohesion as a group. Some of the usual tasks of the Hardyan chorus are still performed here, and very beautifully, as when Mother Cuxsom muses on the death of Susan:

> Well, poor soul; she's helpless to hinder that or anything now . . . And all her shining keys will be took from her, and her cupboards opened; and little things a' didn't wish seen, anybody will see; and her wishes and ways will all be as nothing!

or when Abel Whittle recalls Henchard's end:

> We walked on like that all night; and in the blue o' the morning, when 'twas hardly day, I looked ahead o' me, and I zeed that he wambled, and could hardly drag along. By that time we had got past here . . . and I took down the boards from the windows, and helped him inside. "What, Whittle," he said, "and can ye really be such a poor fond fool as to care for such a wretch as I!"

But such passages, fewer here than in Hardy's earlier novels, are really no more than occasional grace notes. In the main, the rustics are viewed in a hard and realistic light; their moral seediness and decay reflect the social changes portrayed through the dominant line of plot. One could almost speak of the events at Mixen Lane as a sub-plot, the darkened reflection through plebeian grotesquerie of the main strand of action.

Yet it surely must be the common experience of Hardy's readers that in *The Mayor of Casterbridge* it is Henchard himself who is the unremittent center of interest. He is that rarity in modern fiction: an integral characterization, a figure shown not through a dimension of psychology or an aspect of conduct, but at a single stroke, in his full range of being. Henchard neither grows nor changes; and we do not really come to understand him any better as the novel progresses. We do not need to. For we know him immediately and completely, through an act of intuitive apprehension. He appears before us through those gestures of conduct and speech which realize his uniqueness: a man exemplifying the heroism and futility of the human will. For a novelist to have created this image of character is a very great achievement—it adds to the stock of archetypal possibilities that inhabit our minds.

Of all his novels Hardy liked best *The Woodlanders,* which appeared in 1887, a year after *The Mayor.* Though never an object of much critical attention, it has remained a favorite with those readers who respond to the nuances of minor English fiction without being overly concerned about the novel as moral criticism or epistemological scrutiny. Hardy said of *The Woodlanders* that it enabled him to "hold my own in fiction, whatever that may be worth." His estimate was correct.

There are very real pleasures to be had from reading *The Woodlanders,* even if not quite the pleasures most of Hardy's critics have found. The material of the book is quickly available, and there are fewer barriers of credence or disappointments with language than in the greater novels. All *The Woodlanders* requires is a few sharp discriminations, so that its permanent values can be brought into relief. For like the woods and the woodlanders it portrays, this book has a quietly vibrant life shaded and half-hidden beneath the level of one's eye.

The Woodlanders is hardly, I think, the pastoral romance critics have often declared it to be. Some conventions of pastoral are present, if not always persuasively employed: there is, for one thing, the parallel between a hierarchy of social status and a hierarchy of moral qualities. But if we think of *Under the Greenwood Tree* as Hardy's finest pastoral, it becomes clear that a useful description of *The Woodlanders* will have to employ other terms. Pastoral implies a stylized bucolic setting drawn from a distance—a cosmopolitan willing of the natural. By contrast *The Woodlanders,* beneath a flimsy superstructure of plot, offers a realistic picture of country life, one that recedes from the active cultivation of farming into an alert dependence on the forest. In *The Woodlanders* earth is a place, not an emblem. And the conclusion of the book, all too close to the gritty compromises of actuality, is not what one has come to expect from pastoral. These distinctions matter not as quibbles about *genre,* but as a way, perhaps, toward gaining a better apprehension of what still lives in Hardy's book.

Nor is it profitable to look to *The Woodlanders* for Hardy's usual themes and methods. The clash between a disturbed agricultural world and modern innovation is certainly there, but not as impressively as in *The Return of the Native* or *The Mayor of Casterbridge*. What is missing here is the fierce involvement Hardy has with insurgent figures like Clym Yeobright; indeed, the book suffers in that only one side of Hardy's recurrent social dialectic—the side of the rooted plebeians—comes through with any force. None of the characteristic Hardyan strengths is much in evidence: not the central overpowering character who embodies the tensions of a book, not the compressed scenes in which characters symbolically act out their larger purposes, not even the overarching philosophic sentiment, more mood than statement, which gives the best of Hardy's novels their peculiar resonance.

The Woodlanders is more a leisurely portraiture than a sustained drama. There is—I intend no paradox—a surplus of plot and a shortage of action: Hardy has cumbered himself with Victorian machinery, including blighted loves, drooping coquettes and gothic revengers, but he has not succeeded in dramatizing his materials. Had he really tried to do so, the book would either have become intolerably long (it is already too languid in pace) or it would have required some radical plot surgery. Hardy tells a good portion of the story in passable expository prose and allows his customary devices of coincidence to carry another share of the narrative. It does not much matter, since no mature mind is likely, after the opening chapters, to pay serious attention to the plot. Indeed, the biggest weakness of the novel is a lack of organic connection between plot and picture. Plot goes its own trundling way, while picture is often very beautiful. Much of what is loveliest in *The Woodlanders*—and there are muted delicacies throughout the book—is closer to Hardy's poetry and stories than to his major fiction. Were one to go by internal evidence alone, *The Woodlanders* more than either of the two masterpieces following it would point to Hardy's growing impatience with novel writing.

For a good part of *The Woodlanders,* especially the part occupying its foreground space, is tiresome. The relationship between Felice Charmond, the capricious hedonist, and Fitzpiers, the libidinous physician with metaphysical yearnings, is no more absorbing than a romance of candy sticks; the crucial scene in which the badly treated Giles Winterborne lies shivering with fever outside his own hut because, having yielded it as a shelter for Grace Melbury, he does not wish any word of scandal to pass, seems close to absurd. And not only absurd. It induces in readers unvexed by aspirations to saintliness a response very different from that which Hardy intended: no one, neither man nor dog, should have to be that loyal.

Insofar as the characters are supposed to emerge as individual figures, they are insipid. The strength of the novel lies rather in its revealed sense of all that is shared, all that is *characteristic* in human character; the way men and women, with some dignity and value, can live by received patterns and fixed responses. Marty South and Giles Winterborne, the stoical woodlanders, and even Melbury, the merchant whose plan to better the life of his daughter leads to her ruin: these are type characters but in their typicality convincing and memorable. The strongest portraiture in the novel depends upon Hardy's patient submission to Marty and Giles, just as they in turn live by submission to the woods surrounding them. What *The Woodlanders* shows is how much of human life, even in personal relations, is not at all "personal." Deeply conservative in feeling, the novel evokes a gray and muted poetry of mundane existence, and this flows through the individual figures even as it seems to be apart from and greater than themselves.

About Marty and Giles there hangs a faint aura of idealization, and clearly Hardy so intended it. Otherwise, there could be no reason for accepting characters so pleasingly unadulterated by "personality." The mournful passivity of Marty and Giles may trouble us; the critical cult that has grown up around Marty, a mere sketch of a girl compared to Tess Durbeyfield, may strike us as a bore. But the strength with which Marty and Giles move into their fate; their admirable refusal to regard themselves as spectacles for self-appraisal; the unity they exhibit between person and role—all this comes as a decided relief from the endless clatter about individuality which fills modern literature and life.

For considerable stretches Hardy suspends the motions of his plot and lingers before the woods and its people. Then the novel lives, beautifully. The interpenetration of nature and humanity

is sketched in halftones, without the intellectual straining that
mars the more ambitious novels:

> Giles had a marvellous power of making trees grow. Although he
> would seem to shovel in the earth quite carelessly, there was a sort
> of sympathy between himself and the fir, oak, or beech that he was
> operating on; so that the roots took hold of the soil in a few days . . .
> The holes were already dug, and they set to work. Winterborne's
> fingers were endowed with a gentle conjurer's touch in spreading
> roots of each little tree, resulting in a sort of caress under which the
> delicate fibres all laid themselves out in their proper direction for
> growth. He put most of these roots toward the southwest; for, he
> said, in forty years' time, when some great gale is blowing from that
> quarter, the trees will require the strongest holdfast on that side to
> stand against it and not fall.
> "How they sigh directly we put 'em upright, though while they're
> lying down they don't sigh at all," said Marty.

Giles's touch is that of a master workman, while Marty's is a
shade more romantic, as if to care for the being as well as the
nurture of the tree. And here is Winterborne walking with his
apple-mill:

> He looked and smelt like Autumn's very brother, his face being sun-
> burned to wheat-colour, his eyes blue as cornflowers, his sleeves and
> leggings dyed with fruit-stains, his hands clammy with the sweet
> juices of apples, his hat sprinkled with pips, and everything about
> him that atmosphere of cider which at its first return each season has
> such an indescribable fascination for those who have been born and
> bred among the orchards.

The language is intimate, unpretentious, concrete. There are
other passages dramatizing the relation between nature and men—

> The plantations were always weird at this hour of eve . . . The
> smooth surface of glossy plants came out like weak, lidless eyes; there
> were strange faces and figures from expiring lights that had somehow
> wandered into the canopied obscurity; while now and then low peeps
> of the sky between the trunks were like sheeted shapes, and on the
> tips of boughs sat faint cloven tongues.

—passages in which Hardy yields a little to rhetorical bravura,
as in the phrase about "canopied obscurity," but then recovers
in the metaphoric exactness of the following clause.

Learning to push aside the overgrowth of plot and look beneath it at the measured life of the woodland, we can value the

fidelity with which Hardy has drawn his portrait. And at that point, a little surprisingly, *The Woodlanders* can be taken as a novel of manners, expertly distinguishing among the grades of status and prestige in the world of Little Hintock—grades that may seem minute to an external observer but are fateful to its inhabitants. Power, deference, class barriers, prestige rankings, snobbism: all are here, drawn not to high relief or with the stress of indignation, but quietly and modestly.

In the fine opening chapter Marty South must sell her hair for two gold sovereigns staring at her like "a pair of jaundiced eyes on the watch for an opportunity"—and then see the hair adorn the landowner Felice Charmond. The Melburys, preening themselves on their town-educated daughter, come to Giles's party and arriving too early, father and stepmother cheerfully pitch in to help with the food but keep Grace from joining them: " 'Tisn't quite so much in your line," says the doting father, "as it is in your stepmother's and mine." Speaking to his wife about his fears that Grace will sink into the lethargic ways of Little Hintock, Melbury says: "Fancy her white hands getting redder every day, and her tongue losing its pretty up-country curl in talking, and her bounding walk becoming the regular Hintock shail-and-wamble!" No, replies Mrs. Melbury, "She may shail, but she'll never wamble." And toward the end, when Grace has been half broken by her marriage to Fitzpiers and turns back to the faithful Giles, there occurs a splendid bit of incident dramatizing the sense of social distinction between them. Giles invites the girl to a tavern for a meal, and she, "in a mood of the greatest depression," observes that while clean and respectable enough it is a simple place "with its knives and steel forks, tin pepper-boxes, blue salt-cellars, and posters advertising the sale of bullocks against the wall. . . ."

The two strengths of *The Woodlanders*—faithful portraiture and touches of mundane poetry—meet in the final pages. Grace has to accept a reunion with Fitzpiers, not in some romantic or sacrificial climax, but with the weariness of a commonplace, all-too-realistic adjustment. This strand of the story Hardy handles with a cool restraint: Grace's discovery that she feels nothing very special upon learning her husband has betrayed her, Fitzpiers' use of his sexuality to work his way with her and finally Grace's nagging little revenge in demanding that he give up both smoking and metaphysics. The ways of the world may not be Hardy's deepest concern, but when he needed to, he knew them well enough.

The poetry—somber, gray, flitting—is in the voices of the defeated and the resigned. As Marty South mourns over the grave of Giles Winterborne——

"Now, my own, own love . . . you are mine, and only mine; for she has forgot 'ee at last, although for her you died! But I—whenever I get up I'll think of 'ee and whenever I lie down I'll think of 'ee again. Whenever I plant the young larches I'll think that none can plant as you planted; and whenever I turn the cider wring, I'll say none could do it like you. If ever I forget your name let me forget home and heaven! . . . But no, no, my love, I never can forget 'ee; for you was a good man, and did good things!"

——eloquence and integrity come finally together.

VI

Let the Day Perish

As a writer of novels Thomas Hardy was endowed with a pre-cious gift: he liked women. There are not, when one comes to think of it, quite so many other nineteenth century novelists about whom as much can be said. With some, the need to keep returning in their fiction to the disheveled quarters of domesticity causes a sigh of weariness, even at times a suppressed snarl of dis-content; for, by a certain measure, it must seem incongruous that writers intent on a fundamental criticism of human existence should be sentenced to indefinite commerce with sex, courtship, adultery and family quarrels. Hardy, by contrast, felt no such impatience with the usual materials of the novel. Though quite capable of releasing animus toward his women characters and casting them as figures of destruction, he could not imagine a universe without an active, even an intruding, feminine principle. The sexual exclusiveness of nineteenth century American writing would have been beyond his comprehension, though probably not beyond his sympathy.

Throughout his years as a novelist Hardy found steadily in-teresting the conceits and playfulness of women, the elaborate complex of stratagems in which the sexual relationship appears both as struggle and game. He liked the changefulness, sometimes even the caprice, of feminine personality; he marveled at the seemingly innate capacity of young girls to glide into easy adaptations and tactical charms. And he had a strong appreciation of the manipulative and malicious powers that might be gathered beneath a surface of delight. Except perhaps with Sue Bridehead, he was seldom inclined to plunge into the analytic depths which mark the treatment of feminine character in George Eliot's later novels; but if he did not look as deeply as she did into the motivations of feminine character, he was remarkably keen at apprehending feminine behavior. He had observed and had watched, with uneasy alertness. The range of virtuosity which other writers had believed possible only in a stylized high society or sophisticated court, Hardy, in his plain and homely way, found among the country girls of southwest England.

Throughout Hardy's fiction, even in his lesser novels, there is a curious power of sexual insinuation, almost as if he were not locked into the limits of masculine perception but could shuttle between, or for moments yoke together, the responses of the two sexes. This gift for creeping intuitively into the emotional life of women Hardy shared with a contemporary, George Gissing, though he was quite free of that bitter egocentrism which marred Gissing's work. And at the deepest level of his imagination, Hardy held to a vision of the feminine that was thoroughly traditional in celebrating the maternal, the protective, the fecund, the tender, the life-giving. It was Hardy's openness to the feminine principle that drew D. H. Lawrence to his work and led him to see there, with some justice, a kinship with his own. One may speculate that precisely those psychological elements which led Hardy to be so indulgent toward male passivity also enabled him to be so receptive to feminine devices. He understood and could portray aggression; but at least as a writer, he did not allow it to dominate or corrode his feelings about the other sex—and that, incidentally, is one reason he does not care to pass judgment on his characters. The feminine admixture is very strong in his work, a source both of his sly humor and his profound sympathy.

It is in *Tess of the D'Urbervilles* that this side of Hardy comes through with the most striking vitality. The book stands at the center of Hardy's achievement, if not as his greatest then certainly his most characteristic, and those readers or critics who cannot

accept its emotional ripeness must admit that for them Hardy is
not a significant novelist. For in *Tess* he stakes everything on his
sensuous apprehension of a young woman's life, a girl who is at
once a simple milkmaid and an archetype of feminine strength.
Nothing finally matters in the novel nearly so much as Tess
herself: not the other characters, not the philosophic underlay,
not the social setting. In her violation, neglect and endurance,
Tess comes to seem Hardy's most radical claim for the redemp-
tive power of suffering; she stands, both in the economy of the
book and as a figure rising beyond its pages and into common
memory, for the unconditional authority of feeling.

   Tess is one of the greatest examples we have in English literature of how a writer can take hold of a cultural stereotype and,
through the sheer intensity of his affection, pare and purify it
into something that is morally ennobling. Tess derives from
Hardy's involvement with and reaction against the Victorian
cult of chastity, which from the beginning of his career he had
known to be corrupted by meanness and hysteria. She falls. She
violates the standards and conventions of her day. And yet, in
her incomparable vibrancy and lovingness, she comes to represent a spiritualized transcendence of chastity. She dies three times,
to live again:—first with Alec D'Urberville, then with Angel
Clare, and lastly with Alec again. Absolute victim of her wretched
circumstances, she is ultimately beyond their stain. She embodies
a feeling for the inviolability of the person, as it brings the absolute of chastity nearer to the warming Christian virtue of charity. Through a dialectic of negation, Tess reaches purity of spirit
even as she fails to satisfy the standards of the world.

   Perhaps because she fails to satisfy them? Not quite. What we
have here is not the spiritual sensationalism of the Dostoevsky
who now and again indulges himself in the notion that a surrender to licentiousness is a necessary condition for spiritual re-
birth. Hardy's view is a more innocent one, both purer and less
worldly. He does not seek the abyss nor glory in finding it. He
is not a phenomenologist of the perverse. But as a man deeply
schooled in the sheer difficulty of life, he does recognize that
there is a morality of being as well as of doing, an imperative
to compassion which weakens the grip of judgment. Once educated to humility, we do not care to judge Tess at all: we no

longer feel ourselves qualified. And that, I think, is a triumph of the moral imagination.

In staking out these claims for *Tess of the D'Urbervilles* I recognize that Hardy's vision of Tess can hardly satisfy the rigorous morality of Protestantism which was a part of his heritage. Other forces are at work, both pre- and post-Christian: the stoicism of the folk ballad, from whose wronged heroines Tess descends, and the moral experiment of romanticism. Hardy could no more avoid the conditioning influence of romanticism than a serious writer can now avoid that of modernism; it was part of the air he breathed. His romanticism enabled Hardy to break past the repressions of the Protestant ethic and move into a kindlier climate shared by Christian charity and pagan acceptance; but it was also romanticism, with its problematic and perverse innovations, which threatened his wish for a return to a simple, primitive Christianity. In *Tess of the D'Urbervilles* the romantic element appears most valuably as an insistence upon the right of the individual person to create the terms of his being, despite the pressures and constraints of the external world. Yet, because Tess is a warmhearted and unpretentious country girl barely troubled by intellectual ambition, Hardy's stress is upon the right of the person and not, as it will be in *Jude the Obscure*, upon the subjective demands of personality. Sue Bridehead anticipates the modern cult of personality in all its urgency and clamor; Tess Durbeyfield represents something more deeply rooted in the substance of instinctual life.

There are, to be sure, instances of self-indulgent writing in this novel which can be described as late-romantic, even decadent, but the controlling perception of Tess is restrained and, if one cares to use such terms, "healthy." Tess demands nothing that can be regarded as the consequence of deracination or an overwrought will; she is not gratuitously restless or neurotically bored; she is spontaneously committed to the most fundamental needs of human existence. Indeed, she provides a standard of what is right and essential for human beings to demand from life. And because we respond to her radiant wholeness, Tess stands somewhat apart from, nor can she be seriously damaged by, the romantic excesses into which Hardy's writing can lapse. Tess is finally one of the great images of human possibility, conceived in the chaste, and chastening, spirit of the New Testament. Very few proclaimed believers have written with so complete a Christian sentiment as the agnostic Thomas Hardy.

Simply as a work of fiction, *Tess of the D'Urbervilles* is singularly direct in its demands. It contains few of the elements we have come to know and expect in nineteenth century novels. There is little interplay of character as registered through nuances of social manners or the frictions of social class. None of the secondary figures has much interest in his own right, apart from his capacity to illuminate and enlarge the experience of Tess; all of them seem, by Hardy's evident choice, to be dwarfed beside her. The passages of philosophic comment, about which I will say more on a later page, surely do not provide a center of concern for the serious modern reader. And while the social setting—a setting that, in its several parts, forms a history of rural England leveled in space—comes to be quite essential for the development of the action, finally it is not to the world in which Tess moves, nor even the world Tess may symbolize, that we yield our deepest assent.

As for the plot, it seems in isolation a paltry thing, a mere scraping together of bits and pieces from popular melodrama: a pure girl betrayed, a woman's secret to be told or hidden, a piling on of woes that must strain the resources of ordinary credence. Whether Hardy was deliberately employing the threadbare stuff of melodrama in order to transcend it, or whether he shared in the emotional premises of such fiction but through his peculiar genius unconsciously raised it to the level of abiding art (as Dickens repeatedly did), is very hard to say. Perhaps, in the case of a writer like Hardy, it is a distinction without much difference.[1]

1. "There is no absolute divorce," writes Joseph Warren Beach in a keen paragraph, "between 'literature' proper and the literature of the dime novel. Themes which receive their crudely sentimental and melodramatic treatment in the one are sure to appear above the surface, somewhat refined, it may be, but recognizable. Meredith, when he put forth *Rhoda Fleming*, showed in his chapter headings a consciousness that he was writing somewhat in the manner of *East Lynne*. . . . *Tess of the d'Urbervilles* came at a time when, in serious literature, especially in plays, a great deal of attention was being paid to the subject of the *déclassée*—the woman who would come back, the woman who lives under 'the shadow of a sin,' the woman who has to pay for 'one

There is just enough plot loosely to thread together the several episodes that comprise the book, yet surely it is not here that one looks for Hardy's achievement. *Tess of the D'Urbervilles* can, in fact, profitably be regarded as a fiction in the line of *Pilgrim's Progress* rather than in the line of Jane Austen's and George Eliot's novels, for its structure is that of a journey in which each place of rest becomes a test for the soul and the function of plot is largely to serve as an agency for transporting the central figure from one point to another. *Tess* is clearly not an allegory and no one in his senses would wish that it were, but its pattern of narrative has something in common with, even if it does not directly draw upon, Bunyan's fiction. There are four sections or panels of representation: Tess at home and with Alec; Tess at Talbothays and with Angel; Tess at Flintcomb-Ash and again with Alec; Tess briefly happy with Angel and then in her concluding apotheosis at Stonehenge. None of these panels is quite self-sufficient, since narrative tension accumulates from part to part; but each has a distinctiveness of place, action and tone which makes it profitable to think of the novel as episodic. One is reminded of a medieval painting divided into panels, each telling part of a story and forming a progress in martyrdom. The martyrdom is that of Tess, upon whom everything rests and all value depends.

The novel opens with several compact vignettes. The first chapter, in which John Durbeyfield is told that he comes from an ancient but decayed aristocratic family, presents through comedy the dislocation which is to serve as pressure for Tess's odyssey. The second chapter, in which Tess, a healthy farm girl but "not handsomer than the others," is seen at the rite of "club-walking," has a double value: it quickly introduces the village of Marlott in the gentle Vale of Blackmoor, where something still remains of an independent yeomanry, small land holdings

---

false step.' *The Second Mrs. Tanqueray* will suffice to suggest the currency of a theme which is treated by such other notable hands as Oscar Wilde and Henry Arthur Jones. So that Hardy's subject was timely from the point of view of the 'high brow' as well as popular in the original sense of the word. And that one of his novels which is most satisfying to the critic for the beauty and seriousness of its art is at the same time the one to make, from the time of its first appearance, an appeal to the widest circle of readers."

and traditional rural ways, yet where the old rituals have been shorn of their significance and reduced to pleasant customs. Tess, "a mere vessel of emotion untinctured by experience," has passed the Sixth Standard in a National School, but this should not be taken to suggest that she has been cut off from the life of Marlott. Indeed, the Sixth Standard is rapidly becoming part of that life. Hardy provides this piece of information about — Tess's schooling in order to make more plausible her role as a country girl, not a mere dumb victim of incomprehensible social forces (as are her three young friends in the later portions of the book), but a figure with some articulateness and awareness. Her education underscores her representativeness, for there is just enough of it to endow her with consciousness while not enough to make her estranged.

—A few pages later, for the first time, Tess takes the center of the stage: she is driving the family wagon in the dark of night, because her shiftless father has gotten drunk and the family's beehives must be delivered to Casterbridge. Dozing off, Tess fails to hear the mail-cart "with its two noiseless wheels, speeding along these lanes like an arrow," and in the ensuing accident the Durbeyfield horse, the family's main economic asset, is killed. Out of remorse and guilt, Tess then agrees to her mother's scheme that she visit the rich Trantridge D'Urbervilles who will make her fortune. That these cousins are not authentic offshoots of the aristocratic line, but *arriviste* bourgeois who have bought their way into the gentry and appropriated the name as a decoration, is a fine stroke.

The trap has been sprung for Tess, be it a trap of fatality, social pressure, family sloth or all at once. Throughout the remainder of the book, Hardy will employ a pattern of hunting images, as John Holloway has nicely observed. Tess will be "harried from place to place at what seems like gradually increasing speed." Finally, "when the hunt is over, Tess is captured on the sacrificial stone at Stonehenge, the stone where once, like the hart at bay, the victim's throat was slit with the knife. With these things in mind, Hardy's much abused quotation from Aeschylus ('in Aeschylean phrase, the President of the Immortals had finished his sport with Tess') takes on a new meaning and aptness."

Thus far, in the first few chapters, Tess has not been cast in a strongly individual mold, except possibly during the poignant, if overburdened, conversation with her little brother Abraham as to whether "we be on a blighted star." She is shown in the ease of her natural surroundings, a long-cultivated and soft-featured rural landscape, but also in the discomfort of her social place, an idle crumbling family and a growing poverty that forces her to surrender her independence and appeal to her rich "cousins." As it happens—and Hardy is clearly starting to weave a social fable here—the rich cousin is Alec D'Urberville, shown at the outset as a stagy villain who greets Tess with the standard melodramatic gambit: "Well, my Beauty, what can I do for you?" The theatricality is deliberate. In this novel Hardy will achieve something that is rare in fiction: a fusion of theater and truth.

To prepare for the monstrousness of Alec's betrayal as well as to set off Tess from the subordinate figures that will surround her, Hardy starts to fill in the portrait of his heroine. We are still far from the depth that will characterize the later Tess, but we do now see her in characteristic health and country bloom. There is the marvelous passage in which Alec, during their first meeting, plies her with strawberries, insisting that he himself pop them in her mouth and meanwhile adding rose blossoms "to put in her bosom." One of those symbolic miniatures at which Hardy is so masterful, the passage radiates with suggestions of dominance, patronage, sexuality. Tess, stirred and bewildered, "obeyed like one in a dream."

The texture darkens a little, but only a little, when Alec drives Tess from her cottage to his mansion and begins to make advances to her. For if there is something ominous in the air, there is also fun and youthful zest in their sparring—Hardy's gift for evoking the play of flirtation seldom fails him. And the writing itself is notably delicate and vivacious. Forced to kiss Alec, Tess "unconsciously" wipes "the spot on her cheek that had been touched by his lips" and then, to prevent another embrace, tricks him into stopping the wagon so that she can jump off:

"Now then, up again. What's the matter?"
The hat was in place and tied, but Tess had not stepped forward.

"No sir," she said, revealing the red and ivory of her mouth as her
eye lit in defiant triumph; "not again, if I know it!"

"What—you won't get up beside me?"

"No; I shall walk."

" 'Tis five or six miles yet to Trantridge."

"I don't care if 'tis dozens. Besides, the cart is behind."

"You artful hussy! Now, tell me—didn't you make that hat blow
off on purpose? I'll swear you did!"

Her strategic silence confirmed his suspicion.

Then D'Urberville cursed and swore at her, and called her everything he could think of for the trick. . . .

By the close of the incident Tess is still huffily refusing all
pleas to remount. But, adds Hardy with a touch of slyness, "she
did not object to his keeping his gig alongside her; and in this
manner, at a slow pace, they advanced toward the village of
Trantridge." It is a clash of pride and purpose, and its suggestion that Tess is not quite indifferent to Alec's commonplace
charms adds a humanizing note: Tess is to be more than a stiff
bundle of virtue. An equally affectionate feeling for the change-
ability of human response is shown in another passage between
Tess and Alec, in which he is teaching her to whistle:

"Now try," said D'Urberville.

She attempted to look reserved; her face put on a sculptural severity. But he persisted in his demand, and at last, to get rid of him, she
did put up her lips as directed for producing a clear note; laughing
distressfully, however, and then blushing with vexation that she had
laughed.

He encouraged her with "Try again!"

Tess was quite serious, painfully serious by this time; and she tried
—ultimately and unexpectedly emitting a real round sound. The momentary pleasure of success got the better of her; her eyes enlarged,
and she involuntarily smiled in his face.

At this point Tess has a touch of Pamela, and later she will
have still more of Clarissa.

Hardy manages the seduction scene with a tact not always
characteristic of his novels. With so much tact, indeed, that
readers have often supposed Tess to be a victim of rape—though
the sequel is surely no rape, Hardy declaring that Tess "had been
stirred to confused surrender awhile . . ." The concluding passage of mournful reflection—"But, some might say, where was
Tess's guardian angel? where was the providence of her simple

faith?"—serves in this novel an over-all purpose to which I shall return, as well as the local purpose of what is called in film-making a "dissolve." We are led back, away from the event, so that we may regard it with the brooding helplessness which for Hardy is the ultimate register of trouble.

In any case, the overture is now done.

The Tess we next meet is a transformed young woman, "a person who did not find her especial burden in material things." There has been a fall from innocence, and in some ways—Hardy is by no means the first to notice this irony—it has been a fortunate fall. Tess's eye is now keener, her tongue sharper, her mind quicker. Innocence lost, she takes upon herself the weight of awareness. Her freedom will be steadily diminished, as she steps along the markings of fate; yet it is only now that she gains another freedom, since only now can she grasp the significance of choice. The book begins to mobilize and direct large masses of tension which, until the last page, will make the reading of it an experience slow and grueling, a drain upon emotion.

As Tess leaves Alec, she breaks into lucid and passionate speech such as could, in the earlier chapters, only have been anticipated:

> ". . . Well, if you didn't wish to come to Trantridge why did you come?"
> She did not reply.
> "You didn't come for love of me, that I'll swear."
> " 'Tis quite true. If I had gone for love o' you, if I had ever sincerely loved you, if I loved you still, I should not so loathe and hate myself for my weakness as I do now! . . . My eyes were dazed by you for a little, and that was all."
> He shrugged his shoulders. She resumed—
> "I didn't understand your meaning till it was too late."
> "That's what every woman says."
> "How can you dare to use such words!" she cried, turning impetuously upon him, her eyes flashing as the latent spirit . . . awoke in her. "My God! I could knock you out of the gig! Did it never strike your mind that what every woman says some women may feel?"

The situation is trite enough, as are most of the central crises of human experience, but the force of speech, and the intensity of represented life which it conveys, is remarkable. Still more so is another passage on the following page:

. . . D'Urberville alighted, and lifted her down bodily in his arms, afterwards placing her articles on the ground beside her. She bowed to him slightly, her eye just lingering in his; and then she turned to take the parcels for departure.

Alec D'Urberville removed his cigar, bent towards her, and said— "You are not to go away like that, dear? Come!"

"If you wish," she answered indifferently. "See how you've mastered me!"

She thereupon turned round and lifted her face to his, and remained like a marble term while he imprinted a kiss upon her cheek —half perfunctorily, half as if zest had not yet quite died out. Her eyes vaguely rested upon the remotest trees in the lane while the kiss was given, as though she were unconscious of what he did.

"Now the other side, for old acquaintance' sake!"

She turned her head in the same passive way, as one might turn at the request of a sketcher or hairdresser, and he kissed the other side, his lips touching cheeks that were damp and smoothly chill as the skin of the mushrooms in the field around.

The writing is rich with compressed significance. Tess bowing slightly to Alec, perhaps with ironic contempt, perhaps with recognition that, in some detested way, he has established a hold over her—it is from detail of this kind that a novel is made. Alec going through the motions of his dominance, half-languid but still appreciative of the prize he has had—this too is very fine. And then the comparison of Tess's cheeks with the skin of mushrooms closes the passage with a reverberating simile: as if her cheeks now had something of the inert sponginess, the yielding lifelessness of the plant.

Tess once more alone, there quickly follows another of those telling brief incidents which in Hardy's work gather together the symbolic purport of the narrative. Tess encounters the slightly crazed preacher who paints his signs of loveless theology "placing a comma after each word, as if to give pause while that word was driven well home to the reader's heart—

THY, DAMNATION, SLUMBERETH, NOT . . ."

The words do drive "well home" into Tess's heart, but she answers with an unexpected resilience of mind: "Pooh—I don't believe God said such things." It thereby becomes clear that Tess is not at all a broken woman; she has suffered, but as she "throbbingly resume[s] her walk," she cannot, if she would, suppress the life-force that surges through her. Returning to her mother, she cries out: "Why didn't you tell me there was danger in men-folks?" and is answered with a cool mixture of sluttishness and peasant fatalism: "Well, we must make the best of it . . . 'Tis nater, after all, and what do please God." Tess will find no help here, as she will find little anywhere. On this ironic downbeat Chapter XII concludes, a triumph of Hardy's mature art.

The narrative voice now draws sharply away from Tess the individual, and for an interval we see her mainly from a distance, in the rhythms of sickness and recovery, which as Hardy describes them seem almost impersonal, since so often repeated in the experience of the race. These abrupt transitions from intimacy to distance and then back again to intimacy are used by Hardy to reinforce Tess's representative nature:

> She felt that she could do well to be useful again—to taste anew sweet independence at any price. The past was past; whatever it had been it was no more at hand. Whatever its consequences, time would close over them; they would all in a few years be as if they had never been, and she herself grassed down and forgotten. Meanwhile the trees were just as green as before; the birds sang and the sun shone as clearly now as ever. The familiar surroundings had not darkened because of her grief, nor sickened because of her pain.

To renew herself through work, Tess goes to the Talbothays dairy, and in the pages that follow there can be found some of the most remarkable writing in Hardy's—for that matter, in all of English—fiction. At Talbothays both the natural world and Tess, who is part of that world yet distinct from it, come into ripe bloom. An ease of rhythm, a summer drowse, overtakes everything. Unexpended youth brings with it hope "and the invincible instinct toward self-delight." Tess, "warmed as a sunned cat," heals and opens. Working quietly on the farm; finding comfort in dairyman Crick's generosity and his wife's steadiness; immersing herself in the green life of the place; enjoying the camaraderie of her fellow-workers and the tales they tell; falling in love with Angel Clare, who seems all seriousness and refinement, to be worshiped in his purity where Alec had been despised for his designs—Tess reaches a radiant fullness. She and the land come together, in a metaphoric boldness:

> Amid the oozing fatness and warm ferments of the Froom Vale, at a season when the rush of juices could almost be heard below the

hiss of fertilization, it was impossible that the most fanciful love should not grow passionate. The ready bosoms existing there were impregnated by their surroundings.

All of Tess's sexuality comes into readiness, but it is a sexuality superbly at ease with itself; she is the only one of Hardy's heroines who does not use it to manipulate or crush men. In her unaffectedly sexual charms, she is quite without self-consciousness:

> The outskirts of the garden in which Tess found herself had been left uncultivated for some years, and was now damp and rank with juicy grass which sent up mists of pollen at a touch; and with tall blooming weeds emitting offensive smells—weeds whose red and yellow and purple hues formed a polychrome as dazzling as that of cultivated flowers. She went stealthily as a cat through this profusion of growth, gathering cuckoo-spittles on her skirts, cracking snails that were underfoot, staining her hands with thistle-milk and slug-slime, and rubbing off upon her naked arms sticky blights which, though snow-white on the apple-tree trunks, made madder stains on her skin; thus she drew quite near to Clare, still unobserved of him.
>
> Tess was conscious of neither time nor space. The exaltation which she had described as being producible at will by gazing at a star, came now without any determination of hers; she undulated upon the thin notes of [Angel's] secondhand harp, and their harmonies passed like breezes through her, bringing tears into her eyes. The floating pollen seemed to be his notes made visible . . . Though near nightfall, the rank-smelling weed-flowers glowed as if they would not close for intentness, and the waves of colour mixed with the waves of sound.

In this eden of sensuousness Tess and Angel enact the rites of courtship, but with the faintest foreshadowing of disaster:

> At these non-human hours [it is dawn] they could get quite close to the waterfowl. Herons came, with a great bold noise as of opening doors and shutters, out of the boughs of a plantation which they frequented at the side of the mead; or, if already on the spot, hardily maintained their standing in the water as the pair walked by, watching them by moving their heads round in a slow, horizontal, passionless wheel, like the turn of puppets by clockwork.
>
> They could see then the faint summer fogs in layers, woolly, level, and apparently no thicker than counterpanes, spread about the meadows in detached remnants of small extent . . .
>
> Or perhaps the summer fog was more general, and the meadows lay like a white sea, out of which the scattered trees rose like dangerous rocks. Birds would soar through it into the upper radiance, and

hang on the wing sunning themselves, or alight on the wet rails sub-
dividing the mead, which now shone like glass rods. Minute diamonds
of moisture from the mist hung, too, upon Tess's eyelashes, and
drops upon her hair, like seed pearls. When the day grew quite
strong and commonplace these dried off her; moreover, Tess then
lost her strange and ethereal beauty; her teeth, lips and eyes scintil-
lated in the sunbeams, and she was again the dazzlingly fair dairymaid
only, who had to hold her own against the other women of the world.

The metaphor of "pollen" weaves through the courtship
scenes, linking natural fecundity and human desire:

The country custom of unreserved comradeship out of doors during
betrothal was the only custom [Tess] knew, and to her it had no
strangeness; though it seemed oddly anticipative to Clare till he
saw how normal a thing she, in common with all the other dairy-
folk, regarded it. Thus, during this October month of wonderful
afternoons they roved along the meads by creeping paths which
followed the brinks of trickling tributary brooks . . . They were never
out of the sound of some purling weir, whose buzz accompanied their
own murmuring, while the beams of the sun, almost as horizontal
as the mead itself, formed a pollen of radiance over the landscape.

Idyllic as they are, these scenes are never allowed to become
mere idylls, for the courtship is being conducted within a community that registers and approves:

Some of the dairy-people, who were also out of doors on the first
Sunday evening after their engagement, heard [Tess's] impulsive
speeches, ecstasized to fragments, though they were too far off to hear
the words discoursed; noted the spasmodic catch in her remarks,
broken into syllables by the leapings of her heart, as she walked
leaning on his arm; her contented pauses, the occasional little laugh
upon which her soul seemed to ride—the laugh of a woman in company with the man she loves and has won from all other women—
unlike anything else in nature. They marked the buoyancy of her
tread, like the skim of a bird which has not quite alighted.

Surely it was passages like these which prompted D. H. Lawrence to say about Hardy that "his feeling, his instinct, his sensuous understanding is . . . apart from his metaphysic, very
great and deep, deeper than that, perhaps, of any other English
novelist. Putting aside his metaphysic, which must always ob-
trude when he thinks of people, and turning to the earth, to
landscape, then he is true to himself." To which it needs only
be added: a passionate woman is the blessing of literature.

What keeps the Talbothays section from sliding into pantheist sentimentalism is the firmness with which Hardy grounds it in the commonplace world of human labor. The action is set within a recognizable milieu, and Tess is a woman who works with her hands. Benign as the atmosphere of Talbothays may be, personal as the relationship between dairyman Crick and his workers remains, there can be no doubt that in coming to Talbothays Tess has taken another step in her social descent: she is a hired hand and the work itself is seasonal. In a few months, the workers will scatter and their community dissolve. (It is notable, by the way, that in contrast to Tess neither Alec nor Angel does meaningful work: Alec is a wastrel, Angel a dilettante. Neither lives under the lash of necessity, neither defines himself through craft or occupation.)

There are moments when Tess and Angel go off into the woods, apart from the places of settlement, but most of the time they are shown within the bounds of structured society. Nothing about Talbothays is "primitive," and nothing "wild" or asocial in the manner of *Wuthering Heights*. The Talbothays farm is not a place of fantasy pitted against a decadent or corrupt civilization; it is itself representative of a phase in civilized existence. Centuries of effort have had to pass before the civilization of Talbothays could be achieved, though only a few decades of technological change would be required to destroy it. Rhapsodic and lyrical this section of *Tess of the D'Urbervilles* is meant to be, but the rhapsody celebrates a love of earthly creatures and the lyricism has nothing to do with primitivist negations. For a few months, Tess reaches an ecstasy resting upon commonplace human experience—and that is precisely what makes the ecstasy so remarkable.

Hardy's conception of Angel Clare is not, by itself, to be faulted: a timid convert to modernist thought who possesses neither the firmness of the old nor the boldness of the new. Scene by scene, as the action works itself out, Angel comes to seem the complement of Alec; indeed, the parallels might be trying, if they were not so strictly subordinated to the presentation of Tess herself. Alec assaults Tess physically, Angel violates her spiritually. Alec is a stage villain, Angel is an intellectual wretch. Alec has a certain charm, in his amiable slothful way;

Angel bears an aura of tensed moralism. What they share is an incapacity to value the splendor of feeling which radiates from Tess. Each represents a deformation of masculinity, one high and the other low; they cannot appreciate, they cannot even *see* the richness of life that Tess embodies. Yet there are important differences. At least Alec does not pontificate, or wrap himself in a cloak of principles. He may not be admirable but he can be likable, simply because commonplace vice is easier to bear than elevated righteousness. And as Lawrence has shrewdly noticed, Alec "seeks with all his power for the source of stimulus in women. He takes the deep impulse from the female . . . he could reach some of the real sources of the female in a woman, and draw from them . . . [But Angel, as] the result of generations of ultra-Christian training, [has] an inherent aversion to the female . . ." Together the two men represent everything in Hardy's world, and not his alone, which betrays spontaneous feeling and the flow of instinctual life.

Angel's priggishness is not only hard to take, it is sometimes hard to credit. That he should condemn Tess for her sins directly after confessing his own, may not—in light of what we know about his character and his culture—be entirely implausible. But when seen in the context of the whole book, this seems another of those instances where Hardy abuses his plot in order to make clear what is already quite evident. Nor can one be certain that Hardy sees Angel for the insufferable prig he is—not because Hardy feels anything but dislike toward everything Angel stands for, but because at this point in the narrative Hardy is so caught up with Tess and her ordeal, he seems almost ready to share in her refusal to judge her adored lover.

Where Hardy's art can be brought into more serious question is in the famous sleepwalking scene. It is a set-piece that bears a relation to Hardy's work somewhat like the death of Little Joe to Dickens's. The incident is affecting, it is bold, it is brilliant in conception. Angel, having learned about Tess's past, refuses to go to bed with her on their wedding night; but during a moment of sleepwalking, when his inhibitions are somewhat at rest, he carries her to a stone coffin and places her there lovingly. This piece of action can be seen as a forceful projection of Angel's psychology, in which love and death are sadly compounded. That Tess should submit to such a ghastly dumb show, and submit with all the trustfulness which marks her character, is also telling. That Tess should then lead the stricken Angel back to the house and that Hardy, plunging deeper and deeper into risk, should remark that Tess walks barefoot in the chill night while Angel is in his woolen socks (he would be!)—all this can be accepted as an expressionist strategy for acting out inner states of feeling.

Yet even if we accept this strategy as a way of coping with those incidents in Hardy's fiction which are as improbable as they are crucial, there remain serious difficulties. Hardy is frequently lacking in tact. Almost obsessively, he needs to pile gratuitous excess on top of initial improbability. The idea of the sleepwalking, as it turns out, is not quite enough for him, and to add still another *frisson*—though, if we respond at all, our nerves are by now sufficiently strained—Angel must be shown carrying Tess across a narrow footbridge threatened by autumnal flood, "a giddy pathway for even steady heads." The detail itself hardly matters, but it may be just enough to break the current of conviction. In the large, then, the sleepwalking incident strikes one as a perilous touch of genius; it also suggests that genius can be quite compatible with bad taste.

About the sequence at Flintcomb-Ash, however, there is almost no disagreement. Even those critics and readers who question Hardy's place as a novelist are likely to acknowledge the disciplined power of this section. The writing is harsh and compact, absolutely without self-indulgence; there is frequent metaphoric intensification; every word is directed toward a fierce rendering of the sterility of place and the brutality of labor. Nothing in Zola or Dreiser surpasses these pages for a portrayal of human degradation—a portrayal compassionate through its severe objectivity.

The land is barren and flinty, the very opposite of Talbothays. The atmosphere is hushed, death-like. The weather is cruel, apocalyptic. And Tess has been reduced to an agricultural proletarian, working not for a benevolent dairyman but for an unseen landowner, under the nervous prodding of a foreman and the shock of the new farm machines. Mechanization, impersonality, alienation, the cash nexus, dehumanization—all these tags of modern thought, so worn and all too often true, are brought to quickened reality in Tess's ordeal at Flintcomb-Ash. What Marx wrote about the working day and the outrage of female labor becomes tangible and immediate. Tess as a woman, Tess as a distinctive person hardly exists; she has become a factor in the process of production.

The engineman who works the new threshing machine (that "red tyrant . . . the woman had come to serve") is presented with a Dickensian vividness. Hardy describes him not as a person but as a threatening force, a function:

> By the engine stood a dark motionless being, a sooty and grimy embodiment of tallness, in a sort of trance, with a heap of coals by his side; it was the engineman. The isolation of his manner and colour lent him the appearance of a creature from Tophet, who had strayed into the pellucid smokelessness of this region of yellow grain and pale soil, with which he had nothing in common, to amaze and to discompose its aborigines.
> . . . He was in the agricultural world, but not of it. He served fire and smoke; these denizens of the fields served vegetation, weather, frost, and sun. He travelled with his engine from farm to farm . . . He spoke in a strange northern accent; his thoughts being turned inwards upon himself, his eye on his iron charge . . . holding only strictly necessary intercourse with the natives, as if some ancient doom compelled him to wander here against his will in the service of his Plutonic master. The long strap which ran from the driving-wheel of his engine to the red thresher under the rick was the sole tie-line between agriculture and him.

Flintcomb-Ash is like a vision of hell, for Hardy what London was for Dickens:

> After this season of congealed dampness came a spell of dry frost, when strange birds from behind the North Pole began to arrive silently on the upland of Flintcomb-Ash; gaunt spectral creatures with tragical eyes—eyes which had witnessed scenes of cataclysmic horror in inaccessible polar regions of a magnitude such as no human being had ever conceived, in curdling temperatures that no man could endure . . . These nameless birds came quite near to Tess and Marian . . . With dumb impassivity, they dismissed experiences which they did not value for the immediate incidents of this homely upland —the trivial movements of the two girls in disturbing the clods with their hackers so as to uncover something or other that these visitants relished as food.

. . . There came a moisture which was not of rain, and a cold which was not of frost. It chilled the eyeballs of the twain, made their brows ache, penetrated to their skeletons, affecting the surface of the body less than its core.

These ghastly evocations are heightened by the swede-grubbing, by the "myriads of loose white flints in bulbous, cusped and phallic shapes" which are dug up in the ground, and by the fields which have "a complexion without features, as if a face, from chin to brow, should be only an expanse of skin. The sky wore, in another colour, the same likeness; a white vacuity of countenance with the lineaments gone." It is Hardy's wasteland. And Tess, broken with fatigue, assumes the largeness of martyrdom:

A panting ache ran through the rick. The man who fed was weary, and Tess could see that the red nape of his neck was encrusted with dirt and husks. She stood at her post, her flushed and perspiring face coated with the corn-dust . . . She was the only woman whose place was upon the machine so as to be shaken bodily by its spinning . . . The incessant quivering, in which every fibre of her frame participated, had thrown her into a stupefied reverie in which her arms worked on independently of her consciousness . . .
Whenever Tess lifted her head she beheld always the great upgrown straw-stack with the men in shirt-sleeves upon it, against the gray northern sky; in front of it the long red elevator like a Jacob's ladder, on which a perpetual stream of threshed straw ascended, a yellow river running up-hill, and spouting out on the top of the rick.

Weaving through the Flintcomb-Ash sequence is a line of symbolic action—though to call it "symbolic" is to risk minimizing its strong immediacy—in which Alec d'Urberville, shed of religion and gone back to his calling of tempter, keeps appearing and reappearing at the swede-field, prepared to rescue Tess if only she will forget the husband who had left her. At this point Alec appears in a double guise: he is both kinder and crueler to Tess than is anyone else, both more humane and sinister. The tribute he pays Tess is that he always finds her interesting and wishes steadily to be near her—one glimpse of her eyes, he tells her during his phase as preacher, and he is undone! Only he among the figures surrounding her offers Tess and the disabled Durbeyfields any help. Yet it is also he who comes to seem a kind of devil, embodying the amiable sloth, the slackness of will and value, which is the devil's word. Tess succumbs to him and, succumbing, hates him; there is a frightful intimacy in their conversation, the intimacy of sinners. That Tess finally murders Alec does not, as one yields oneself to the momentum of the book, seem nearly so implausible or disconcerting as any number of earlier and less violent incidents. The murder is an act of desperate assertion which places Tess in the line of folk heroines who kill because they can no longer bear outrage, but it is also an act toward which our responses have been trained by Hardy to move past easy approval or easy rejection, indeed past any judgment. Given all that has happened, we accept the killing of Alec with a feeling that approaches relief, if only because we know that it signifies an end to Tess's journey. The murder of Alec is, I think, easier to credit than the sleepwalking scene with Angel, for the sleepwalking is eccentric, a stroke quite special to Hardy's imagination, while the killing is traditional, part of the accepted heritage that has come down to us through popular and literary channels.

There remains the interval in which Tess and Angel briefly come together as husband and wife, living, as it were, suspended from time, and then the climax at Stonehenge, staged by Hardy with a sharp eye for chiaroscuro effects. At once joyful and anxious, the reunion of Tess and Angel provides a rest in the accumulating tension of the novel: it reminds one, on a small scale, of the scene in Siberia where Zhivago and Lara have a short time of happiness before their enforced separation. After this interval, we are ready for the climax. Stonehenge is a place emanating inexplicable grandeurs and horrors: the scene is blunt in its demands, enormously ambitious in its grasp. Hardy's writing it very quiet, almost mere notation, as Tess fades from life. It is a scene that can best be understood and accepted in the terms proposed by John Holloway when he writes that Hardy's novels require "a special mode of reading. The incidents in them which strike us as improbable or strained or grotesque invite (this is not to say that they always deserve) the kind of response that we are accustomed to give, say, to the Dover Cliff scene in *Lear*. Admittedly, Hardy has local failures; but incidents like the one at Stonehenge are at some distance from the probable and the realistic. Almost, it is necessary for them to be unrealistic, in order that their other dimension of meaning, their relevance to the larger rhythms of the work, shall transpire."

I have gone into such considerable detail of analysis and excerpt primarily because, of all Hardy's novels, *Tess* has the richest narrative texture and depends most upon that texture for its cumulative effects. It is the kind of novel in which the commanding design is relatively simple and the artistic realization is mostly a consequence of the depth and intensity with which the design has been worked out.

Where, then, is the center of interest in this book? There have appeared in recent years the thoughtful studies of *Tess* by English critics Douglas Brown and Arnold Kettle, which see Tess as victim of a social disintegration that has been caused by the coming of industrialism to the countryside. Brown's stress is traditionalist and Kettle's Marxist, but both critics, while warning against the dangers of allegorical dryness, tend to read the book as a social fable—that is, a narrative in which attention is steadily being directed to a scheme of social relations behind the foreground events.

Tess, writes Brown, "is the agricultural predicament in metaphor, engaging Hardy's deepest impulses of sympathy and allegiance." In so reading the novel, Brown stresses the care with which Hardy fixes the action in the context of country ritual, even if a ritual fallen into neglect, half-forgotten and decadent; the novel is bounded by an early scene that describes the May-walking and a late scene that describes the uprooting of the Durbeyfields—but also of large numbers of other farm people—on Old Lady Day. Kettle writes that *Tess* has "the quality of a social document. It has even, for all its high-pitched emotional quality, the kind of impersonality that the expression suggests. Its subject is all-pervasive, affecting and determining the nature of every part. It is a novel with a thesis . . . and the thesis is true. The thesis is that in the latter half of the last century the disintegration of the peasantry—a process which had its roots deep in the past—had reached its final and tragic stage."

Now it would be foolish and ungenerous to deny that both critics are saying something valuable about *Tess*. Both are pointing, Brown with more subtlety than Kettle, to the superbly rendered social frame which makes Tess what she is and in which she acts out her ordeal. Though, like the greatest characters in literature, she lives beyond the final pages of the book as a permanent citizen of the imagination, Tess is inconceivable except as a Wessex girl rooted in Wessex particulars—and these particulars form part of the social substance which concerns Brown and Kettle. Whenever Hardy ventures upon his expressionist set-pieces and pictorial stylizations in trying to magnify the stature of Tess, the effort depends, first of all, on having grounded the story in commonplace social reality. And not only Tess as a country girl but the other figures—Alec as a sleazy *arriviste,* Angel as a neurotic moralist, Joan Durbeyfield as a good-natured slattern—gain their initial credence through their representativeness. That, to begin with, is how fictive individuals are created.

Yet I feel that, no matter how helpful and enriching this critical approach to *Tess* may be, it does not bring us to the vital heart of the book. The case is somewhat as with Kettle's reading of *Wuthering Heights,* in which he persuasively demonstrates that the action takes place not in a mythic cloud but in nineteenth century England, that Heathcliff is not merely a figure of satanism but a man determined to revenge social snobbery, and that throughout the book issues of class power and relationships are significant. All true; yet what is missing is precisely that which makes *Wuthering Heights* so remarkable a work. What is missing is the ravenous and deathly love between Heathcliff and Catherine, set in the very foreground, dominating everything near it, and certain to be regarded by a reader unburdened by theses as the center of the book.

Similar judgments hold for *Tess of the D'Urbervilles.* When the book is fully alive, forming a self-sufficient area of the imagination, I cannot for a moment believe that Tess is "the agricultural predicament in metaphor" or that she represents "the disintegration of the peasantry." These may well be elements contributing to her reality as a character in a novel, but they are not quite the reality itself. For when the book is indeed fully alive, we have no wish to look beyond her or to think of her as representing anything whatever; we are fully engaged with the motion and meaning of her behavior. Closer than Brown or

Kettle to the heart of the book is the analysis offered by Dorothy Van Ghent: "The dilemma of Tess is the dilemma of morally individualizing consciousness in its earthy mixture. The subject is mythological, for it places the human protagonist in dramatic relationship with the nonhuman and orients his destiny among preternatural powers. The most primitive antagonist of consciousness is, on the simplest premise, the earth itself. It acts so in *Tess*, clogging action and defying conscious motive. . . ." This is fine; except that here too one suspects a thematic overload. Does the novel itself, as distinct from certain trends in contemporary criticism, enforce the mythological reference? If placing a human protagonist in dramatic relationship to the nonhuman makes a novel "mythological," is there a significant work of Western literature which is not "mythological"? And if as I suspect, there is not, where then can one locate the usable boundary of the description?

What matters in *Tess of the D'Urbervilles*, what pulses most strongly and gains our deepest imaginative complicity, is the figure of Tess herself. Tess as she is, a woman made real through the craft of art, and not Tess as she represents an idea. Marvelously high-spirited and resilient, Tess embodies a moral poise beyond the reach of most morality. Tess is that rare creature in literature: goodness made interesting. She is human life stretched and racked, yet forever springing back to renewal. And what must never be forgotten in thinking about her, as in reading the book it never can be: she is a woman. For Hardy she embodies the qualities of affection and trust, the powers of survival and suffering, which a woman can bring to the human enterprise. The novel may have a strong element of the pessimistic and the painful, but Tess herself is energy and joy, a life neither foolishly primitive nor feebly sophisticated. Though subjected to endless indignities, assaults and defeats, Tess remains a figure of harmony —between her self and her role, between her nature and her culture. Hardy presents her neither from the outside nor the inside exclusively, neither through event nor analysis alone; she is apprehended in her organic completeness, so that her objectivity and subjectivity become inseparable. A victim of civilization, she is also a gift of civilization. She comes to seem for us the potential of what life could be, just as what happens to her signifies what life too often becomes. She is Hardy's greatest tribute to the possibilities of human existence, for Tess is one of the greatest triumphs of civilization: a natural girl.

Simply as a fictional character, she is endlessly various. She can flirt, she can listen, she can sympathize, she can work with her hands. Except when it is mocked or thwarted, she is superbly at ease with her sexuality. In no way an intellectual, she has a clear sense of how to reject whatever fanatic or pious nonsense comes her way. After pleading with the vicar to give a Christian burial to her illegitimate child, she answers his refusal with the cry: "Then I don't like you! and I'll never come to your church no more!" A mere instance of feminine illogic? Not at all; for what Tess is saying is that a man so seemingly heartless deserves neither human affection nor religious respect. And she is right. Her womanly softness does not keep her from clear judgments, and even toward her beloved Angel she can sometimes be blunt. "It is in you, what you are angry at, Angel, it is not in me," she pointedly tells him when he announces that he cannot accept her. The letter she sends Angel during the Flintcomb-Ash ordeal is a marvelous expression of human need: "The daylight has nothing to show me, since you are not here . . ." At least twice in the book Tess seems to Hardy and the surrounding characters larger than life, but in all such instances it is not to make her a goddess or a metaphor, it is to underscore her embattled womanliness.

The secondary figures in the book have useful parts to play, but finally they are little more than accessories, whose task is not so much to draw attention in their own right as to heighten the reality of Tess. Only one "character" is almost as important as Tess, and that is Hardy himself. Through his musing voice, he makes his presence steadily felt. He hovers and watches over Tess, like a stricken father. He is as tender to Tess as Tess is to the world. Tender; and helpless. That the imagined place of Wessex, like the real places we inhabit, proves to be inadequate to a woman like Tess—this, if message there must be, is the message of the book. The clash between sterile denial and vital existence occurs repeatedly, in a wide range of episodes, yet through none of them can Hardy protect his heroine. And that, I think, is the full force of his darkness of vision: how little can be done for Tess.

If we see Hardy's relation to Tess in this way, we can be a

good deal more patient with the passages of intermittent philosophizing that dot the book. These passages are not merely inert bits of intellectual flotsam marring a powerful narrative. They are evidence of Hardy's concern, tokens of his bafflement before the agony of the world. At best, if not always, the characters in *Tess* are not illustrations or symbols of a philosophic system; at best, if not always, the philosophic reflections comprise a gesture in response to the experience of the characters. It is Hardy ruminating upon the destruction of youth and hope—and if we thus see Hardy's role in his narrative, we can grasp fully the overwhelming force of the lines from Shakespeare with which he prefaces the book: *". . . Poor wounded name! My bosom as a bed/Shall lodge thee."* It is her only rest.

In Hardy's diary for 1888 there appears a note for "a short story of a young man who could not afford to go to Oxford." It would deal with "his struggles and ultimate failure. Suicide. There is something this world ought to be shown, and I am the one to show it . . ." Six years later the projected story had grown into a novel, Hardy's last and most bitter, *Jude the Obscure.* By 1895, the year *Jude* came out, Hardy was in his mid-fifties, an established writer who had composed two great novels and several of distinction. But he was more than a famous or honored writer. For the English-speaking world he had become a moral presence genuinely affecting the lives of those who read him.

When Hardy first printed *Jude the Obscure* as a monthly serial in *Harper's Magazine* between December 1894 and November 1895, he agreed to cut some of its most vital parts: those which showed Jude to be harried by sexual desire, others reporting that Jude and Sue Bridehead did finally go to bed together, and still others displaying Hardy's gift for a muted but humorous earthiness. In the serial Jude and Sue did not have a child; more demurely, they adopted one. Arabella, when she got Jude back and flooded him with liquor, ended the evening by tucking him into bed in a spare room. Today such mutilations by a serious writer would provoke an uproar of judgment; but Hardy, not being the kind of man who cared to languish in a garret, did what he had to do in order to sell the serial rights. In any case, he knew that his true novel, the one later generations would read and judge him by, was soon to appear in hard covers.

Some months later, when the book came out, it stirred up a storm of righteousness. Many of the reviewers adopted a high moral tone, denouncing Hardy's apparent hostility to the institution of marriage while choosing to neglect the sympathy he showed toward people caught up in troublesome relationships, whether in or out of marriage. One true-blooded Englishman, the Bishop of Wakefield, publicly announced that he "was so disgusted with [the book's] insolence and indecency that I threw it into the fire." To which Hardy added that probably the bishop had chosen to burn the book because he could not burn the author.

Later, writing to his friend Edmund Gosse, Hardy denied that the novel was "a manifesto on the marriage question, although, of course, it involves it." This is precisely the kind of distinction that most of the contemporary reviewers neither could nor wished to understand: they were, like most reviewers of any age, blunt-minded journalists who demanded from a work of art that it confirm the settled opinions they already had. What Hardy was getting at in his letter to Gosse is an idea now commonly accepted by serious writers: that while a work of fiction may frequently raise social and moral problems, the artist's main intention is to explore them freely rather than take hard-and-fast public positions. In his 1895 preface to *Jude the Obscure* Hardy made quite clear his larger purpose in composing the book:

> . . . to deal unaffectedly with the fret and fever, derision and dis-
> aster, that may press in the wake of the strongest passion known to
> humanity; to tell, without a mincing of words, of a deadly war
> waged between flesh and spirit; and to point the tragedy of unful-
> filled aims.

Nor were these new concerns for Hardy. In his earlier novels he had already shown what a torment an ill-suited marriage can be; he had known himself, through much of his first marriage, the dumb misery that follows upon decayed affections. By the 1890s, when England was beginning to shake loose from the grip of Victorian moralism, the cultivated minority public was ready for his gaunt honesty, even if the bulk of novel readers was not.

That marriage had become a *problem*, that somehow it was in crisis and need of reform, was an idea very much in the air. During the 1890s the notorious Parnell case, involving an adultery suit against the leader of Irish nationalism, split the English-speaking world into hostile camps but also forced a relatively candid discussion of the realities of conjugal life. The plays of Ibsen were being performed in English translation during the years *Jude* was written, and their caustic inquiry into the evasions and repressions of middle-class marriage may have found an echo in Hardy's book. And through the late 1880s Hardy had been reading the work of Schopenhauer and von Hartmann, pessimistic German philosophers who had recently been translated into English; he did not need their help, or anyone else's, in order to reach his "twilight view" of man's diminished place in the universe, but he did find in their philosophic speculations a support—he might have said a confirmation—for his own temperamental bias.

Hardy's last novel was not quite the outcry of a lonely and embittered iconoclast that it has sometimes been said to be. *Jude* displeased official opinion, both literary and moral; it outraged the pieties of middle-class England to an extent few of Hardy's contemporaries were inclined to risk; but it also reflected the sentiments of advanced intellectual circles in the 1890s. Thus while it is true that *Jude* was not meant to be "a manifesto on the marriage question," the book could hardly have been written fifteen or twenty years earlier. Coming at the moment it did, *Jude* played a part in the modern transformation of marriage from a sacred rite to a secular and thereby problematic relationship—just as those nineteenth century writers who tried to salvage Christianity by scraping it of dogma and superstition unwittingly helped to undermine the whole structure of theism.

Jude the Obscure is Hardy's most distinctly "modern" work, for it rests upon a cluster of assumptions central to modernist literature: that in our time men wishing to be more than dumb clods must live in permanent doubt and intellectual crisis; that for such men, to whom traditional beliefs are no longer available, life has become inherently problematic; that in the course of their years they must face even more than the usual allotment of loneliness and anguish; that in their cerebral overdevelopment they run the danger of losing those primary appetites for life which keep the human race going; and that courage, if it is to be found at all, consists in a readiness to accept pain while refusing the comforts of certainty. If Hardy, excessively thin-skinned as he was, suffered from the attacks *Jude* brought down upon his head, he should have realized—as in his moments of shrewdness he did —that attack was precisely what he had to expect. For he had threatened his readers not merely in their opinions but in their deepest unspoken values: the first was forgivable, the second not.

In its deepest impress *Jude the Obscure* is not the kind of novel that compels one to reflect upon the idea of history, certainly not in the ways that Tolstoy's *War and Peace* or Stendhal's *The Red and the Black* do. Nor is it the kind of novel that draws our strongest attention to the causes, patterns and turnings of large historical trends as these condition the lives of a few centered characters. The sense *Jude* leaves one with, the quality of the pain it inflicts, has mostly to do with the sheer difficulty of human beings living elbow to elbow and heart to heart; the difficulty of being unable to bear prolonged isolation or prolonged closeness; the difficulty, at least for reflective men, of getting through the unspoken miseries of daily life. Yet to grasp the full stringencies of Jude's private ordeal, one must possess a strong historical awareness.

The English working class, coming to birth through the trauma of the Industrial Revolution, suffered not merely from brutality, hunger and deprivation, but from an oppressive snobbism, at times merely patronizing and at other times proudly violent, on the part of the "superior" social classes. By the middle of the nineteenth century a minority of intellectuals and reformers had begun to display an active sympathy for the workers: they could not live in peace while millions of countrymen lived in degradation. But meanwhile, and going as far back as the late eighteenth century, something far more important had begun to happen among the English workers themselves—the first stirrings of intellectual consciousness, the first signs of social and moral solidarity. Workingmen began to appear who sought to train their minds, to satisfy their parched imaginations, to grasp for themselves a fragment of that traditional culture from which Western society had coldly locked them out.

The rise of the self-educated proletarian is one of the most remarkable facts in nineteenth century English history. Frequently this new man discovered himself through the trade union and socialist movements, which brought to him a sense of historical mission, an assignment of destiny and role; but he could also be found elsewhere. Struggling after long hours of labor to master the rudiments of learning, he flourished in the dissident chapels which had shot up in England beyond the privileged ground of the Anglican Church; in the lecture courses and night schools that were started by intellectual missionaries; in little reading "circles" that were formed amidst the degradation of the slums. For some of these men education meant primarily a promise of escape from their cramped social position; for others, no doubt a minority, it could approximate what it meant to Jude Fawley —a joy, pure and disinterested, in the life of the mind.[2]

English fiction was slow to absorb this remarkable new figure, just as it was slow to deal with the life of the working class as a whole. There are glimpses of the self-educated worker in the novels of George Gissing; he appears a bit more fully in the "Five Towns" fiction of Arnold Bennett, and still more impressively in D. H. Lawrence's early novels; and in recent years, as he begins to fade from the social scene, he is looked back upon with nostalgia in novels about the early English Labor movement written by Raymond Williams and Walter Allen.

Now Jude Fawley is not himself a character within this tradition. But he is close to it, a sort of rural cousin of the self-educated worker; and I think it can be said that unless the latter had begun to seem a significant type in late nineteenth century England, Hardy could not have imagined as strongly as he did the intellectual yearnings of Jude. That in his last novel Hardy should have turned to a figure like Jude is itself evidence of a major

---

2. In 1912 Hardy remarked, with forgivable pride, that "some readers thought . . . that when Ruskin College was . . . founded it should have been called the College of Jude the Obscure." Ruskin College at Oxford was the first English college designed to enable needy but gifted working-class boys to attend a university.

shift in outlook. The fixity of Hardy's rural attachments was, in the previous Wessex novels, so deep as to provide him with something equivalent to a moral absolute, a constant of moral security through which to set off—yet keep at a manageable distance—those of his characters troubled by unrest. But Hardy, by the point he had reached in *Jude the Obscure,* could no longer find in the world of Wessex a sufficient moral and emotional support. His feelings had come to a pained recognition that Wessex and all it stood for was slipping out of his fingers, changing shape beyond what he remembered from his youth, receding into history. And as for Jude, though he comes from the country, he spends most of his life in the towns. The matter upon which Jude's heart and mind must feed, the matter which rouses him to excitement and then leaves him broken, is the intellectual disturbance of modern life—and that, for good or bad, can be found only in the towns. Not born a worker, and without the political interests which usually spurred the self-educated proletarian to read and study, Jude nevertheless shares in the latter's passion for self-improvement, as well as in the pathos of knowing that never can he really know enough. Jude is Hardy's equivalent of the self-educated worker: the self-educated worker transplanted into the Wessex world. So that when Hardy first conceived of Jude in that notable clause, "a young man who could not go to Oxford," he was foreshadowing not merely one man's deprivation but the turmoil of an entire social group.

Socially, Jude hovers somewhere between an old-fashioned artisan and a modern worker. The kind of work he does, restoring old churches, pertains to the traditional English past, but the way he does it, hiring himself out for wages, points to the future. His desire for learning, both as a boy trying to come by a Greek grammar and then as a man walking awestruck through the chill streets of Christminster (Oxford), is portrayed by Hardy with enormous sympathy. But to stress this sympathy is not at all to share the view of some critics that Hardy is so deeply involved with Jude's yearnings, he cannot bring to bear upon them any critical irony. What but somberly ironic is the incident in which Jude receives a crushing reply from the Christminster master to whom he has applied for advice, and what but devastatingly ironic is the scene in which Jude drunkenly flaunts his Latin before the good-natured uncomprehending artisans at the Christ-minster tavern? Jude is a thoroughly individualized figure, an achievement made possible by Hardy's balance of sympathy and distance; but Jude's personal drama is woven from the materials of historical change, the transformation and uprooting of traditional English life.

The same holds true for Sue Bridehead. She is a triumph of psychological portraiture—and to that we shall return. But the contours of her psychology are themselves shaped by a new historical situation. She could not possibly appear in a novel by Jane Austen or Dickens or Thackeray; her style of thought, her winsome charms and maddening indecisions, are all conditioned by the growth of intellectual skepticism and modernist sensibility. She is the first major anticipation in the English novel of that profoundly affecting and troublesome creature: the modern girl. If she could not appear in an earlier nineteenth century novel, she certainly could in a twentieth century one—the only difference would probably be that now, living in her neat brownstone apartment in Manhattan or stylish flat in London and working for a publishing house or television company, she would have learned to accept a "healthier" attitude toward sex. Or at the least, she would have learned to pretend it.

In the last third of the nineteenth century, the situation of women changed radically: from subordinate domesticity and Victorian repression to the first signs of emancipation, leading often enough to the poignant bewilderments of a Sue Bridehead. So that while Sue, like Jude, is an intensely individualized figure, she is also characteristic of a moment in recent history; indeed, the force with which Hardy has made her so uniquely alive depends a great deal on the accuracy with which he has placed her historically.

Between Jude and Sue there is a special closeness, and this too has been historically conditioned. It is the closeness of lovers, but more than that. It is the closeness of intellectual companions, but more again. In Jane Austen's *Pride and Prejudice* Elizabeth Bennet and Mr. Darcy make their way past comic misunderstandings to a happy marriage, for they share a sense of superior cultivation and, with the additional advantage of status, can expect to keep themselves in a semi-protected circle, a little apart from the dull but worthy people surrounding them. At home in their society, they can yet maintain a comfortable distance from it. In Emily Brontë's *Wuthering Heights* Heathcliff and Cathy, in their moments of ecstasy, cut themselves off from common life, neither accepting nor rebelling against society, but refusing the very idea of it. In George Eliot's *Middlemarch* Dorothea Brooke and Lydgate, the two figures who should come together but through force of circumstances and vanity do not, envision a union in which they would struggle in behalf of those serious values their society disdains. They know the struggle would be difficult, but do not regard it as impossible. But by *Jude the Obscure* there is neither enclave nor retreat, evasion nor grasped opportunity for resistance. Jude and Sue are lost souls; they have no place in the world they can cherish or to which they can retreat; their goals are hardly to be comprehended in worldly terms at all. Lonely, distraught, rootless, they cling to one another like children in the night. Exposed to the racking sensations of homelessness, they become prey to a kind of panic whenever they are long separated from each other. The closeness of the lost—clutching, solacing and destroying one another—is a closeness of a special kind, which makes not for heroism or tragedy or even an exalted suffering, but for that somewhat passive "modern" sadness which suffuses *Jude the Obscure*.

Now it would be foolish to suppose that the social history of nineteenth century England can be neatly registered in this sketch of changing assumptions from Jane Austen to Thomas Hardy—though by 1900 there was, I think, good reason for cultivated persons to feel more estranged from their society than their great-grandparents might have felt in 1800. What can plausibly be assumed is that there were serious historical pressures behind the increasingly critical attitudes that nineteenth century English novelists took toward their society. Hardy comes at the end of one tradition, that of the solid extroverted English novel originating mostly with Henry Fielding; but he also comes at the beginning of another tradition, that of the literary "modernism" which would dominate the twentieth century. In personal background, novelistic technique, choice of locale and characters, Hardy remains mostly of the past; but in his distinctive sensibility, he is partly of the future. He moves somewhat beyond, though he does not quite abandon, the realistic social novel such as George Eliot and Thackeray wrote, and by *Jude the Obscure* he is composing the kind of fiction about which one is tempted to employ such terms as expressionist, stylized, grotesque, symbolic distortion and a portrait of extreme situations. None of these is wholly to the point, yet all suggest that this last of Hardy's novels cannot be fully apprehended if read as a conventional realistic work. Not by its fullness or probability as a rendering of common life, but by its power and coherence as a vision of modern deracination— so must the book be judged. It is not a balanced or temperate work; it will not satisfy well-adjusted minds content with the blessings of the wholesome; it does not pretend to show the human situation in its many-sidedness. Committed to an extreme darkness of view, a promethean resistance to fatality, *Jude the Obscure* shares in the spirit of the Book of Job, whose author seems also to have been a pessimist. In the history of Hardy criticism *Jude the Obscure* provides a touchstone of taste: the older and more traditional critics, loving Hardy for the charm and comeliness of his Wessex portraiture, have usually disparaged the book as morbid, while the more recent and modern critics are inclined to regard its very starkness as a sign of truth.

To present *Jude the Obscure* as a distinctively modern novel is surely an exaggeration; but it is an exaggeration I think valuable to propose, since it helps to isolate those elements which make the book seem so close to us in spirit. There is, in regard to *Jude the Obscure,* an experience shared by many of its readers: we soon notice its fragility of structure, we are likely to be troubled by its persistent depressiveness and its tendency to prompt a fate already more than cruel, yet at the end we are forced to acknowledge that the book has moved and shaken us. This seeming paradox is almost impossible to explain if *Jude* is regarded as a conventional realistic novel; it becomes easier to account for if the book is read as a dramatic fable in which the traditional esthetic criteria of unity and verisimilitude are subordinated to those of a distended expressiveness.

In Hardy's earlier novels, as in most of nineteenth century English fiction, characters tend to be presented as fixed and synthesized entities, as knowable public events. They function in a social medium; they form the sum or resultant of a set of distinguishable traits; they act out, in their depicted conduct, the consequences and implications of these traits; and their very "meaning" as characters in a novel derives from the action to which they are entirely bound. In a book like *The Mayor of Casterbridge* the central figure, Michael Henchard, becomes known to us through his action: what he does is what he is. It would be impudent to suppose that in writing *The Mayor* Hardy did not realize that human beings have a complex inner life, or that there are discrepancies between one's inner and outer, private and public, experience. Of course he knew this, and so did such novelists as Fielding, Jane Austen and Thackeray. But in their work, as a rule, the inner life of the characters is to be inferred from their public behavior, or from the author's analytic synopses.

By *Jude the Obscure* Hardy is beginning to move away from this mode of characterization. He is still quite far from that intense hovering scrutiny to which James subjects his figures, nor does he venture upon that dissolution of public character into a stream of psychic notation and event which can be found in Virginia Woolf and James Joyce. Yet we are made aware, while reading *Jude the Obscure,* that human character is being regarded as severely problematic, open to far-reaching speculative inquiry, and perhaps beyond certain knowledge; that the character of someone like Sue Bridehead must be seen not as a coherent force realizing itself in self-consistent public action, but as an amorphous and ill-charted arena in which irrational impulses conflict with one another; and that behind the interplay of events occupying the foreground of the novel there is a series of distorted psychic shadows which, with some wrenching, can be taken to provide the true "action" of the book.

Thinking, for example, of Jude Fawley, we are inclined to see him as a man whose very being constitutes a kind of battlefield and who matters, consequently, more for what happens within him than for what happens to him. He is racked by drives he cannot control, drives he barely understands. Powerfully sexed, drawn immediately to Arabella's hearty if somewhat soiled physical life, Jude is in constant revolt against his own nature. (That revolt comprises a major portion of the novel's inner action "behind" its visible action.) Jude responds far more spontaneously to Arabella than to Sue, for Arabella is unmistakably female and every now and then he needs a bit of wallowing in sex and drink to relieve him from the strain of his ambition and spirituality. At the same time Jude is forever caught up with Sue, who represents an equivalent or extension of his unsettled consciousness, quick and brittle as he is slow and cluttered, and therefore all the more attractive to him, as a vivid bird might be to a bear. The two of them are linked in seriousness, in desolation, in tormenting kindness, but above all, in an overbred nervousness. Theirs is a companionship of the nerves.

At least in part, Jude seems an anticipation of modern rationality struggling to become proudly self-sufficient and thereby cutting itself off from its sources in physical life. Though he is born in the country and lives mostly in towns, Jude could soon enough adapt himself to the twentieth century city: his mental life, in its creasing divisions and dissociations, is that of the modern metropolis. Destined to the role of stranger, he stops here and rests there, but without community, place or home. His frustration derives not so much from a denial of his desires as from their crossing and confusion; and as he struggles to keep in harmony his rumbling sensuality, his diffused ambition and his high ethical intent, one is reminded a little of St. Augustine's plaint to God: "Thou has counselled a better course than thou hast permitted."

Even more than Jude, Sue Bridehead invites psychological scrutiny; indeed, she is one of the great triumphs of psychological portraiture in the English novel. Sue is that terrifying specter of our age, before whom men and cultures tremble: she is an *interesting* girl. She is promethean in mind but masochist in character; and the division destroys her, making a shambles of her mind and a mere sterile discipline of her character. She is all intellectual seriousness, but without that security of will which enables one to live out the consequences of an idea to their limit. She is all feminine charm, but without body, without flesh or smell, without femaleness. Lacking focused sexuality, she casts a vaguely sexual aura over everything she touches. Her sensibility is kindled but her senses are mute. Quite without pride in status or self, she is consumed by vanity, the vanity of the sufferer who takes his suffering as a mark of distinction and bears a cross heavier than even fate might demand. Sue cannot leave anything alone, neither her men nor herself: she needs always to be tampering and testing, communicating and quivering. D. H. Lawrence, quick to see in Sue Bridehead the antithesis of his idea of the woman, writes of her with a fascinated loathing:

> She is the production of the long selection by man of the woman in whom the female is subordinate to the male principle. . . .
> Her female spirit did not wed with the male spirit . . . Her spirit submitted to the male spirit, owned the priority of the male spirit, wished to become the male spirit. . . .
> One of the supremest products of our civilization is Sue, and a product that well frightens us. . . .
> She must, by the constitution of her nature, remain quite physically intact, for the female was atrophied in her, to the enlargement of the male activity. Yet she wanted some quickening for this atrophied female. She wanted even kisses. That the new rousing might give her a sense of life. But she could only *live* in the mind . . .
> Here, then, was her difficulty: to find a man whose vitality could infuse her and make her live, and who would not, at the same time, demand of her a return of the female impulse into him. What man could receive this drainage, receiving nothing back again? He must either die or revolt.

Yet one thing more, surely the most important, must be said about Sue Bridehead. As she appears in the novel itself, rather than in the grinder of analysis, she is an utterly charming and vibrant creature. We grasp directly, and not merely because we are told, why Jude finds himself unable to resist Sue. Hardy draws her with a marvelous plasticity, an affectionate yet critical attentiveness. She is happily charming when she first encounters Jude at the martyr's cross: "I am not going to meet you just there, for the first time in my life! Come farther on." She is pathetically charming when she escapes the training school and, dripping wet, comes to Jude's chambers. And there is even charm of a morbid kind when she rehearses in church with Jude the wedding she is soon to seal with Phillotson. "I like to do things like this," she tells him, "in the delicate voice of an epicure in emotions"—and in that remark lies a universe of unrest and perversity.

What has been said here about the distinctively "modern" element in *Jude the Obscure* holds not merely for its characterization but also for its narrative structure. The novel does not depend primarily on a traditional plot, by means of which there is revealed and acted out a major destiny, such as Henchard's in *The Mayor of Casterbridge.* A plot consists of an action purposefully carved out of time, that is, provided with a beginning, sequence of development and climax, so that it will create the impression of completeness. Often this impression comes from the sense that the action of a novel, as given shape by the plot, has exhausted its possibilities of significant extension; the problems and premises with which it began have reached an appropriate terminus. Thus we can say that in the traditional kind of novel it is usually the plot which carries or releases a body of meanings: these can be profound or trivial, comic or tragic. *The Mayor of Casterbridge* contains a plot which fulfills the potential for self-destruction in the character of Henchard—but it is important to notice that in *this* kind of novel we would have no knowledge of that potential except insofar as we can observe its effects through an action. Plot here comes to seem inseparable from meaning, and meaning to inhere in plot.

When a writer works out a plot, he tacitly assumes that there is a rational structure in human conduct, that this structure can be ascertained, and that doing so he is enabled to provide his work with a sequence of order. But in "modernist" literature these assumptions come into question. In a work written on the premise that there is no secure meaning in the portrayed action, or that while the action can hold our attention and rouse our feelings, we cannot be certain, indeed must remain uncertain, as to the possibilities of meaning—in such a characteristically modern work what matters is not so much the plot but a series of *situations,* some of which can be portrayed statically, through tableaux, set-pieces, depth psychology, and others dynamically, through linked episodes, stream of consciousness, etc. Kafka's fiction, Joyce's novels, some of Faulkner's, like *The Sound and the Fury*—these all contain situations rather than plots. *Jude the Obscure* does not go nearly so far along the path of modernism as these works, but it goes as far as Hardy could. It is consequently a novel in which plot does not signify nearly so much as in his more traditional novels.

With a little trouble one could block out the main lines of a plot in *Jude the Obscure*: the protagonist, spurred by the dominant needs of his character, becomes involved in a series of complications, and these, in turn, lead to a climax of defeat and death. Yet the curve of action thus described would not, I think, bring one to what is most valuable and affecting in the novel—as a similar kind of description would in regard to *The Mayor of Casterbridge.* What is essential in *Jude,* surviving and deepening in memory, is a series of moments rather than a sequence of actions. These moments—one might also call them panels of representation—tend to resemble snapshots rather than moving pictures, concentrated vignettes rather than worked-up dramatic scenes. They center upon Jude and Sue at critical points of their experience, at the times they are together, precious and intolerable as these are, and the times they are apart, necessary and hateful as these are. Together, Jude and Sue anticipate that claustrophobic and self-destructive concentration on "personal relationships" which is to be so pervasive a theme in the twentieth century novel. They suffer, as well, from another "modern" difficulty: that of thoughtful and self-reflective persons who have become so absorbed with knowing their experience, they become unable to live it. Their predicament is "tragic" in that deeply serious and modern sense of the word which teaches us that human waste, the waste of spirit and potential, is a terrible thing. Yet a tragedy in any classical sense *Jude* is not, for it directs our attention not to the fateful action of a looming protagonist but to the inner torments of familiar contemporaries. In classical tragedy, the hero realizes himself through an action. In the modern novel, the central action occurs within the psyche of the hero. And *Jude,* in the last analysis, is a novel dominated by psychology.

It is not the kind of book that can offer the lure of catharsis or the relief of conciliation. It does not pretend to satisfy the classical standard of a composure won through or after suffering: for the quality it communicates most strongly is that of naked pain. Awkward, subjective, overwrought and embittered, *Jude the Obscure* contains moments of intense revelation, at almost any point where the two central figures come together, and moments of glaring falsity, as in the botched incident of Father Time's death. (Botched not in conception but in execution: it was a genuine insight to present the little boy as one of those who were losing the will to live, but a failure in tact to burden him with so much philosophical weight.) Such mixtures of psychological veracity and crude melodrama are characteristic of Hardy, a novelist almost always better in parts than the whole. Yet the final impact of the book is shattering. Here, in its first stirrings, is the gray poetry of modern loneliness, which Jude brings to apotheosis in the terrible words, *"Let the day perish wherein I was born, and the night in which it was said, There is a man child conceived."*

VII

An Iliad of Europe

THE IDEA FOR *The Dynasts* had been germinating in Hardy's mind for at least thirty years before he published the work, its first part in 1904, its second in 1906, and its third in 1908. The book brought together the philosophical concerns of his maturity with a fascination he had felt for the Napoleonic wars since early childhood. During the years when it seemed likely that Napoleon would invade England, Dorset had been shaken out of its usual course of life; volunteer companies had been formed, arrangements for signaling the approach of a French fleet worked out and the population alerted to its duties in defense. Hardy grew up at a time when these great events were still fresh in the memories of many people in Dorset, and as a boy, he heard endless stories of excitement and comedy, quite as William Faulkner in his boyhood heard somewhat similar stories about the Civil War. There is a vivid passage of recollection in the preface to *The Trumpet Major*:

> An outhouse door riddled with bullet holes, which had been extemporized by a solitary man as a target for firelock practice when the landing was hourly expected, a heap of bricks and clods on a beacon hill, which had formed the chimney and walls of a hut occupied by the beacon keeper, worm-eaten shafts and iron heads of

pikes for the use of those who had no better weapons, ridges on the
down thrown up during the encampment, fragments of volunteer
uniform, and other such lingering remains, brought to my imagination in early childhood the state of affairs at the date of the war more
vividly than volumes of history could have done.

In 1875, the year in which he interviewed survivors of Waterloo
at Chelsea Hospital, Hardy noted:

Mem; a Ballad of the Hundred Days. Then another of Moscow.
Others of earlier campaigns—forming altogether an Iliad of Europe
from 1789 to 1815.

Seven years later there occurs another memorandum:

Write a history of human automatism or impulsion—namely an
account of human action in spite of human knowledge, showing how
very far conduct lags behind the knowledge that should really
guide it.

And in 1886:

The human race to be shown as one great network or tissue which
quivers in every part when one point is shaken, like a spider's web
if touched. Abstract realisms to be in the form of Spirits, Spectral
Figures, etc.

When the first part finally appeared in 1904, the critical recep-
tion was decidedly lukewarm. The *Spectator's* reviewer said, with
some justice, that the Spirits "conduct their espionage in the
spirit of a very young man who has just begun to dabble in metaphysics and is imperfectly acquainted with terminology." Others,
including Max Beerbohm in a fine notice, were more sympathetic.
By the time of the First World War, the critical response had
changed remarkably, perhaps under the influence of patriotic
sentiment, and *The Dynasts* came to be regarded as a major work.

It is a chastening experience to reflect upon this shift in
literary taste. Sensitive poet-critics like Lascelles Abercrombie and
Edmund Blunden have declared *The Dynasts* a masterpiece, yet
at the present moment the work seems to have few enthusiastic
critics and, I would surmise, not many more readers. So rapid
and extreme a shift in opinion ought to persuade us to avoid
critical absolutism and call into question our own historically
shaped preferences. For nothing could be more parochial than
to suppose that having gotten past the middle of the twentieth

century we necessarily have better taste than the cultivated readers of a few decades ago.

Perhaps one clue to the problem lies in Hardy's wish that
The Dynasts be read as "an Iliad of Europe" reflecting "the real,
if only temporary, thought of the age." This note was taken up by
Abercrombie, who praised the book in terms not very different
from those with which Pound's *Cantos* and Eliot's *Wasteland*
have been praised in our day. He accepted as valid Hardy's claim
that *The Dynasts* encompassed the thought of the age and con-
cluded that this, among other reasons, entitled it to high admiration. That *The Dynasts*, its idiosyncrasies of form and diction
notwithstanding, does reflect the deterministic scientism of the
late nineteenth century is beyond dispute. And there's the rub.
"The real . . . thought of the age" usually turns out to be all
too temporary and what is perhaps worse, among a later generation of readers, less a matter for violent dispute than indifference.
(The sense of moral and intellectual crisis which prompted
Hardy to his philosophical ventures is another matter: *that* remains entirely urgent and relevant.) We are today not much
concerned with questions of ultimate causation. Our problems
seem closer to home, more within ourselves than the cosmos. The
lesson might be that a work of literature enamored of the most
advanced opinions of the time in which it has been composed
runs the danger of quick obsolescence. There will always be new
advanced opinions.

Reading *The Dynasts* yields the unexpected consequence of
making one attentive to a kind of criticism little practiced these
days: the criticism of *genres*, a study of literature through close
differentiation of its kinds and their appropriateness for achiev-
ing particular ends. It is a criticism that lends itself to sterility,
the scholasticism of replacing a living response to a work of art
with a fixed category for its classification. Yet I think that if seen
as a strategy for adjusting responses to texts rather than texts to
responses, it can be a useful approach. And in regard to *The
Dynasts*, an indispensable one.

Precisely what kind of work *The Dynasts* is seems hard to say.
Hardy describes it as an "epic-drama," in three parts, nineteen
acts, and one hundred and thirty scenes, covering a time span of
about ten years. It is roughly the length of at least two full-sized

novels; it is written mainly in verse, with a wide range of meters though predominantly blank verse; it contains hundreds of characters, some merely glimpsed and others, like Napoleon, Nelson, Pitt, Alexander, Wellington and Josephine encountered frequently. At intervals there appears a battery of spectral voices, hovering over the action like philosophic harpies and returning again and again to the same solemn ruminations, mostly to the effect that little good can come from human effort and even less possibility for freedom be found within it. The most important of these voices is the Spirit of the Years, who speaks for Hardy's fatalistic mechanism by stressing the inflexible predetermination of historical events as these operate through an impersonal Will (sometimes called "the Great Foresightless" and other times merely "It"). Flanking the Spirit of the Years are the Spirit of the Pities and the Spirit Ironic, the first closest in compassionate voice to the traditional Greek chorus, though only at an ineffective distance, and the second, quite as if itself human, regarding the earthly holocaust as a bitter joke. It might be said that the Spirit of the Years represents fatality and the surrounding Spirits futility: the former what must and has been ordained to be, the latter what is or can be felt along a spectrum of helplessness. Among these Spirits there seems to be occurring a continual debate, but in fact it does not involve a dialectic of change and modulation; there is almost nothing but a fixed recitation of inflexible positions and attitudes.

One thinks, then, about problems of *genre* not out of a fastidious wish to categorize *The Dynasts,* but because difficulties in reading the work create puzzlement over its nature and the varieties of response it invites. So that if we can even tentatively describe the kind of work it is, we may succeed in dismissing false expectations and accept whatever pleasures can legitimately be had.

At the very outset it becomes clear that the pleasures associated with prose fiction will be in short supply. There is a narrative line, but one which is known entirely in advance, so that little if any suspense is possible, and which is virtually lacking in the disciplines of plot, so that little if any development is possible. A string of incidents chronologically arranged, even if it follows a curve of actual events, does not yet comprise a structured action.

Many of these incidents are dependent for their meaning and shape upon a remembered course of history, almost always unsatisfactory in an imaginative work because insufficiently selective, but here especially unsatisfactory because excessively complex and chaotic. Many of these incidents are also redundant, most notably those items of battle resting upon Hardy's innocent faith in the excitement he can arouse by references to the way "the left" of one general outflanks "the center" of another. What we have here is at best a chronicle or a panorama, not a disciplined narrative.

Only one thing could give coherence to so vast an undertaking, and that would be a controlling myth, such as can be found in traditional epic, or a moral ideology, such as appears in *War and Peace*. The Spirits, in their moaning rhythms of reflection, are meant to provide precisely this element; but they do not, and I believe, they cannot. For, by virtue of the philosophic premises from which they rarely can break free, they are necessarily inert. They are spectators not participants, they muse but do not move, they appear but cannot act. What could at most be claimed is that there are two related lines of action and significance in *The Dynasts,* the terrestrial and the spectral; but as Abercrombie, with his admirable honesty, must admit: "The two circles of drama [the Spirits above and the humans below] are not geometrically struck. They touch each other several times"—which, in a work of such enormous scope, is not very often. When "the two circles of drama" do indeed touch, they break the integument of Hardy's thought, which requires that the Spirits remain aloof, in a grandeur of isolation; and when, more frequently, "the two circles of drama" remain apart, there can be no persuasive *dramatic* reasons —regardless of the intellectual motive—for steadily juxtaposing a historical action which has at least a potential of dynamism with a spectral observation which soon becomes fixated in its own premises.

Nor is there much gratification to be had from the portrayal of the earthly characters. Hardy's panoramic method—quite apart from the philosophic intent which makes the whole performance seem frigid—necessarily enforces distance. All is to be seen as inexorable process and settled procession; all is by prearrangement but without a motivating arranger—which, at least esthetically, is to have the worst of all possible views of the world. Yet certain figures in *The Dynasts* do achieve moments of vividness, if only because Hardy is a great writer despite all the preconceptions he erects in the path of his gift. He may claim to regard the population of *The Dynasts* as mere puppets of "It," but he cannot help depicting them on occasion as spontaneous and active human beings. Napoleon rushes out to meet Marie-Louisa's carriage soon after she crosses into France, just as if he were a boy eager with love; Nelson speaks poignantly at the moment of his death; Queen Louisa of Prussia tries to charm the French conqueror into leniency toward her beaten country. But in the main Hardy's commitment to spectacle and fixed posture is strongly at variance with the very idea of fictional characterization, and in this work it is usually the first that dominates. With some pleasing exceptions, men are shown from a distance, as negligible factors in a historical charade and not as human beings to be studied and revealed. Hardy's plan for covering in more or less equal segments an enormous span of history does not leave him, despite the length of *The Dynasts*, enough space to write with intensity and scenic fullness about particular characters and events. An overextension of scope precludes concentration in detail—so that one might say with equal pertinence that the work has too much or not enough detail.

And the pleasures of poetry? Even the warmest defenders of *The Dynasts* will usually admit that little of the verse has distinction. Edmund Blunden writes with a delicacy that is touching: "Blank verse makes the principal fabric [of *The Dynasts*], and is not always equal to the task, unless we regard the numerous passages which amble along and betray the author's uninterested transcriptions of unavoidable historical information as proper to the full scheme of a chronicler." If, in a long English poem, blank verse is to carry interest over the inevitable plateaus of the ordinary, there must be, at the least, an over-all structural firmness, some moments of local vivacity and a command of "middle" diction, neither high eloquence nor colloquial scrappiness. None of these, in my judgment, is sufficiently present in *The Dynasts*, though it is the lack of the third, a usable "middle" style, that seems the most damaging. It is a lack which the crushing spell of Shakespeare has made almost unavoidable, for under that spell the stately rhythm of blank verse quickly slips into bombast. A passage like the following, in which the dying Nelson speaks to his aide Captain Hardy, suggests the extent not merely of debt but of decline:

> Ay, thus do little things
> Steal into my mind, too. But ah, my heart
> Knows not your calm philosophy!—There's one—
> Come nearer to me, Hardy.—One of all,
> As you well guess, pervades my memory now;
> She, and my daughter—I speak freely to you.

The blank verse spoken by the Spirits reads at times like an undiscovered language, not quite English or any other:

> Spirit of the Years:
> These are the Prime Volitions,—fibrils, veins,
> Will-tissues, nerves, and pulses of the Cause,
> That heave throughout the Earth's compositure.
> Their sum is like the lobule of a Brain
> Evolving always that it wots not of;
> A Brain whose whole connotes the Everywhere
> And whose procedure may but be discerned
> By phantom eyes like ours . . .

Hardy's liking for neologisms and archaisms becomes downright wanton in the more pretentious sections of *The Dynasts*, perhaps because the absence of intellectual development and philosophic tension forces him to linguistic straining. So that the Spirit of the Years can speak in a strange patois:

> Hold what ye list, fond unbelieving Sprites,
> You cannot swerve the pulsion of the Byss,
> Which thinking on, yet weighing not Its thought,
> Unchecks its clock-like laws.

Is *The Dynasts* then an epic? Hardy calls it an "epic-drama." To notice that the work lacks the strong positive hero who in traditional epic contains the aspirations of a people; that, despite its intermittent appeal to English pride in defeating Napoleon, it can hardly be said to release a set of compelling national values (Hardy treats the English victory with decided realism, stressing the role of English gold in propping up the Continental allies; which would be fine for a realistic novel but damaging to the exalted tone necessary for an epic)—this is not to indulge in a criticism of categorical preconceptions, but to suggest how the work fails to satisfy the expectations raised by both Hardy's label and the magnitude of his composition. By contrast *War and Peace*, though written in prose and cast as a novel, does take on certain qualities of epic. Tolstoy communicates the *fullness* of the Russian experience in repelling Napoleon as Hardy, with both his greater and more diffuse ambitions, does not do for the English in *The Dynasts*. *War and Peace* profits from a perspective which allows Tolstoy to be closely implicated with historical events while also rising above them in behalf of national goals and moral values. Hardy's motivating philosophy is monistic, but in the actual composition of his work he falls into a hopeless split between the terrestrial and the spectral, two static and dramatically unrelated realms.

More important still is the fact that an epic is a work resting primarily on the *activity* of one or more central figures, men who change history or through their "chosenness" begin a new portion of history. *The Aeneid* is preeminently a work of this kind. And even if one accepts the questionable modernist interpretation of *The Iliad* as an anti-heroic poem, the idea of heroic action and heroic will continues to play a central role in Homer. *The Dynasts*, however, is dedicated to an idea of human helplessness, the idea that men are mere refractions of impersonal force. Even if Hardy were more skillful than he is in evading his set notions, there would still follow a certain listlessness of presentation.

If *The Dynasts* comes to seem, upon inspection, more an anti-epic than an epic, similar doubts arise as to the second term in Hardy's title. *The Dynasts* lacks the concentration of drama, but more important, the animating persuasion that there is or can be meaningful conflict. Now, in practice, some of the terrestrial scenes do take on dramatic quality; and if the work as a whole is flawed by the absence of organic connection between the worldly figures and the otherworldly specters, locally this often proves to be an advantage. For the human figures can then behave as if there were in fact no such paralyzing force above them as the Immanent Will; as if, indeed, their own wills signified.

There are two other and perhaps more important ways in which *The Dynasts* fails as drama. The death of Satan, wrote Wallace Stevens, was a tragedy for the imagination; had he been writing with Hardy's book in mind, he might have added, so too was the death of God. For whatever the theological or metaphysical merits of traditional Christianity and mechanistic determinism, there can be no doubt that for a dramatic poem aspiring to fundamental revelations about the cosmos, and trying to present a celestial cast which will be roughly equivalent to that of Christian myth, a God-created world is greatly preferable to one driven by "It." A world of purpose provides norms by which to measure conduct; an It-made world underscores the pointlessness of trying to secure norms anywhere but from the experience they are supposed to guide.

Let me say clearly that I am not at all endorsing the tiresome notion of certain "traditionalist" critics that the denial of a personal god signifies that the universe must necessarily be devoid of poetry. What I am saying is that Hardy could not succeed, nor could anyone else, in writing a large-scale work in which the idea of Christianity has been abandoned but an effort is made to preserve pale duplicates of its heavenly population. Everyone knows about Jehovah in the Bible, not just the author or authors of the Bible; but Hardy's spectral figures are the abstractions of an intellectual, which makes them seem both private and eccentric insofar as they must be introduced to his readers and must remain forever unknown to his characters.

In a naturalistic or even realistic novel Hardy's conception would be quite usable, for there the center of interest would be not a view of the universe but the struggle of men to survive in its alien space. But Hardy's theory of Immanent Will does not lend itself to a composition dealing with the larger issues of human destiny and suprahuman intervention, since it can only be stated or worse, repeated; it cannot be developed dramatically. God has a history. He stayed Abraham's hand, He punished Sodom, He sent a son to earth, He may even have done something more recently. But at least until that dim time foreseen at the close of *The Dynasts* when "It" will have taken on a measure of consciousness, and thereby become susceptible to all the difficulties Hardy found in the God of Theism, the "Great Foresightless" can only appear as an inert and inscrutable force, a dead weight of foredesign without the intent of design. At least for literature, "It" will never be able to compete with Jehovah.

Yet this very difficulty in representing the Immanent Will

drives Hardy toward a recurrent anthropomorphism. His use of the word "Will" suggests as much, since what he really has in mind is characterized above all by the absence of will. But his imagination boggles at what his mind proposes, and, as a writer obsessed with a need for meaning, he smuggles in a strand of teleology. The purposeless drive of the "It" to produce events comes to seem a despiritualized version of the creating God, or alternately, as an effort, such as many nineteenth century writers undertook, to endow dumb nature with potential spirit. Even if toward the end of the work we suspect that the Immanent Will is a kind of metaphysical spawning-ground for a personal God who has been abandoned but may yet, after aeons of good conduct, be allowed to return, "It" is a concept peculiarly recalcitrant to literary treatment. Hardy is not to be blamed for the intellectual dilemma that is here manifested. He was too serious a man simply to "use" the idea of God which for earlier writers had been an unquestioned reality; and that is entirely to his credit. What he might have considered, however, was the advisability of even attempting a cosmic "epic-drama" once there was no place in it for God.

Previous writers trying to embody, as distinct from merely comment on, supernatural creatures have sensed that to make such creatures plausible they must be shown as possessing some human characteristics. The Greeks understood this instinctively, and so did Milton. Fallen or not, the angels in *Paradise Lost* can be apprehended only insofar as they have a certain human admixture: otherwise they would be beyond our grasp. The Spirits in *The Dynasts,* however, are neither living creatures nor pure abstractions; they are disembodied voices without the powers of gods or the passions of men, forever stalled in the rut of a predetermination which seems more the work of their creator than of the cosmos. Hardy tries to adapt to his purposes something like Milton's celestial machinery, but what he is forbidden by his premises to create is anything like Milton's rigorous celestial life.

Our process of elimination grows disconcerting. What *is The Dynasts*? One critic, John Wain, has come up with an answer both startling and ingenious:

> Despairing of the conventions of fiction, poetry, and drama as he understood them, Hardy gathered his strength and leapt into an

entirely new imaginative area. He wrote his huge work in accordance
with the conventions of an art that had not yet been invented: the
art of the cinema.

... *The Dynasts* anticipates the cinema because the imagination
that went into its making was of the same kind that goes into the
making of a film. Though it introduces characters speaking to one
another, it is not dramatic. The devices it uses most centrally—
panoramic views dissolving into close-up, for instance—are cinematic.
The presiding eye is that of the film camera, called into being by the
imagination of a major writer before it existed in the physical world.
The Dynasts is neither a poem, nor a play, nor a story. It is a
shooting-script.

... This bold originality, the creation at one stroke of a new perspective, stamps *The Dynasts* as the work of a major artist.

This is charming—but is it true? or useful? I doubt it, since to
regard *The Dynasts* as a shooting-script is not yet to give us any
help as to how, or even whether, the book is to be read. As a
rule, shooting-scripts are not read or meant to be read. They matter insofar as they contribute to a finished work, that is, to the
film as it finally emerges. *The Dynasts,* however, was offered by
Hardy as a finished work in its own right; and if, in this finished
work, there are severe difficulties with regard to diction, structure,
characterization and style, then it is not much help to be told
the work is a kind of shooting-script. Unless, that is, the tacit
message is that *The Dynasts* need no longer be read, except perhaps by film directors in search of material . . . Yet the possibility
of *The Dynasts* ever being filmed is extremely slight; with its
battery of Spirits utterly out of the question. To call the work
a shooting-script is therefore to doom it to a limbo of eternal
unfulfillment, no longer a traditional work of literature yet not
a realized element in a new art form. And meanwhile the difficulties we experienced in reading *The Dynasts* remain—if, that
is, we continue to assume it is a work to be read.

I see no way, then, of escaping the conclusion that *The Dynasts*
is a vast and awkward hybrid, a heroic effort to do what could
not be done within the terms of Hardy's vision. Perhaps a later
generation will discover neglected merit in the work and return
to the estimate of critics like Abercrombie; but right now it
looks very much like a museum piece. No ascription of over-all
significance and structure can remove the excessive number of
local failures. No evidence of local felicities can remove doubt

as to the over-all significance and structure. That there is no satisfactory type-name for *The Dynasts* registers, I think, inescapable difficulties in apprehending and valuing the work: not because we need a label, in itself of no interest, but because we need the discrimination of response that labels are supposed to indicate.

Yet a fact remains. Thomas Hardy is a great writer, a strange genius, and something of his greatness comes through in any work he takes seriously. Not even his own will, in this work far more preemptory than the Immanent Will, can completely thwart his creative powers.

There are excellent touches: warm, ironic, odd. When a dumb show reveals the Milan Cathedral, the Spirit of the Pities asks, "What is the creed that these rich rites disclose?" and the Spirit of the Years answers with a piquant remark:

> A local cult, called Christianity,
> Which the wild dramas of the wheeling spheres
> Include, with divers other such, in dim
> Pathetical and brief parentheses . . .

The Russian troops come upon French soldiers frozen to death on the plains. Kutuzoff refers to them as "frost-baked meats" and an officer remarks:

> They all sit
> As they were living still, but stiff as horns;
> And even the colour has not left their cheeks,
> Whereon the tears remain in strings of ice.

The Prince of Wales must speak at a public assembly and, tongue-tied, he turns to Sheridan for words. The wit supplies some lines that begin

> If heat be evidence of loyalty,
> This room affords it without question . . .

Taunted by a Lord that the Prince's "outpouring tastes suspiciously like your brew, Sheridan . . . How d'ye sell it a gallon?" Sheridan replies

> I don't deal that way nowadays. I give the recipe, and charge a duty on the gauging. It is more artistic, and saves trouble.

Napoleon, home from the Russian fiasco, tells his queen that he nevertheless intends to gild the dome of the Invalides, "in best gold leaf, and on a novel pattern." His explanation implies a shrewd sense of the Parisians:

> To give them something
> To think about. They'll take to it like children,
> And argue in the cafés right and left
> On its artistic point.—So they'll forget
> The woes of Moscow.

And toward the end, surveying the battlefield of Waterloo before blood has yet been spilt, the Chorus of the Years exhibits Hardy's powers of sympathetic identification with the speechless of the earth:

> Yea, the coneys are scared by the thud of hoofs,
> And their white scuts flash on their vanishing heels,
> And swallows abandon the hamlet-roofs.
>
> The mole's tunnelled chambers are crushed by wheels,
> The lark's eggs scattered, their owners fled;
> And the hedgehog's household the sapper unseals.
>
> The snail draws in at the terrible tread,
> But in vain; he is crushed by the felloe-rim;
> The worm asks what can be overhead,
>
> And wriggles deep from a scene so grim,
> And guesses him safe, for he does not know
> What a foul red flood will be soaking him!

If there were but more of such passages. If Hardy had been less enchanted with the ideas of his time and more by the powers of his imagination. If he had only been able to let his philosophic notions lie at rest, or let them go, or let them go hang.

VIII

The Lyric Poems

HARDY BEGAN AS A POET and ended as a poet. His *Collected Poems,* which does not include *The Dynasts,* comes to more than eight hundred closely printed pages, and except during the middle period of his career, from about 1872 to 1890, he kept producing verse with professional regularity. These poems range in quality from a mass of routine work to a small portion that is distinguished and occasionally great. But commonplace or inspired, Hardy continued to turn out poems with the steadiness of a painter who even in dry periods chooses to keep his hand in through persistent sketching. An inexperienced eye may regard such sketches as repetitive to the point of sterility, but the painter's reply would surely be that small ventures in craft are being tested, as his hope might be that even in journeywork there remains a chance for an unforeseen breakthrough.

The sheer quantity of Hardy's verse is discouraging. Who but a scholar or another poet can be expected to read through the *Collected Poems,* on the alert for the slender margin of Hardy's greatness? Nor is bulk the only impediment to the modern reader. Coming to Hardy's poems rather far into the twentieth century, we have to put aside the expectations to which we have been trained by modernist writing. Complex dialectic, willed disorder, mythic parallels, plunges into and out of faith, exposures of personal dissolution, city blues, nihilist confessions—none of these, so frequent in twentieth century poetry, is very important to Hardy. He can be read as a precursor of modernism searching for a post-Christian rationale for values, but in tone and temperament he belongs to an earlier time. Moving into the twentieth century and, through the integrity of his negations, helping to make possible its sensibility of problem and doubt, he is finally not of it. That his poems span two cultural eras while refusing to be locked into either is a source of his peculiar attractiveness. For there is something extremely affecting in the way Hardy seems at once near and far, a poet sharing our intellectual trouble yet displaying a composure of temperament we cannot hope to reach: it is somewhat like the pleasure in meeting a very old man who is still alive to the feelings of the young. Auden worshiped Hardy's honesty, Eliot attacked his heresy; yet Hardy prepared the way for both. In the last analysis, however, Auden and Eliot, admirer and opponent, are closer to one another as poets than either is to Hardy, for in Hardy's verse there remains the living evidence of that tradition which they, in their unavoidable self-consciousness, can only name.

The kind of literary development usually found in a major writer is barely visible in Hardy's career. As a poet, he was seldom genuinely youthful. He wrested his ideas during his twenties and thirties, ideas of rationalist liberalism and humane skepticism, and he clung to them into deep old age, like a man still doting on a childhood sweetheart. Over the decades his writing became more assured, even in its frequent clumsiness, so that the aged Hardy writing bad verse tended to imitate himself rather than Shelley or Swinburne. But for the most part his work is consistent in voice and feeling throughout the more than half-century of his career; he writes as a man not brilliant in mind nor dazzling in virtuosity, but now and again blessed with a measure of wisdom and attuned to the controlling rhythms of human experience. Here are lines from an early poem, "Neutral Tones":

> We stood by a pond that winter day,
> And the sun was white, as though chidden of God,
> And a few leaves lay on the starving sod;
> —They had fallen from an ash, and were gray.

Your eyes on me were as eyes that rove
Over tedious riddles of years ago;
And some words played between us to and fro
On which had lost the more by our love.
The smile on your mouth was the deadest thing
Alive enough to have strength to die;
And a grin of bitterness swept thereby
Like an ominous bird a-wing . . .

And here is a passage from a lyric, "The Shadow on the Stone,"
which Hardy wrote some fifty years later:

I went by the Druid stone
That broods in the garden white and lone,
And I stopped and looked at the shifting shadows
That at some moments fall thereon
From the tree hard by with a rhythmic swing,
And they shaped in my imagining
To the shade that a well-known head and shoulders
Threw there when she was gardening.

Between the early and later poem there has occurred, I think,
a subtle shift of rhythm, one that reflects the increasingly ruminative cast of Hardy's mind. Otherwise, we hear the same voice in
both passages. There is the same low-keyed gravity, with its suggestion of the inescapable clash between man's desire and nature's
silence. There is the same modesty of diction which, through patient coaxing, becomes an unmistakable signature. There is the
same rendering, through the movement of phrase and clause, of a
mind yielding and hesitant in memory. There is the same traditional metric, but a metric tripped and halted, so that we are
encouraged to read the verse as a cadenced speech approaching
yet seemingly too restrained for a chant. And there is the same
marsh-gray atmosphere of a natural world grown terribly worn
and old ("Nature," wrote Hardy in one of his notebooks, "is
played out as a Beauty, not as a Mystery.") What we hear in both
of these poems is, or comes close to being, Hardy's characteristic
voice. It is a voice that anyone who has read a dozen of Hardy's
poems will keep forever in memory, as one keeps the voice of
Pope or Eliot, quite apart from whether one likes what is remembered.

Hardy's faults are notorious, and generations of critics have
declared themselves scandalized. His ear was uncertain: some of

his lines drag and crumble, lending themselves neither to song nor fluent speech. At his best Hardy needs to be read aloud, with the reader following the hesitant motions of phrase and clause while trying to preserve the underlying beat of the lines; but anyone who does try to read Hardy aloud will have to go beyond, or move away from, whatever experience he has had in reading modern verse. Hardy's diction is queer, ill assorted and ill tuned: a strange mixture of the "literary" and flat colloquial, of jargon and romantic poesy. Though he toyed a great deal with stanzaic patterns, Hardy's notions as to verse structure tended to be mechanical, as if the elaboration of complicated forms were a virtue in itself. Later poets have been strongly influenced by Hardy, but in no obvious ways and certainly not from respect for his claims as a technician. It is hard to suppose that in the future many writers will be greatly interested in his improvisations of stanzaic patterns or his efforts to write lines of a length and metrical density the English language is hard put to sustain. What can easily be learned from Hardy is not worth the trouble, and what is very much worth the trouble can hardly be learned at all.

We can extend the indictment. Hardy held to a limited vision of life, unskeptical of his skepticism and after a time, cozy in his doubt. His country mind had suffered an overwhelming trauma of belief during his early years and then, once adjusted to the consequences, he never again risked exposure to ideas that might threaten his peace of mind. His advanced opinions became fixed coordinates of dogma, held with the innocence of the pious rural churchgoer which in a somewhat earlier time he would certainly have been. As a result, large quantities of experience have trouble in breaking past the defenses of his mind; the convictions to which he clings with naive integrity keep him from engaging with the variousness of life and changes in thought; his poems tend to become vehicles for the rehearsal of settled views. Hardy's skepticism shares in the qualities of the village faith it rejects; his belief in the unavoidability of loss can be read in a good many of his poems as a simplistic inversion of Victorian optimism. Immanent Will can prove to be quite as comfortable an object of piety as Almighty God. The scathing assaults upon untested convictions, the playfulness and deviousness of mind we have come to expect in modern poetry—these are not here, not here at all.

Yet now and again Thomas Hardy is a great poet, a master who lives for us as none of his contemporaries can. He is one of the few indispensable poets in English—and this I mean literally: one of the few it would be painful to lose. For not only does he please and delight, he also transforms our entire sense of the human situation. He changes the world. Slowly his flaws as a writer become marks of distinction: like character without physical advantage revealing itself as a mode of beauty. His voice seems to rise from the depths of time, bearing the weight, the sameness and the frightening waste of all human effort. His range is limited, but his penetration deep. Whole areas of experience are shut to him, and whole scales of response; but what he knows and what he says are fully his, untarnished by vanity or pretense.

Any critic can, and often does, see all that is wrong with Hardy's poetry, but whatever it is that makes for his strange greatness is much harder to describe. Can there ever have been a critic of Hardy who, before poems like "The Going" and "During Wind and Rain," did not feel the grating inadequacy of verbal analysis and the need to resort to such treacherous terms as "honesty," "sincerity," and even "wisdom"? We hesitate before such roomy descriptions; we are right to hesitate; and we have, finally, no choice but to use them.

The experience contained in Hardy's poems, or better yet, the experience from which they derive and with which they seem profoundly continuous, is quite ordinary. Much of his poetry stems from private sources and has its private reverberations, but soon the merely intimate is put aside, with a quiet resignation, and what remains in the best of his poems is austere and objective, a sharing in common fate. As a writer Hardy responded most finely to the small events of daily life, because he knew that in their sum these small events comprise our destiny. But if the events are small and the dramas miniature, they are filtered through his consciousness with an enormous patience—the kind of patience that follows upon the appearance and exhaustion of intensity. I shall quote the first stanza of "A Broken Appointment," not quite Hardy at his greatest but in the opening and closing lines extremely distinguished. The genesis of these lines may lie in

Hardy's own experience, but they speak for the constant course
of human disappointment:

> You did not come,
> And marching Time drew on, and wore me numb.—
> Yet less for loss of your dear presence there
> Than that I thus found lacking in your make
> That high compassion which can overbear
> Reluctance for pure lovingkindness' sake
> Grieved I, when as the hope-hour stroked its sum,
> You did not come.

Rhetorically these lines are somewhat more elevated than is
usual with Hardy, so that they suffer a certain affectation of
grandeur that is a recurrent risk in blank verse; but the periodic-
ity of the second of the two sentences, with the brilliant rhythm
in the next to the last line, as it serves to graph the speaker's intensifying command of his recollections, is surely a triumph. So
too is the "hope-hour," one of Hardy's homely coinages. That the
"hope-hour" strikes a "sum" is an instance of Hardy's capacity
for compressing into a single clause the experience of the race
(the clock striking and no lover arriving makes the stroke sound
heavily, like a sum of hours endured—and between "hope-hour"
and "sum" there is a link of irony, each being precisely right yet
in heavy friction with one another). The experience evoked here
is common enough, but the attitude taken toward it is by no
means so. Hardy is expressing that compassion for frailty which
supersedes moral judgment, a compassion he is rightly prepared
to extend to himself. He recognizes that if we are to survive and
gather some affection, we must have with our love a little allowance for inadequacies, a little "lovingkindness."

Hardy can be said to represent a new kind of poet in English.
He is not the satanic desperado or fallen angel of the romantic
tradition, nor the learned and authoritative culture-spokesman
favored by classicism. He is one of the few major English poets
whose origins are plebeian and values throughout his life also
plebeian; and what is more important, he is a poet whose work
is importantly shaped by those origins and values. In saying this
I do not mean to suggest a programmatic social bias, for whatever class resentments Hardy felt in his youth were largely burned

off by the time he turned back to poetry in the 1890s. Nor do I mean to suggest that he was in any usual sense a realist—as, in a twentieth century context, the plebeian emphasis would often imply. When Hardy tried to compose realistic miniatures of drama or character, poems that might be read as scenarios for unwritten stories, he was not nearly so successful as many of his critics claim. His plebeian sensibility and his realism are important elements in the poetry, but only seldom do they appear as a social bias or a commitment to a particular subject. They emerge, instead, as a complete refusal to accept a posture of superiority toward any living creature or defenseless object. For Hardy, the poet is a man neither separate from nor superior to common flesh. He *assumes* the connection between poetry and ordinary life, and writes about those areas of experience Wordsworth proposed to enter but in which he could never claim Hardy's knowledge or ease. Above all, Hardy's plebeian stress comes through as a profound democracy of the feelings, an incomparable courtesy to all he sees and touches.

Hardy's mind had been unsettled by the intellectual dislocations of the nineteenth century, unsettled enough to lend a permanent touch of anxiety to his poems yet not enough to destroy his awareness of what it is that binds all men together. Though he could understand and even share in the pain of deracination, he was never in danger of succumbing to it. The result is a poetry which at its best is knotted with the particulars of historical immediacy yet beautifully eased by the continuities of tradition. Without the sense that he was living through a major historical transformation, Hardy's poetry could sink, as in his second-rank pieces it often did, to mere local detail and passive recording. Without the support of an inherited tradition, Hardy's poetry could sink, as again it often did, to the eccentricities of an autodidact, the provincialism of a man who had once been to the city.

In our actual reading of the poems we are not likely to be directly concerned or moved by his fusion of contemporary and traditional styles of perception. It matters in the poetry as an enabling force, one that allows Hardy to bring his encompassing sympathy to bear upon a chosen situation and to examine it from both a minute closeness and the distance of timelessness. And what matters even more is Hardy's recognition that there

cannot be an easy reconciliation between historical awareness
and the inherited values of a traditional society: the two must
be kept in something approximating a balance of tension. A
good part of what we mean in saying that Hardy is a "sincere"
or "honest" poet has to do with his refusal to bring together in
words what must remain separate in experience.

Hardy's major poetry is marked by a splendid patience, a
tender caring for and affinity with his subjects. If sometimes detached, he is never indifferent. He watches and waits, but in
waiting, does not draw apart from the suffering of others and
himself. He makes no accusations and permits himself few judgments: he is one of us. In Hardy's refusal of moralism there is
something morally exhilarating; it is, I think, a source of that
subdued glow of humaneness which brightens his pages. Transcending the barrier of his metaphysical improvisations, Hardy
settles upon the recurrence of longing and loss, desire and failure,
endurance and fatigue; above all, on the terms of honorable survival, how a man learns to accept sorrow without expecting, or
perhaps even wishing, to lessen his pain. Hardy's humaneness has
little in common with anything so dubious as pity, for a writer
who does not presume to judge will rarely be tempted by pity.
The best of his poems embody a vision both hard and fraternal,
which derives from brooding upon the most terrible facts of
existence while refusing the sentimentalism of despair. He is the
poet, as I. A. Richards has well remarked, "who has most steadily
refused to be comforted. The comfort of forgetfulness, the comfort of beliefs, he has put these both away. Hence his singular
preoccupation with death; because it is in the contemplation of
death that the necessity for human attitudes . . . to be self- supporting is felt most poignantly." In the poem "A Night of Ques-
tionings" there are a few lines which read like a bare summary
of Hardy's outlook. A group of "dead men" ask the wind, "What
of the world now?" and the wind replies:

> Men still
> Who are born, do good, do ill
> Here, just as in your time;
> Till their leaves the locust hath eaten,
> Leaving them bare, downbeaten;
> Somewhiles in summer glow,

Somewhiles in winter snow:—
No more I know.

The writing slips into flat assertiveness, but there are phrases and rhythms which point to Hardy's best work. In the fifth of these lines the word "downbeaten" comes as a shock of compression, with some of the power that the clause "as the hope-hour stroked its sum" does in "A Broken Appointment." These are tokens of Hardy's accomplishment.

It is a most uneven accomplishment, requiring some radical discriminations of judgment and selection. Not all of his critics agree, of course, and one of the best among them, Mark Van Doren, insists that

> No poet more stubbornly resists selection. And this has not been to Hardy's advantage in the field where reputations are made. There is no core of pieces, no inner set of classic or perfect poems, which would prove his rank. Perhaps no poem of Hardy's is perfect; indeed, there is no great poet, in whom imperfection is easier to find. Yet he is a great poet, and there are those who love him without limit even though they will admit his thousand failures and defects. With such persons it is the whole of him that registers and counts; one thing they would be reluctant to admit, namely that out of his *Collected Poems* a *Selected Poems* might be put together which would contain everything pertaining to his essence . . .

These sentiments are admirable, and far to be preferred to the sophisticated condescension that has marked a good portion of recent Hardy criticism. But it is hard to agree entirely. For while the whole of Hardy's "world" needs to be known by his readers, one is likely to be satisfied with a good deal less than the entirety of the poems. In their bulk, they create a landscape of imagination that is both rich and barren, beautiful and dead. To know the contours of this "world" is to see how some of the poems complement one another, half-hidden connections are unexpectedly revealed, and a consistency of atmosphere—the Hardyan weather —is established, to which one may succumb even while knowing that many of the individual pieces are threadbare. Yet this is but the beginning of a serious involvement with Hardy's poems, which in my own experience means a slow, steady and deepening return to a few dozen lyrics. The background of the total work

surely helps, but only if kept where backgrounds should be. Van
Doren is also right in saying that some minor lyrics, like "The
Blinded Bird" and "Let Me Enjoy," can suddenly strike one in
new and pleasing ways. But such small adjustments, while always desirable, do not really affect the issue. Hardy's poems require sharp discriminations, not in order to indulge in joyless
dismissals, but to reach the firm ground of pleasure and praise.
An inner set of "perfect poems" there may not be, but an inner
set most strongly displaying his gifts there certainly is.

   The kind of poem for which Hardy is perhaps best known is
that which borrows from the ballad tradition. His ballad-tales
and ballad-sketches, adapting an old form to a new setting, are
frequently charming; but to say this is already a way of suggesting their limitations. Unstrained and chivalrous, they offer
tribute to the pieties of the immediate past and the ways of
timeless human conduct; they assume a range of association
which nothing but a shared culture can provide; they are
uniquely and inexpressibly English. In "The Dead Quire," a
hard yet humorous sketch of the long-dead Mellstock choir rising
on Christmas Eve to sing an old hymn, Hardy brings together a
somewhat quizzical sensibility with an expert knowledge of Wessex details:

> The singers had followed one by one,
> Treble, and tenor, and thorough-bass;
> And the worm that wasteth had begun
>   To mine their mouldering place.
>
>   * * *
>
> When nigh without, as in old days,
> The ancient quire of voice and string
> Seemed singing words of prayer and praise
>   As they had used to sing:
> *While shepherds watch'd their flock by night,—*
> Thus swells the long familiar sound
> In many a quaint symphonic flight—
>   To, *Glory shone around.*

   Some of Hardy's ballads are also satisfying as verse equivalents
to his pastoral fiction, or, as in "A Trampwoman's Tragedy" and
"A Sunday Morning Tragedy," efforts to place a relatively modern subject within the bounds of a traditional form. In both of
these strong narratives, the rustics are not the auxiliary figures or

diverting clowns of Hardy's novels; they stand at the center of
things, agents of a swift plunge into doom. The writing is taut,
braced in "A Trampwoman's Tragedy" into an intricate stanza
in which the refrain comes, forebodingly, in a shortened second
line:

> Now as we trudged—O deadly day,
> O deadly day!—
> I teased my fancy-man in play
> And wanton idleness.
> I walked alongside jeering John,
> I laid his hand my waist upon;
> I would not bend my glances on
> My lover's dark distress.

Yet it is not, I think, in poems of this kind that Hardy's genius
comes to blossom. The very touches of personal sensibility which
make some of his lyrics so remarkable serve in the ballads to
soften and confuse. There is, in them, either too much or too
little of Hardy: too much if one looks back to the austerity of
the great ballads, too little if one looks forward to modern psychological portraiture. And it is a trouble with Hardy's ballads
that, unavoidably, they do make us look either backward or forward. For Hardy was trying something that may well be impossible: he was trying to give a personal flavor to a form that
achieves its finest effects through impersonality. He could not
write a poem that would be like, or would be dependent upon, a
traditional ballad. The linked temptations thereby besetting him
were a drop into anecdotal gossip or a deviation into character-
drawing. Exactly to the point is a passage from Evelyn Wells's
The Ballad Tree: "It is in objectivity, that veil behind which
generations of folk poets have hidden themselves, that the modern imitator fails. He finds it hard to avoid interpretation; a
moral, a personal reaction, or a reflection from his own experience slips out . . . The supernatural becomes a source of subjective wonder and marvel, made deliberately eerie to evoke horror.
The bounds of the simple ballad are thus broken down by the
dual interest in action and emotion."

There is a stanza in "A Sunday Morning Tragedy" which illus-
trates this weakness almost too well. A shepherd speaks, offering
a woman his nostrum, usually applied to animals, for ending the

pregnancy of her unmarried daughter:

> " 'Tis meant to balk ill-motherings"—
> (Ill-motherings! Why should they be?)—
> If not, would God have sent such things?"
> So spoke the shepherd unto me.

The parenthesis is damaging: "he finds it hard to avoid interpretation . . ." If Hardy intends the poem to be read as though it were indeed a ballad, his intervention violates the ballad tone; if he wishes it to be read with a modern stress, his comment is too pat to convey psychological or moral interest.

Another kind of poem for which Hardy has won applause, probably too much of it, is the dramatic vignette, notably in the groups entitled "War Poems," "Time's Laughingstocks," and "Satires of Circumstance." Few of these short poems invite a close second reading, for there is something decidedly mechanical and self-satisfied in their regular drops into irony. Whatever pleasure they can yield comes mostly from a first exposure, the bare quick recurrence of human delusion in sketch after sketch.

The primary claim for such writing must be as a poetry of experience, a poetry resting on a faithful attention to things as they are and structured through a cogent organization of detail. It is a very difficult kind of poetry to write, since the aim of the poet must be to achieve some fresh insight or complex reflection about human affairs by means of a severely limited and hence not very complex action. In trying to write the dramatic vignette, the poet subjects himself to severe deprivations: story without plot, portrayal without depth, suggestion without supporting context. The dangers in such poetry are, consequently, an excessive reliance upon mere anecdote and a mannerist proliferation of items—both of which are assumed to carry a heavy charge of implied meaning. To the first of these dangers Hardy succumbed more frequently than to the second, though there is not much evidence that he was strongly aware of either.

The writing of such poems seems to have been for Hardy an emotional convenience or shortcut, reflecting his conclusions about the way things are, his ideas about the nature of experience, so fixedly and with such an amiable relish in his "pessimism," as virtually to cancel out the experience itself. Meant as dramatic embodiments, these poems often decline into mere illustrations for a settled opinion. And often enough, for a familiar opinion. At a first reading they can perhaps yield a mild *frisson*, but when read in bulk they draw attention to their dominating formula rather than the material that is supposed to be rendered through use of the formula. For students of Hardy's "philosophy" they provide neat prefabrications; for readers of poetry, thin anecdotes and the aura of disenchantment. Crowded though they are with melodrama and disaster, these poems do not contain enough: they are diagrammed, not imagined. Among all the "Satires of Circumstance" only one sketch, "Over the Coffin," goes beyond that mechanical irony which in Hardy's inferior work serves as a tic of complacence:

> They stand confronting, the coffin between,
> His wife of old, and his wife of late,
> And the dead man whose they both had been
> Seems listening aloof, as to things past date.
> —"I have called," says the first. "Do you marvel or not?"
> "In truth," says the second, "I do—somewhat."
>
> "Well, there was a word to be said by me! . . .
> I divorced that man because of you—
> It seemed I must do it, boundenly;
> But now I am older, and tell you true,
> For life is little, and dead lies he;
> I would I had let alone you two!
> And both of us, scorning parochial ways,
> Had lived like the wives in the patriarchs' days."

No extravagant claims need be made for this little poem, nor need we hesitate to admit that in the second stanza the writing becomes somewhat puffy and slack. But there are modest successes to be registered: an initial sharpness of conception which is given a wry turn in the concluding couplet, and the brilliant phrase, "as to things past date," which keeps us from lending complete assent to the first wife and thereby mordantly qualifies the meaning of the whole incident. The final implication of the poem is more complex—I mean thereby to suggest, less clever—than any of its lines might indicate.

To recognize, or measure, the limitations of Hardy's dramatic poems one need only compare them with a similar group of poems by Edwin Arlington Robinson. Robinson too had expe-

rienced a loss of faith and its subsequent discomforts, but except
for occasional flights into a nebulous transcendentalism, he tried
to keep his eye upon the actualities of human experience. There
is a psychological closeness and moral complication in Robinson's dramatic poems which Hardy as poet cannot match—despite
the fact that in any total reckoning Hardy is surely the greater
poet. More willing than Hardy to submit to the multiplicity and
variety, even the sheer waywardness, of human experience, Robinson is thereby readier to allow the material of his little dramas
to emerge according to their own impetus, their inner logic. The
problem here is that of literary tact, perhaps the most difficult
and elusive problem faced by a writer: to what extent should he
yield himself to his unavoidable urge for shaping his work in
accordance with his beliefs, and to what extent should he resist
that urge in favor of the autonomy of the world, the *difference*
of everything beyond his self? In Hardy's dramatic poems one
is aware of a quietly insistent philosophical will, imposing itself
upon, sometimes even crushing, his rendered situations. And as
a result one cannot find in his dramatic poems the psychological
finesse of Robinson's "Eros Turannos" or the analytic refinement
of "The Wandering Jew."

To these strictures, two qualifications need to be added. First,
it is not the mere presence of formula itself which causes most
of Hardy's dramatic poems to fail, since in his best work he also
employs formulas of sorts. Why then should a characteristic
Hardy formula—say, the destructive consequences of a minor
misunderstanding—lead to such radically different results in different poems? A speculation, if no more, is possible. Hardy was
essentially a poet of conservative temperament, pleased to return
again and again to a few themes, a few tones. The formula he
might employ in approaching one of these themes served him
as a constant, a well-used habit of imagination. What kind of
poem would emerge from a particular use of the formula would
depend mainly on the pressure Hardy brought to bear upon it.
In his major poems there is an enormous weight of felt experience, an intelligence active, discriminating and self-aware, which
breaks out of or overwhelms the originating formula. We may
therefore say that what is decisive is not the mere presence of
the formula, but the use to which, in any particular poems, it

can be put, the extent to which its familiar comforts enable Hardy to gain unfamiliar perception. Second, there are dramatic poems by Hardy about which a criticism must be made sharply different from the one I have just noted. To represent possible or plausible incidents for their own sake is an aim dubious enough in prose fiction; but anything like this aim is quite pointless in a short poem, where the development of action, situation and character possible to writers of fiction is not available. If some of Hardy's dramatic poems fail through rigidity of pattern, others fail through triviality of content, an accurate enough recording of inconsequential event. We read Hardy's dramatic poems; recognize the situation to which they point; sometimes respond in ways they invite. But seldom do we feel impelled to return to them.

There is another group of poems that brings us somewhat closer to the heart of Hardy's achievement: it is the group in which he improvises dialogues with an abandoned God. These are most curious poems, semi- or pseudo-theological fables written in the absence of a secure theology, in which the voice of a God no longer believed in yet strongly commiserated with, joins the voices of men and sometimes a chorus of "Spirits" from the dead to deplore the radical inequities of the cosmic order. The deity who speaks in these poems tends to be distracted and distressed, uncertain as to the provenance or meaning of his creation, and quite as bewildered by the eternal moral quandaries as are the human beings he presumably created. In a "neutralized" universe stripped of intent and value, man has been left helpless and God defenseless. For (and I continue roughly to paraphrase Hardy) God cannot answer our questions as to the reasons for creation and we do not know what to make of his guilt as the author of creation.

While the intellectual assumptions behind such poems are certainly grave, Hardy's tone in writing them is by no means always solemn. In poems like "The Subalterns" and "Channel Firing" there is a wry and touching humor: deity, "Spirits" and men both dead and alive prove equally helpless before the riddles of time and fatality. It is amusing to be told that the questions which torment human beings also torment their putative creators, and it helps establish the Hardyan tone, a democracy of comradeship in a shared plight. These are not poems that invite close doctrinal inspection, for their premise is the collapse of doctrine and their method the loose personification of the dilemmas faced by unbelievers who have grown up in a world of belief. One cannot suppose that anything like these poems will ever again be written, or that a historical occasion for writing them will ever recur—and that, I think, is one reason, if not the major reason, for a strong interest in them. There is something quite as awesome in historical uniqueness as in historical recurrence.

For having written such poems Hardy has been severely rated by critics in the Eliot line, who regard them as tritely heretical and intellectually feckless. They look with distaste upon what one of them, R. P. Blackmur, called Hardy's lack of "emotional discipline and the structural support of a received imagination" (by which immensity I take Blackmur to mean the complex of symbols and myths associated with the Christian tradition). Yet it might be remembered that we cannot always choose the situation in which we live out our lives; that for Hardy, as for many other nineteenth century writers, the loss of faith was an experience of the utmost consequence, not a mere frivolity or pretext for a wanton emotionalism; and that his effort to improvise voices, personifications and fables which might replace Christian authority was undertaken in a spirit of humility testifying not merely to the hold Christianity continued to exert upon his mind but also the depth to which its values had penetrated his very being.

There is another quality to these poems that makes them utterly winning: I refer to their quality of innocence. (Middleton Murry, in a superb remark, once said of Hardy that "the contagion of the world's slow stain had not touched him.") The issues to which these poems point or upon which they impinge are difficult and complex enough, but the way in which Hardy approaches them—a compassion for creator and created alike which never slips into blasphemy or mere cleverness—displays at its strongest the purity of his countryman's soul. A sophisticated urban mind might blanch at the prospect of enrolling God among his spokesman and then making the deity subject to our familiar disabilities; but all this is done by Hardy with entire good feeling, the charm of natural piety and the tact of a man to whom considerations of hierarchy, whether mundane or celestial, are entirely foreign.

Some of these odd mythological poems, like "The Masked Face" and "New Year's Eve," are failures which slide into the dreariness of rehearsed opinion. The voices may be those of God, men and Spirits, but the words are too much those of Hardy. Given his limited powers of conceptual development and almost complete incapacity for the play of dialectic, Hardy could seldom versify statements of his ideas with much distinction. Despite the dogmas of certain critics, a poetry of statement can be written, and written well: but not by Hardy. He could sense complexities better than state them, and he was best at showing their entangling implications for human conduct. He writes most effectively when his mind has been set in motion by some intellectual difficulty and then turns back—though what I must put here as sequence was in actuality simultaneous—to a remembered or imagined situation which serves him as an emblem of the difficulty. As the idea "melts" into the rendered experience, so that in the course of the poem the two seem as if one, there occurs a gradual upheaval of Hardy's deepest yearnings, pieties and sympathies.

A good many of Hardy's critics have assumed that his beliefs were impediments he had to overcome in order to reach his true poetry. No doubt; in some sense, that must be true for all writers. But it is also true that impediments can be energizing, and whatever it is that blocks our profoundest speech may also serve as an agent for releasing it. Hardy's beliefs matter deeply to his poetry, for without the pressures they exert upon him, he might never have gone beyond the mild *genre* pictures of William Barnes. Hardy's beliefs matter, but not as raw hunks of doctrine we must accept or deny; they matter as irritants, provocations and stimulants for the release of his sensibility. He takes his beliefs with complete seriousness, and so must we; it would be foolish to deny that our attitudes toward his poetry are strongly affected by the extent of our accord with its substructure of belief; yet in reading his best poems, as perhaps in reading all successful poetry, an appropriate response must soon transcend issues of doctrine. Transcend, not remove.

In "The Subalterns" there speaks a series of "Spirits," each in
his own clipped stanza—"the leaden sky," "the North," "Sickness," and "Death." All confess themselves helpless agents of
"laws in force on high." Then, in the fifth and concluding stanza,
the one upon which the point of the poem depends, Hardy
speaks in his own voice:

> We smiled upon each other then,
>   And life to me had less
> Of that fell look it wore ere when
>   They owned their passiveness.

The tone here is a mixture of Hardy's characteristic modesty
and a somewhat saddened self-irony. I say "self-irony" because
even as Hardy finds a consolation in the thought that the "Spirits" of destruction have confessed themselves as helpless as their
victims, he recognizes how little and unavailing that consolation
finally is. Indeed, how little and unavailing any consolation must
be. Still—he says in effect—that is the best men can do, and since
there is no other way out, we had better learn to accept this "kinship" with whatever power it is that will soon turn us into dust.
Something very different from and a good deal more subtle than
romantic pantheism or conventional stoicism is here at work.
The resolving voice is the voice of the mature Hardy, a poet
supremely honest before his dilemmas and failures, no matter
what the cost.

This is the note Hardy sustains through the group of poems
in which he speaks directly out of his own situation and with
an intensely personal accent that has been freed from the dis-
tempers of egotism. I have in mind poems like "The Oxen," or
the touching first stanza of "The Impercipient," in which Hardy
observes a cathedral service and, far from claiming any superiority as an "emancipated" modern, recognizes the extent of his
losses while refusing to allow these to lure him into a faith his
mind has already rejected:

> That with this bright believing band
>   I have no claim to be,
> That faiths by which my comrades stand
>   Seem fantasies to me,
> And mirage-mists their Shining Land,
>   Is a strange destiny.

A bit later I shall want to qualify what is suggested by the phrase, "an intensely personal voice," in describing Hardy's lyrics; but here it is purity and directness of feeling, a complete freedom from pose, that needs to be remarked. The last line of the stanza I have just quoted may seem, upon a casual reading, somewhat flat and "prosaic." Yet if one enters into the spirit and situation of the speaker, recognizing his kinship with the men who have remained believers (for they are "comrades" still, they form a "band" from which he sees himself as properly if painfully excluded), then the word "strange," with the strong stress Hardy's metric enforces, seems right, a very powerful stroke. It needs also to be remarked, in opposition to a frequent critical opinion, that in his short lyrics Hardy commands a surprising range of tone, from the contemplative melancholy which is his best and deepest note to occasional moments of playfulness and joy. There is the lover's ecstacy of "When I Set Out for Lyonnesse," which, through a pleasing interplay of three- and four-beat lines, takes the form of a chant-like and enchanted repetition:

> When I set out for Lyonnesse,
> A hundred miles away,
> The rime was on the spray,
> And starlight lit my lonesomeness
> When I set out for Lyonnesse
> A hundred miles away.
>
> * * *
>
> When I came back from Lyonnesse
> With magic in my eyes,
> All marked with mute surmise
> My radiance rare and fathomless,
> When I came back from Lyonnesse
> With magic in my eyes!

There is the splendid song, "Great Things," celebrating in successive stanzas "sweet cyder," "the dance," and "Love," and concluding with a stanza that fuses rapture and reflection, through a metric that in the crucial fifth line collapses the rhythm of song (e.g., the spondaic "Joy-jaunts"), slows into the hesitation of speech, and then surges to a concluding lilt:

> Will these be always great things,
> Great things to me? . . .
> Let it befall that One will call,
> "Soul, I have need of thee":

> What then? Joy-jaunts, impassioned flings,
>   Love, and its ecstacy,
> Will always have been great things,
>   Great things to me!

There is Hardy's special fondness for a chiarosouro of scene
and feeling, as in "An August Midnight," a poem that succumbs
at its end to didactic flatness but in its opening placement of
detail is remarkably fine. Some of this detail may stir a comparison with Frost's "Design," but only enough to mark the great
distance between the two poets, since Hardy's relation to the
strangeness of physical matter is finally an inclusive one while
Frost's is not:

> A shaded lamp and a waving blind,
> And the beat of a clock from a distant floor:
> On this scene enter—winged, horned and spined—
> A longlegs, a moth, and a dumbledore;
> While 'mid my pages there idly stands
> A sleepy fly, that rubs its hands . . .
>
> Thus met we five, in this still place,
> At this point of time, at this point in space . . .

And then a sharp lyric about the survival into old age of the
fires of youth, in its rhythm (especially that of the second stanza)
reminiscent of Emily Dickinson, but in its capacity for fusing
sadness and ecstacy into a coherent encounter with time, unmistakable as Hardy's:

> I look into my glass,
> And view my wasting skin,
> And say, "Would God it came to pass
> My heart had shrunk as thin!"
>
> For then, I, undistrest
> By hearts grown cold to me,
> Could lonely wait my endless rest
> With equanimity.
>
> But Time, to make me grieve,
> Part steals, lets part abide;
> And shakes this fragile frame at eve
> With throbbings of noontide.

Perhaps the most impressive, surely the most uncanny, of these
personal lyrics is "Transformations," a poem which may at first

seem little more than a romantic fancy but actually is tough-spirited and dryly ironic:

> Portion of this yew
> Is a man my grandsire knew
> Bosomed here at its foot;
> This branch may be his wife,
> A ruddy human life
> Now turned to a green shoot.
>
> These grasses must be made
> Of her who often prayed,
> Last century, for repose;
> And the fair girl long ago
> Whom I often tried to know
> May be entering this rose.
>
> So, they are not underground,
> But as veins and nerves abound
> In the growths of upper air,
> And they feel the sun and rain,
> And the energy again,
> That made them what they were!

That "philosophy" of Hardy which too frequently lured him into frigid assertion is here dissolved into a genuine vision of an ultimate mixture of flesh and dust. Each of the first two stanzas breaks into two groups of three lines, providing within a sequence of time instances of transformation; the final stanza moves in a single curve of statement, one that does not willfully attempt to dissolve the fact of death into a mere idea, but contains a somber recognition that no matter what transformations lie ahead, our dissolution is irrevocable. A "fair girl" may be "entering this rose"—she can, with all the unnerving implications of that verb, enter it only insofar as she ceases to be. The woman who, last century, prayed for repose, may indeed have found it, but there is no hint of any solace that makes her death the less terrible. And the point is clinched by the final word of the poem, which shows Hardy to have been intent upon undermining whatever possibilities of religious or pantheist sentimentalism his earlier lines may have stirred.

Hardy is here following the pattern of the consolation poem but at crucial points shatters it through ironic deflation: life after death is what you wish? well yes, but a kind of life that will no more ease your vanity or fears than the thought of eternal nothingness. Not only does the language work toward this effect, but also an interweaving of red and green images, subordinating our desires to natural life, and the three-beat lines, neatly clipping the stories of the dead into quick and efficient summary. Hardy is writing here out of his deepest sources, at once anonymous and intimate; and with the tact he sometimes won, he brings together primitive and modernist strangeness, both rallied against the receding powers of Christianity.

Heartlessly moving past such wonderful poems as "The Darkling Thrush," "Neutral Tones" and "During Wind and Rain," I wish finally to look at the group of elegies Hardy composed in 1912–13, called "Veteris vestigia flammae." These poems, written shortly after the death of his first wife, are painfully grounded in Hardy's own experience. What had begun as a marriage of joy had become a marriage of quarreling and heavy silence. Mrs. Hardy seems to have been subject to mild derangements, and almost as distressing was her snobbery, which drove her to condescend toward Hardy's origins and to repeat publicly her wish that they might return to the glitter of London rather than be stuck away in Dorset. Though as private in source as any writing could be, these marvelous poems are quite independent of the events that stirred Hardy to write them, and they can be read with pleasure by someone entirely ignorant of their place in Hardy's own experience. "The verses came," wrote Hardy, "it was quite natural. One looked back through the years and saw some pictures; a loss like that makes one's old brain vocal." In his seventies Hardy opened himself to passion.

What came back to him was the whole tragic entanglement of a relationship sustained through forty years and in the end gone dead. The regrets haunting his memory are declared in "The Going" with a poignancy few English poets have ever matched:

> Why, then, latterly did we not speak,
> Did we not think of those days long dead,
> And ere your vanishing strive to seek
> That time's renewal? We might have said,
>   "In this bright spring weather
>   We'll visit together
> Those places that once we visited."

> Well, well! All's past amend,
> Unchangeable. It must go.
> I seem but a dead man held on end
> To sink down soon . . . O you could not know
> That such swift fleeing
> No soul foreseeing—
> Not even I—would undo me so!

The deepest note struck in these poems is not regret but the recapture of experience. Focused and intensified, regret leads to an opening of memory, a flooding return, sometimes almost a hallucination of *seeing* the past as a structure beneath the tracings of memory. The experience rendered is a kind of second life achieved through imagination, in which the speaker, never deluding himself, knows perfectly well that it is ghosts and bloodless presences to which he yields himself, yet welcomes and savors the unshackling of memory, even the pain it brings him. At times it is a pain so fierce as to provoke him into a mild complaint:

> Why do you make me leave the house
> And think for a breath it is you I see
> At the end of the alley of bending boughs
> Where so often at dusk you used to be;
> Till in darkening dankness
> The yawning blankness
> Of the perspective sickens me!

But the complaint dissolves: Hardy waits for the delusion of return, the gesture of ghosts, and in "After a Journey" speaks in direct incantation:

> I see what you are doing: you are leading me on
> To the spots we knew when we haunted here together,
> The waterfall, above which the mist-bow shone
> At the then fair hour in the then fair weather,
> And the cave just under, with a voice still hollow
> That it seems to call out to me from forty years ago,
> When you were all aglow,
> And not the thin ghost that I now frailly follow!

The struggle to remember and to salvage the debris of life—achieved in these lines through a rhythm of turn and return, offer and withdrawal, till it reaches the triumphant simplicity of the penultimate line, set off in its brevity and finality—this struggle to remember leads Hardy beyond the merely contingent and toward those elements of his experience that are not his alone and finally not even his at all. What begins with an obscure private hurt ends with the common wound of experience. The writing is free of posture, whether to heroism or abasement; it bends neither to the luxury of anger nor the irrelevance of judgment; and it is utterly past condolence. The speaker shuts out the world beyond him, murmuring as if no one were near, neither flesh nor answering voice. Talking to himself and his dead wife, he summons the life they had. And as he muses to himself, the enlargement of his memory seems almost to regain for him the presence of his life. "You are past love, praise, indifference, blame," he tells her in "Your Last Drive," and all he wishes now is to hold fast to their time as it was, without any retouching. Grief, regret, pain are neither brushed away nor willfully magnified. They fill the scene in quiet, and then lead past themselves, to a final dry clarity.

In this group of elegies as they appear in the *Collected Poems*, there is, I think, a loose kind of structural pattern. Four major poems carry the development of feeling. There is an opening cry in "The Going," an utter forlornness in "The Voice," then an ecstatic recapture in "After a Journey" and finally a partial acceptance and diminuendo in "At Castle Boterel." About these great poems there coil themselves a series of lesser pieces, usually written in three-beat lines, serving as variations in feeling and recollection. The sequence is broken by the shock of "The Haunter," a poem in which the dead woman herself suddenly speaks out, with some bitterness but more assuagement. She cannot answer "the words he lifts me":

> When I could answer he did not say them:
>   When I could let him know
> How I would like to join in his journeys
>   Seldom he wished to go.
> Now that he goes and wants me with him
>   More than he used to do,
> Never he sees my faithful phantom
>   Though he speaks thereto.

She appears again in "The Phantom Horsewoman" and "The Spell of the Rose," in which she also returns to the "misconceits" that bedeviled them but ends with a question:

And would that now I knew
What feels he of the tree I planted,
And whether, after I was called
To be a ghost, he, as of old,
Gave me his heart anew.

The resolution, if indeed there is one, comes in the final poem, "Where the Picnic Was," in which the speaker is drained of ecstasy and little remains but repetition of the external act which had before led to inner illumination:

I slowly climb
Through winter mire,
And scan and trace
The forsaken place
Quite readily.

In the major poems of this group, the speaker, as he commands the past or sinks back into the present, ruminates upon wastes of experience, the gestures refused and opportunities missed. He leaves behind him the treacheries of poetic display and "expression": it is too late for vanity or defense. What is left—and this forms the most stirring motif in the whole group of poems—is the moment of overwhelming relief when there is no longer any need for self-deception and nothing to claim for oneself but the truth of memory. This surrender brings pain and through pain, composure. It yields, in Hardy's poems, a purification of self and a marvelous openness to the shades and nuances of the past. In "At Castle Boterel" there are joys remembered beyond loss:

It filled but a minute. But was there ever
A time of such quality, since or before,
In that hill's history? To one mind never,
Though it has been climbed, foot-swift, foot-sore,
By thousands more.

Primaeval rocks form the road's steep border,
And much have they faced there, first and last,
Of the transitory in Earth's long order;
But what they record in colour and cast
Is—that we two passed.

Or, as in "The Voice," there can be a surge of anguish, but anguish grasped and contained:

Woman much missed, how you call to me, call to me,
Saying that now you are not as you were
When you had changed from the one who was all to me
But as at first, when our day was fair.

              * * *

       Thus I; faltering forward,
       Leaves around me falling,
Wind oozing thin through the thorn from norward,
       And the woman calling.

In another of these poems, "Rain on a Grave," the past and present move toward a terrible linkage:

       Clouds spout upon her
         Their waters amain
         In ruthless disdain,—
     Her who but lately
        Had shivered with pain
     As at a touch of dishonour
     If there had lit on her
     So coldly, so straightly
       Such arrows of rain . . .

These have been called poems of mourning, and so they are. But they are also something else, perhaps more valuable. Hardy's ultimate concern is not with any immediate emotion, but with the consequences of emotion, survival beyond emotion: how a man lives through what it seems he cannot, and how he learns not to tamper with his grief and not even to seek forgiveness in his own eyes. The kindness Hardy characteristically shows to all creatures he does not deny to himself, for he is free of that version of pride which consists in relentless self-accusation. The speaker in these poems is a man, perhaps a little better or a little worse than others, but not, in any ultimate reckoning, very different. He moves through emotion, for there is no way to live and avoid that, but then he moves a little past it, toward the salvage of poise. And thereby this figure free of the impulse to moralize becomes a moral example, such as few among the more brilliant or complex sensibilities of our age could provide.

The voice that speaks in these poems works through a rhythm by no means simple, a rhythm that registers a mind turning upon its memories, turning in upon itself, turning toward the emptiness ahead, and then to the sum of its apprehensions. But always

turning, through phrases and clauses that carry the motions of
reflection, hesitation, qualification. At the base of these poems
there is sometimes the metric of folk song, but the folk song as
it has been broken into a slow and grave speech, the speech of
contemplation. More often Hardy employs a long, halting line
in which frequent caesura indicate the struggle of the mind to
gather up the remains of memory. The rhythms weave and halt,
resume and rise, drop and come back, as if to create the sense
of a groping speech which clashes with the boundary of the line
and pattern of the stanza but finally bends to their discipline. It
is through these rhythms that Hardy's ultimate quality as a poet
emerges: in the refrain-like lines, very long or short by contrast
to the body of the poem, which call the writing to a break, sometimes a halt, of attention and reconsideration, or in the hints
offered by his indentations, meant to cue the reader as to relative
stresses the lines are to receive. If we speak of Hardy's "ultimate
quality," we must mean that utterly defenseless sincerity which
never stops to reckon the cost of what must be said; but in the
poems themselves this sincerity is realized through his awkward
and drooping rhythms, the music of loss and reconciliation.

Certain artists achieve in old age a style of bareness and bone.
They have come to the heart of what they need to say, and care
little for illustration, nothing for decoration. It is the style of
old age, and if ever it can be reached, it brings a kind of ruth-
less contentment.

The business of the poet, writes T. S. Eliot, "is not to find new
emotions, but to use the ordinary ones." Poetry is "not a turning
loose of emotion, but an escape from emotion; it is not the expression of personality, but an escape from personality. But, of
course, only those who have personality and emotions know what
it means to want to escape from these things." Hardy had personality and he had emotions. By 1912–13 he had come to know what
it meant to want to escape from these things. Imprisoned in a
private affliction, he learned to "escape" from his emotions
through the objectivity and distance of art. That T. S. Eliot, in
his theological fixity, could not grasp the magnificence of these
poems even while providing a critical formula that seems best
to describe them is one of those ironies Hardy would have rel-
ished, he who had written, "Well, well! All's past amend/Un-
changeable . . ."

⊷⦃ IX ⦄⊶

The Last Years

THE LAST FOURTEEN OR FIFTEEN YEARS OF HARDY'S LIFE form a gently declining plane of dignified, quiet, sustained composition and honors enjoyed. Old age fitted Hardy. In a sense that does him no discredit, he had been born old, never quite free—like the little boy in *Jude the Obscure*— of the cares and weight of existence. And as always in his life, though quite ready to accept whatever tributes the world might offer him, Hardy remained staunch and entwined within himself, contemplative, abstracted, withdrawn—even as he was distinguished by a humorous courtesy toward neighbors, friends and unwelcome intruders. He lived his own life, rarely indulging in literary postures and free from the stains of publicity.

The writing of the threnodies about his first wife in 1913–14 formed one of the emotional climaxes of his life; and if it left him purified, it also left him drained. As his memory opened to the time he had had with Emma Hardy, the torment also came back to him and not least of all his fear or suspicion that a streak of insanity had cut through her final years. That she would, nevertheless, always be at the center of his emotional existence he could not doubt. (As late as 1924, when Hardy was eighty years old, he made an entry in his notebook: "E. first met fifty-four years ago.") She had been, as he wrote in his lovely poem, "Beeny Cliff," "The woman whom I loved so, and who loyally loved me." And so he would continue to think of her.

Hardy found it hard to live by himself. He was lonely, disorganized, unable to cope with the minutiae of the day and quite bewildered by the hordes of strangers, many of them Americans, who invaded his privacy in behalf of autographs, mementoes and memorable words. Most important of all, he was by now an old man. The outbreak of the First World War added to his despondency, his "visions ahead of ignorance overruling intelligence and reducing us to another Dark Age." "Why," he burst out to a friend, "does not Christianity throw up the sponge and say, 'I am beaten,' and let another religion take its place?"

In a short time, however, order would be restored to his own life, if to nothing else. In February 1914 Hardy married Florence Emily Dugdale, a young woman who had befriended him and the first Mrs. Hardy some years earlier, had tactfully helped with the research on *The Dynasts*, had faithfully run little errands when Hardy needed a reference, and after Emma's death had managed to restore a livable routine to Max Gate, shooing away the busybodies and shielding Hardy's privacy. At the time of this marriage, Hardy was seventy-three and his bride thirty-five, yet the arrangement was eminently happy and sensible, with the poet profiting from kindly care and his new wife gaining, as she put it, "the right to express my devotion—and to endeavour to add to his comfort and happiness." Hardy was grateful. She had come

> And, spiriting into my house, to, fro
> Like Wind on the stair,
> Cares still, heeds all, and will, even though
> I may despair.

When his book of verse *Moments of Vision* came out in 1917, Hardy inscribed it, "The First Copy/Of the First Edition/To the First of Women/Florence Hardy."

Moments of Vision is a fine work, Hardy the poet recurrently at his best, even if there is nothing in it to compare with the great poems of mourning he had written a few years earlier. And even beyond this point Hardy continued to write verse, publishing four more volumes, the last of which, *Winter Words*, appeared in 1928. He also issued in 1923 *The Queen of Cornwall*, a not very distinguished play on the Tristan and Iseult theme. To the very moment of his death, the writing of verse was an integral part of Hardy's life.

Numerous honors came to him in his late years and he accepted them with easy pleasure and grace. Cambridge awarded him an honorary degree in 1913, and Oxford—the Christminster at the doors of which Jude had knocked in vain—a Doctor of Letters in 1920. Other prizes and recognitions were frequent. Hardy began to be called "the Grand Old Man of English Letters," not perhaps the most comfortable designation for the author of *Jude the Obscure* but harmless enough and pleasing.

Pleasing too were the little pageants and semi-professional performances that were gotten up for him in Dorset, mostly dramatizations of his novels. *Tess of the D'Urbervilles* was staged with some success, *The Mayor of Casterbridge* made into a film. One of Hardy's biographers, Carl Weber, reports that at eighty-four the old man was stricken with an infatuation for a pretty young actress, Gertrude Bugler, who played Tess, and that this caused Florence Hardy considerable distress. Decades earlier, in describing how Time ". . . shakes this fragile frame at eve/With throbbings of noontide," Hardy had seemingly anticipated the tragi-comedy of such a moment.

For many English readers, especially those who had reached or passed middle age, Hardy came to seem more than a distinguished older writer who merited respect for the work he had done in the past. He represented, they felt, a purity of spirit which was inherently precious, and all the more precious during the contaminated post-war years; he seemed like a remembrance, at once fragile and magnificent, of an England gone forever; he was a man to venerate precisely because he remained untouched by the febrile sophistication of the twenties. Hardy had begun his intellectual life as a disciple of agnosticism, and now he seemed like the very embodiment of traditional verities and styles. What won the affection of reflective people throughout the world was, by this point in his career, not merely Hardy's literary achievement in its own right, and certainly not his formal ideas, but a quality of feeling, a modest and brooding serenity, which shone through even the minor poems of his late years.

Nor was it only the aging and the nostalgic who loved Hardy. So flamboyant a representative of the modern spirit as T. E. Lawrence began to make pilgrimages to Max Gate during the early twenties in search of a repose, perhaps a wisdom, he could not discover in his own tormented life. Back from Arabia and subjecting himself to the strange penance of enlistment in the armed forces, Lawrence, as he later wrote to Mrs. Hardy, felt these visits to be "the most honorable stopping place I've ever found." How Lawrence saw the old man he described in a wonderful letter to Robert Graves in 1923:

> The truth seems to be that Max Gate is very difficult to seize upon. I go there as often as I decently can, and hope to go on going there so long as it is within reach . . . Hardy is so pale, so quiet, so refined into an essence: and camp is such a hurly-burly. When I come back I feel as if I'd woken up from a sleep: not an exciting sleep, but a restful one. There is an unbelievable dignity and ripeness about Hardy: he is waiting so tranquilly for death, without a desire or ambition left in his spirit, as far as I can feel it: and yet he entertains so many illusions, and hopes for the world, things which I, in my disillusioned middle-age, feel to be illusory. They used to call this man a pessimist. While really he is full of fancy expectations.
>
> Then he is so far-away. Napoleon is a real man to him, and the country of Dorsetshire echoes that name everywhere in Hardy's ears. He lives in his period, and thinks of it as the great war: whereas to me that nightmare through the fringe of which I passed has dwarfed all memories of other wars. . . .
>
> Also he is so assured. I said something a little reflecting on Homer: and he took me up at once, saying it was not to be despised that it was very kin to *Marmion* . . . saying this not with a grimace as I would say it, a feeling smart and original and modern, but with the most tolerant kindness in the world. Conceive a man to whom Homer and Scott are companions: who feels easy in such presences.
>
> And the standards of the man! He feels interest in everyone, and veneration for no-one. I've not found in him any bowing-down, moral or material or spiritual. . . .
>
> Yet any little man finds this detachment of Hardy's a vast compliment and comfort. He takes me as soberly as he would take John Milton (how sober that name is), considers me as carefully, is as interested in me: for to him every person starts scratch in the life-race and Hardy has no preferences: and I think no dislikes, except for the people who betray his confidence and publish him to the world.
>
> . . . It is strange to pass from the noise and thoughtlessness of sergeants' company into a peace so secure that in it not even Mrs. Hardy's tea-cups rattle on the tray: and from a barrack of hollow

senseless bustle to the cheerful calm of T.H. thinking aloud about life to two or three of us. If I were in his place I would never wish to die: or even to wish other men dead. The peace which passeth all understanding;—but it can be felt, and is nearly unbearable. How envious such an old age is.

One would give a lot to know what, in turn, Hardy thought of Lawrence. All we have is a remark in a letter by Lawrence that Hardy had read a copy of *Seven Pillars of Wisdom* "and made me very proud with what he said about it."

Throughout the twenties a steady parade of literary admirers came to Max Gate or wrote about Hardy in fervent appreciation: Siegfried Sassoon, John Masefield, E. M. Forster, many others. Their impressions of the aged Hardy are often striking. Wrote Llewelyn Powys:

Hardy came in at last, a little old man (dressed in tweeds after the manner of a country squire) with the same round skull and the same goblin eyebrows and the same eyes keen and alert. What was it that he reminded me of? A night hawk? A falcon owl? For I tell you the eyes that looked out of that century-old skull were of the kind that see in the dark.

H. M. Tomlinson remarked that Hardy had kept a quality of childhood and that

Sometimes when talking to him you felt this child was as old as humanity and knew all about us, but that he did not attach importance to his knowledge because he did not know that he had it. Just by chance, in the drift of the talk, there would be a word by Hardy, not only wide of the mark, but apparently not directed to it. Why did he say it? On the way home, or some weeks later, his comment would be recalled, and with the revealing light on it.

In 1927 Leonard Woolf called on Hardy and the old man talked "with great charm and extraordinary simplicity. He was a human being, not 'the great man . . .'" What impressed Woolf most—it was a mixture of elements to be found not only in the man but also in the work—was Hardy's "simplicity and . . . something which is almost the opposite of simplicity." And in the same year Hardy's old friend Edmund Gosse wrote:

He is a wonder, if you like! . . . Very tiny and fragile, but full of spirit and a gaiety not quite consistent in the most pessimistic of poets. He and I collogued merrily of past generations, like two antediluvian animals sporting in the primeval slime.

The end came quietly, unmarred by extreme pain or illness. In January 1928 Hardy slipped away from life.

Several years earlier, on his eighty-first birthday, over one hundred English writers had joined in sending him a tribute:

> In your novels and poems you have given us a tragic vision of life which is informed by your knowledge of character and relieved by the charity of your humour, and sweetened by your sympathy with human suffering and endurance. We have learned from you that the proud heart can subdue the hardest fate, even in submitting to it ... In all that you have written you have shown the spirit of man, nourished by tradition and sustained by pride, persisting through defeat.

Let these words stand.

Works by Thomas Hardy

I. *Novels*

THE POOR MAN AND THE LADY (1868). Never published; and, in its original form, beyond recovery.

DESPERATE REMEDIES (1871).

UNDER THE GREENWOOD TREE—A rural Painting of the Dutch School (1872).

A PAIR OF BLUE EYES (1873).

FAR FROM THE MADDING CROWD (1874).

THE HAND OF ETHELBERTA—a Comedy in Chapters (1876).

THE RETURN OF THE NATIVE (1878).

THE TRUMPET-MAJOR—A Tale (1880).

A LAODICEAN—or, The Castle of the De Stancys. A Story of To-day (1881).

TWO ON A TOWER—A Romance (1882).

THE MAYOR OF CASTERBRIDGE: The Life and Death of a Man of Character (1886).

THE WOODLANDERS (1887).

TESS OF THE D'URBERVILLES: A Pure Woman faithfully Presented (1891).

JUDE THE OBSCURE (1895).

THE WELL-BELOVED—A Sketch of a Temperament (1897).

II. *Collections of Stories*

WESSEX TALES: Strange, Lively, and Commonplace (1888).

A GROUP OF NOBLE DAMES (1891).

LIFE'S LITTLE IRONIES. A Set of Tales with some Colloquial Sketches entitled "A Few Crusted Characters" (1894).

A CHANGED MAN, THE WAITING SUPPER, AND OTHER TALES (1913).

III. *Collections of Poems, and Dramatic Works*

WESSEX POEMS and other Verses (1898).

POEMS OF THE PAST AND PRESENT (1901).

THE DYNASTS. A Drama of the Napoleonic Wars. Three Parts (1904, 1906, 1908).

TIME'S LAUGHING STOCKS AND OTHER VERSES (1909).

SATIRES OF CIRCUMSTANCE. Lyrics and Reveries (1914).

MOMENTS OF VISION and Miscellaneous Verses (1917).

LATE LYRICS AND EARLIER. (1922).

THE FAMOUS TRAGEDY OF THE QUEEN OF CORNWALL AT TINTAGEL IN LYONNESS (1923).

HUMAN SHOWS, FAR PHANTASIES, SONGS AND TRIFLES (1925).

WINTER WORDS, in Various Moods and Metres (1928).

IV. *Essays and Articles*

LIFE AND ART. New York (1925). A collection of essays, notes, and letters not previously printed in book form. Edited with an introduction by E. Brennecke.

Suggestions for Further Reading

The main source of biographical information concerning Hardy remains the two volumes by Florence Emily Hardy: *The Early Life of Thomas Hardy, 1840–1891* (1928) and *The Later Years of Thomas Hardy, 1892–1928* (1930). Other useful biographical works are: Carl L. Weber, *Hardy of Wessex: His Life and Literary Career* (1940); Evelyn Hardy, *Thomas Hardy: A Critical Biography* (1954); Edmund Blunden, *Thomas Hardy* (English Men of Letters, 1942). All of these contain critical sections.

Richard L. Purdy's *Thomas Hardy: A Bibliographical Study* (1954) is valuable for its information about the editions and manuscripts of Hardy's work. The differences between the serial and book form of Hardy's novels are treated in Mary Ellen Chase's *Thomas Hardy from Serial to Novel* (1927).

Hardy's ideas and intellectual background are discussed in William Rutland, *Thomas Hardy: A Study of His Writings and Their Background* (1954) — a book valuable for its information but not very persuasive as criticism. Also dealing with Hardy's philosophical assumptions are Ernest Brennecke's *Thomas Hardy's Universe* (1924) and Harvey Curtis Webster's *On a Darkling Plain* (1947). In John Holloway's chapter on Hardy in *The*

Victorian Sage (1953) there is a first-rate analysis of the way the ideas affect literary techniques. Interesting background information appears in Ruth Firor, *Folkways in Thomas Hardy* (1931).

Some early critical studies still deserve great respect, for while the language of criticism has changed, few critics have written more perceptively than Lionel Johnson, *The Art of Thomas Hardy* (1894), and Lascelles Abercrombie, *Thomas Hardy: A Critical Study* (1912). Douglas Brown's *Thomas Hardy* (1954) is devoted mainly to the "agricultural theme" in Hardy, but it is a fine and sensitive book. D. H. Lawrence's "Study of Thomas Hardy," in *D. H. Lawrence: Selected Literary Criticism*, edited by Anthony Beal (1955), is a brilliant, if at times wayward, study; no student of Hardy can dispense with it. Albert Guerard's *Thomas Hardy* (1964), an enlarged version of a book first published in 1949, contains first-rate criticism of both the fiction and the verse. This study does not discuss Hardy's novels in compact individualized sections, so that it is sometimes cumbersome to discover what Guerard thinks of particular works, but it is full of original insights and observations.

Further interesting material on Hardy's fiction appears in Arnold Kettle, *An Introduction to the English Novel*, Vol. II (1953); Dorothy Van Ghent, *The English Novel: Form and Function* (1953); Joseph Warren Beach, *The Technique of Thomas Hardy* (1922).

Especially helpful to the beginning student or reader is the collection of critical essays appearing in Albert Guerard, *Hardy* (Twentieth Century Views, 1963).

Valuable criticism of the poetry can be found in I. A. Richards, *Science and Poetry* (1926); R. P. Blackmur, *Language as Gesture* (1954); C. Day Lewis, *The Lyrical Poetry of Thomas Hardy* (The Warton Lecture, 1953); F. R. Leavis, *New Bearings in English Poetry* (1932).

INDEX

Index